LYMPNE
AIRFIELD
AT WAR AND PEACE

LYMPNE AIRFIELD
AT WAR AND PEACE

ANTHONY J. MOOR

FONTHILL

Learn more about Fonthill Media. Join our mailing list to
find out about our latest titles and special offers at:
www.fonthillmedia.com

Fonthill Media Limited
www.fonthillmedia.com
office@fonthillmedia.com

First published in the United Kingdom 2014

British Library Cataloguing in Publication Data:
A catalogue record for this book is available from the British Library

Typeset in 10.5pt on 13pt Sabon LT Std
Printed and bound in England

Contents

Acknowledgements

I would like to thank the following people, museums and societies for their assistance, for providing photographs, and for sharing their memories with me: V. Allsop; M. Andrews; R. Badger; K. F. Bartlett; H. Bott; C. Bunyan; P. Capon, Museum of Army Flying; Maisie Conway (née Geal); F. Cruttenden; Keith J. Dagwell; E. P. Dupont; M. Faley, Metal Blade Records USA; Fleet Air Arm Museum, Yeovilton; Fotoflite/Skyfotos; N. Geal; N. Gilbert (Skyways); R. L. Giles; P. H. T. Green; E. Greenstreet; John Henriet; Imperial War Museum; E. Kate; Kent Aviation Historical Research Society; Kent Gliding Club; Kent Libraries & Study Centre; S. Leslie; T. W. Osbourne; B. Pembroke; RAF Museum, Hendon; R. Riding; A. Saunders; Silver City Association; A. Thomas; C. Thomas; J. Vallier (Skyways); J. T. Williams; G. Winter and A. E. Wright.

Introduction

Kent, whose wartime history will always be linked with the Battle of Britain, bore the brunt of Hitler's plans to invade England. Airfields such as Biggin Hill, Manston, Hawkinge and West Malling quite understandably come to mind when the air war over Kent is recalled. However, other airfields deserve to have their place in history recorded, particularly as those who actually worked, fought and flew from them are few in number today.

One such airfield must surely be Lympne – unique in that it had an important role in both world wars and throughout the intervening years. Epic flights were flown from the airfield, set high on an escarpment overlooking Romney Marsh and Hythe. People who were household names at the time spent many hours at Lympne, socialising with members of the public and the flying club, all with one consuming passion – aviation.

These early flights must have inspired many young men who would later fly for their lives with the RAF and other services. Many learnt to fly at the Cinque Ports Flying Club, and numerous flying displays and meetings were held at Lympne. It was a time when aviation captured the imagination of the British public, a time when British aviation was second to none, and an important period when the RAF was expanding. Following the Second World War, air races returned to Lympne and, later, airlines such as Skyways and Silver City operated from this popular airfield.

I hope that the accounts that follow give the reader an interesting insight into the history of Lympne Airfield at war and peace.

Impressions of a Pilot, by Gary Claude Stoker

Flight is freedom in its purest form,
To dance with the clouds which follow a storm;
To roll and glide, to wheel and spin,
To feel the joy that swells within.

To leave the earth with its troubles and fly,
And know the warmth of a clear spring sky;
Then back to earth at the end of the day,
Released from the tensions which melted away.

Should my end come while I am in flight,
Whether brightest day or darkest night;
Spare me no pity and shrug off the pain,
Secure in the knowledge that I'd do it again.

For each of us is created to die,
And within me I know,
I was born to fly.

CHAPTER 1

Early flying in the locality of Lympne; flying display at Westenhanger, 1910

The earliest recorded aviation event within the locality of Lympne took place in 1841, when Richard Gypson, a professional balloonist who originally worked for Vauxhall Gardens near Birmingham and later the Royal Zoological Gardens in London, chose the area for an ascent in his balloon. His first recorded flight had been on 14 May 1832 from London, and he later became the first pilot to use an adjustable gas valve successfully. In 1841, a year after the introduction of the first adhesive postage stamps, Gypson dropped a letter from his balloon at Lympne, which was then delivered to the addressee. His last recorded flight was in October 1849, after which he retired to write his memoirs. Apart from being an 'aeronaut', he claimed to be a nephew of Napoleon. He later stole three pewter tankards from a drinking house in London and was imprisoned for the offence on 25 May 1853, shortly after which he died in poverty. He had, however, contributed to the birth of aviation, which was to be of lasting interest to the public.

Notably, one of the earliest flying displays took place at Westenhanger, situated close to Lympne. It was at the time known for horse racing, and later became Folkestone Racecourse. On Monday 14 September 1910, excited crowds invaded the platform at Folkestone Central station as the 2.45 p.m. train to Westenhanger arrived. So many people were waiting to board the train that the South Eastern & Chatham Railway (SECR) had to lay on a relief service. The casual observer could have been forgiven for thinking some natural disaster had occurred, but the reason for this exodus was a three-day aviation meeting at the racecourse. There had been much speculation as to whether the event would take place. However, the promoters and the racecourse company did reach agreement over

J. B. Moisant's Bleriot monoplane being prepared for take-off from the grounds of Folkestone racecourse Westenhanger near Lympne.

the organisation of the event and financial considerations. An amount of £1,000 was to be guaranteed, most of which was to be raised by an estimated crowd of three thousand people.

The racecourse was an ideal venue for the meeting as there was no need to spend money constructing stands or shelters. Existing marquees were used as cover for both aircraft and aviator. Many airmen had expressed an interest in the flying, but only three took part. Mr G. A. Barnes, who in May that year had won the Brooklands Cup, arrived in his Humber-Bleriot. Employed by the Humber Motor Company as a test pilot, Mr Barnes had previously been a racing motorcyclist. In 1910, the Humber Motor Company at Coventry was constructing Bleriot aircraft under licence. These particular models were powered by a 30 hp, three-cylinder radial engine. The company engineered the complete airframe and engine including propeller in its own workshops and also produced a more powerful four-cylinder engine of 50 hp, which like the radial was equipped with dual ignition.

On 16 August 1910, a well-known American aviator of Spanish descent, John B. Moisant, flew from Paris to London in his Bleriot together with his mechanic, Albert Fileux. This was the first flight across the Channel with a passenger, which received world acclaim. An architect by profession, Moisant had learnt to fly at the Bleriot school in France. The third aviator was Cecil Grace. He arrived later that day in the Bleriot that was earlier flown by Armstrong Drexel in his successful attempt to beat the altitude record.

Flying had been scheduled to commence at 2.30 p.m. and some fortunate members of the public inspected the aircraft prior to flying. Barnes opened the proceedings by wheeling his machine into a field that sloped on the opposite side of the racecourse to the grandstand, the police having great difficulty in preventing some spectators from passing in front of the aircraft. This particular monoplane was smaller than the other two and at the time was reported as being built for speed.

As bad luck would have it, the engine would not start and it was some minutes before she burst into life. Gathering speed, the Bleriot rolled forward, then without warning swerved violently to port, sending two enthusiastic photographers running for their lives. On the second attempt, the machine rose into the air but was unable to clear a hedge bordering the field. Seeing the hedge, Barnes jumped from his seat as the monoplane passed lazily over the obstacle and dropped on the other side. A quick check revealed no damage and on the third attempt he managed to reach a height of no less than 30 feet, which he maintained for some time, circling the racecourse before landing in front of the grandstand. On closer inspection of the engine it was discovered that a fuel pipe blocked with oil had caused the apparent engine failure. Later, during another flight, Barnes thrilled the crowd by flying at high speed over the course, although even then the engine did not sound as though it was running smoothly.

Moisant had been working on his machine during the first display. At last deciding to take off, he had the aircraft wheeled onto the racetrack in front of the grandstand. Impressed by his ascent, the spectators applauded, as he was the only pilot to take off on the narrow stretch of ground between the crowds, rising gracefully into the air. He remained airborne for some twenty-three minutes, completing no fewer than ten circuits and flying an estimated distance of twenty-five miles.

Grace was last to fly his aircraft and was taken to the far side of the racecourse, where he took off without incident. In a short while he had attained an altitude of 500 feet as he turned in front of the grandstand. Circling as he climbed above the astonished spectators, he reached an altitude of 2,500 feet, the roar of the Bleriot's engine fading as he became barely visible. Grace estimated that he was able to maintain a speed of 64 mph at this altitude. As he made his descent he was concerned at the number of people who appeared to be scattered over the area in which he was to land. He quickly climbed again, completing another circuit to allow the crowds to disperse. After twenty-two minutes in the air he landed perfectly. At this juncture in the proceedings Moisant decided that he was prepared to take up passengers, the first two being a Capt. Horden of the Royal Engineers and a young French lady. These flights, which lasted no

Inquisitive crowds gather at the scene of C. G. Barnes undignified landing, shortly after he and his treasured Humber Bleriot parted company.

longer than fifteen minutes each, ended a largely successful opening day to the meeting.

The next day, however, the weather changed. Early in the morning high winds whipped across the racecourse, howling mournfully through the marquees which housed the aircraft, keeping the machines in their shelters. The winds gradually strengthened, bringing showers, and by 2 p.m. were gusting at 50 mph, making flying impossible. However, this did not dampen the enthusiasm of the spectators, and the public transport was crowded as on the previous day. Private cars also brought many people to the meeting, and by 3 p.m. the crowds had reached a total of four thousand people.

On the downs opposite the racecourse many were able to view the events without paying the entry fee. This was not popular with the organisers, who promptly erected a high canvas screen along the side of the racecourse near the Royal Oak Inn. Patiently the crowds waited, hoping for the winds to abate. At about 5 p.m. Moisant walked over to the grandstand where he was pestered by local pressmen and suddenly declared, 'I guess I'm going up in just about fifteen minutes without fail.' True to his word, he later appeared from a marquee clad in his overalls and, amidst cheers of encouragement, climbed into his machine. Just as the aircraft lifted off, the engine cut out, forcing him to land hastily but without damage to him or his mount. His second attempt was more successful, climbing away into the sun and fighting against the strong winds.

A local journalist reported this flight and captured the moment well:

The machine flew towards the eye of the sun. The dazzling golden light streamed around it – still on it flew, 'til one could no longer look at it.

Bleriot monoplane flown by Cecil Grace parked at the entrance to the marquee, a temporary hangar and work shop for the aviators. An interesting view of the aircraft's construction and engine mounting.

> By and by it emerged again from the immense radian and was outlined against the reds and golds, the ochres and all the thousand ever-changing colours of the sunset. Beneath were the contrasted greens of the trees, now dark against the light and over them and around them sped the man enthroned in a machine that carried him above the realms of earth.

This brief description of Moisant's flight that afternoon more than a hundred years ago surely captures the grace and freedom of flight. He had flown as far as Lympne Castle over the Hythe canal, returning to land safely. On being questioned about this, Moisant said that at any other meeting it would have been forbidden to fly in such high winds.

That same day at 6 p.m., much to the surprise of the remaining spectators, Grace took off followed shortly by Moisant. The two aviators proceeded to give perhaps the best display of early aerobatics of the entire meeting, circling each other, diving to earth and rising into the air again. They landed half an hour later, ending an exciting day's flying despite poor weather conditions.

The weather was much brighter on the following day, but the wind was still strong and delayed flying again. Spectators, who outnumbered those of the previous day, enjoyed the music played by the Royal Garrison Artillery Band stationed at Dover. Barnes decided to take off but seemed apprehensive, despite the fact that the wind was not so strong. Throwing grass into the air, he muttered to those nearby, 'I am afraid this wind is too much for me.' These words, his last before taking off, were prophetic. Shaking his head, he climbed into the Bleriot and gave the signal to start the engine. The machine climbed extremely slowly – the engine was not running too well – and almost immediately descended into a field on the opposite side of the racecourse by the railway line. With his engine still running, Barnes kept the machine circling on the ground until he managed to take off again. As he tried to return to the starting point the onlookers were alarmed to see him fighting the controls in an attempt to keep the machine flying. The engine was misfiring and the aircraft careered out of control. Some reports say that he could not cut the engine, as he appeared to be trying to land.

Ahead of him was a clump of trees near the Ashford road, so he decided to jump from the aircraft before it hit the trees. Scrambling from his seat, he put one leg out, getting ready to leap. Then tragedy struck. His weight shifting to one side caused the opposite wing to lift suddenly into the air. Catching his foot in some way, the aircraft climbed 30 feet before the pilot fell to the ground. The Bleriot seemed to stagger in the air before turning on its back and landing upside down not 20 yards from the crumpled body of Barnes.

There were screams from the crowds who watched the accident, helpless to offer any assistance. First on the scene were Cadets Allen and Standen of the St John's Ambulance Brigade. Dr Gilbert, attracted by flag signals from ladies of the British Red Cross Society, was driven to the accident in Barnes' car. On examination, he could tell that the unfortunate pilot had a fractured skull. Unconscious, Barnes was taken back to his marquee and examined further by Dr Eastes, Dr Hackney, Dr Gilbert and Dr Etherington. He had also sustained a broken wrist and was taken to the Royal Victoria Hospital, where he recovered consciousness later that evening.

The aircraft was not badly damaged, but the wheels were buckled and the airframe somewhat distorted. Moisant and Grace continued their display despite the unfortunate incident, Moisant taking off almost immediately after the crash. By this time the wind had abated and Grace, climbing steadily, reached an altitude of 3,600 feet. He could hardly be seen by the spectators. Moisant contented himself by taking up passengers before making a hasty descent when his fuel ran out. Later that evening it was announced that Moisant would be flying alone the following day.

Only a thousand people attended the meeting the following day, so there was a last-minute decision to extend the flying. McCulloch, the organiser, stated that the promoters would be making a financial loss on the meeting which was another reason for the extension – they hoped to

'Jonnie' B. Moisant proudly stands by his Bleriot during a pause in the flying; his trusted Mechanic Albert Filieux is seated in the aircraft.

raise extra money. Even in those days, flying was an expensive pastime and costs had to be met. The weather that day was perfect. Barnes's Bleriot had been taken away, and Grace's machine had been taken back to Eastchurch by road. Incredible though it may seem, this machine took off from Eastchurch that same day – a tribute perhaps to Louis Bleriot, the designer and engineer. Moisant continued to give flights, which lasted from 4 until 5 p.m.

Soon after the meeting, Moisant was to carry out a series of long flights across America, the longest being between New York and St Louis. The following year he competed for the *Daily Mail*'s £10,000 prize, to be won by the pilot who could complete a 1,000-mile 'cross country flight'. An inventor, Moisant had also constructed a monoplane called the Metallique, but admitted that it was too fast an aircraft for learning to fly on. However, the construction had eliminated many wires, which was a step forward in aviation at that time. The possibility of creating a permanent airfield at the Folkestone racecourse was suggested soon after the flying event, but as this would have entailed many trees being cut down and permanent hangars being constructed, the proposal was sadly abandoned.

Later that year, Cecil Grace entered for the £4,000 Baron de Forest prize, offered to a British pilot flying a British machine the furthest distance into continental Europe in a straight line from anywhere in England. Tom Sopwith, the famous aircraft designer and aviator, took off from Eastchurch, followed shortly afterwards by Grace. Flying a Short Farman aircraft at a speed of 60 mph, Grace reached Dover only to find strong winds and thick mist over the Channel, so landed at Swingate Downs. He was not alone – other competitors also waited for clear weather. Four days later, he flew on to Les Baraques, knowing that he could not beat Sopwith. The weather closed in and, determined to fly back to Dover to start another attempt as only nine days were left before the competition ended, he went to see the captain of the SS *Pas de Calais* and suggested he used the ship's smoke as a guide to cross the Channel. Unfortunately the ship sailed late and Grace flew out into the fog alone. The crew of the North Goodwin lightship heard him passing overhead and he was seen by fishermen near the East Goodwin. His goggles and cap were picked up two weeks later on the beach at Mariakerke, Belgium. They were later identified as his by G. C. Golmore, a close friend. Grace was never seen again.

Moisant was killed on the last day of 1910, when his Bleriot stalled during the Michelin International Cup in America. Perhaps Barnes remembered the flying meeting at Westenhanger. In 1914, Lympne and the Romney Marsh area were to play a major role in the First World War.

CHAPTER 2

Establishment of the airfield and the Royal Flying Corps; the railway from Westenhanger; early civil aviation

Following an inspection of the site in October 1915, Lympne was selected for the location of the Machine Gun School, previously at Dover (Swingate Downs) with its HQ at Dymchurch, by officers of 6th Wing Royal Flying Corps (RFC) and the Commander of the Royal Engineers at Dover. The location was chosen as being the driest area available, and also owing to the difficulties of drainage, which the Army engineers informed the RFC would be very hard to overcome if the camp was sited nearer the road. In fact, eleven wooden aircraft workshops were sited close to Aldington Road, almost opposite The County Members public house. Quarters were located on the allotment site over the road, opposite the hangars, in front of April Cottage. The Women's Service was situated in the field between April Cottage and the cliff fir trees. A tin hut, located on the quarry site, was used as a guard room. By 1916, additional land to the east was requisitioned when it was decided that Lympne should become a night Emergency Landing Ground (ELG) for Home Defence purposes. This later became the main area of the aerodrome, incorporating a tented camp on the western edge of Lympne village.

In March 1916, the War Office chose a better site to the north-west of the village between Otterpool Wood (now Harringe Brooks Wood) and the lane to Otterpool Manor. Up until the First World War, the land eventually covered by the airfield belonged partly to Mr Champney, who lived in Otterpool Lane, and partly to Mr Nichols of the Bellevue Estate, which became the Lympne Country Club. The remaining land belonged to Thomas Jones of Holly Bush Farm, which was then part of Lympne Castle Farm, later to become Lympne Hall.

On 19 March, the Home Defence organisation was tested when the Germans launched an aerial attack on the South East. Four Friedrichshafen FF33bs, one Hansa-Brandenburg and a Gotha-Ursinus bombed Dover, Deal and Ramsgate, killing fourteen people and injuring twenty-six. Thirty sorties were flown from Dover, Eastchurch, Isle of Grain and Westgate. This was the biggest 'hit and run' raid up to this date. The German *Flieger-Abteilung* believed that raids at the weekends were less likely to be interfered with by the RNAS and RFC. At the time, orders were given by the Air Board to southern-based training squadrons and units to release aircraft for Home Defence.

During the same raid, No. 8 AAP dispatched several aircraft from Lympne airfield, including Lt D. Armstrong, flying Sopwith Pup B1731, and R.E.8s flown by 2nd Lt S. Crosfield in A3700, 2nd Lt E. Carpenter, and 2nd Lt C. A. Rogers in A4711, aided by 2nd Lt H. D. Crompton flying A4713, without any attacks on enemy aircraft being recorded.

It was no surprise to the RFC at Lympne when an F.E.2b flown by 2nd Lt R. Collis and Flt Sgt A. C. Emery of the Aircraft Acceptance Park (AAP) at Lympne were ordered to take to the air. Unfortunately, despite their enthusiasm, not one enemy aircraft was located. Worse still, they had to land in France. By the end of June 1916, the Home Defence Group was allocated S.E.5s and Sopwith Pup aircraft, both being popular with those who flew them. It was decided that the two best aircraft available at Lympne would be held back until later, during evening raids, although they were too far away to defend London.

However, on 13 July 1916, orders were received at Lympne to assist with daylight raids along with other training units, such as No. 2 AAP at nearby Wye. Aircraft at Lympne were held in reserve, awaiting orders. At 6.40 p.m. Lt G. W. Gathergood, a pilot serving with the AAP, took off to join in the hunt for Gotha bombers of *Kagohl 3*. Turning south to avoid London, covered by fog and cloud, the German aircraft flew over Kent, dropping their bombs on Lympne. The main attack concentrated on Folkestone and Shorncliffe Army Camp. Meanwhile Lt Gathergood, flying DH.5 B347, landed back at Lympne at 7.50 p.m. Nearby Hythe became No. 1 (Auxiliary) School of Air Gunnery, and part of this unit operated from Lympne as the Advanced Air Firing School.

No. 8 (Lympne) AAP was formed on 1 September 1917 from the existing AAP unit at Lympne. Its role was to ferry aircraft over to France, modifying aircraft required by the HQ expedition. Some forty aircraft a month would be flown to France, until the AAP unit at Hawkinge was fully operational. Pilots ferrying aircraft to the front in France would land at Lympne to receive final instructions. They would then fly their allotted aircraft across the Channel to No. 1 Aircraft for onward delivery. The ferry pilots would

Christmas was always celebrated in style, in 1916 a party was arranged for OR's (Other Ranks) in their mess hut, under the watchful eye of Senior NCO's and Officers. At the far end on the wall a poster reads '*Happy Xmas to you all – but not 'Bill'*', a reference to Kaiser Wilhelm.

Thought to be a photograph taken at Lympne, airmen of the RFC and women of the WRAF on parade on 31 May 1918. Women serving with the RNAS or RFC were given the option to transfer to the WRAF, when the RAF was formed on 1 April 1918.

be picked up at St Omer by an old Handley Page aircraft that would stagger back to Lympne with twenty-five or more pilots crammed into the fuselage, where they would return by train or car to their own pools.

As early as November 1916, the idea of such a unit was discussed with a view to eliminating the waste of time that ensued when the weather was unfavourable to the supply of aircraft, especially during the winter months. It was proposed to obtain machines from the manufacturer and construct them at Lympne. Once completed, they would be flown direct to France, thus ensuring the supply of aircraft to the Expeditionary Force with the least possible delay. In order to do this, erecting sections were required. It was proposed to start with one section, plus a store and an accounting sub-section. The newly formed unit would deal with fifty aircraft a month; when this number was exceeded another section would be formed. The unit took charge of large numbers of RFC machines destined for France, which, following final mechanical checks and refuelling, took off to join similar units on the Continent. To assist navigation, two large crosses had been cut into the chalk cliffs at Folkestone and near Cap Gris Nez – a great help to pilots crossing the English Channel.

A railway line had been constructed for the purpose of bringing supplies and aircraft parts up to the airfield at Lympne. The route of the spur line passed over the A20 road close to Elm Farm, curving south from between the footbridge and loading dock, then skirting the east boundary of the racecourse, terminating at an east–west siding and head-shunt on the eastern side of the engineering site, opposite The County Members public house. The branch was built by or under the direction of Royal Engineers from Longmoor. The only locomotive permitted on the line was an SECR P Class 0-6-0T locomotive based at Ashford. The line was for goods traffic, loads usually being disassembled aircraft, and trains were limited to ten wagons. In 1922, the railway track was taken out of use and lifted. However, the following advertisement appeared in the *Surplus* on 1 January 1921: 'Wagons for sale – twelve 2 ft gauge wagons at Lympne Aerodrome.' These wagons were most probably used to shift spoil in construction work. No narrow-gauge locomotives are known to have operated at this site. Today, there is no evidence of the line's existence to be found, apart from on a layout of the airfield, drafted for the purpose of land requisition, in files at the National Archives.

By December 1916, the planned development of a School of Aerial Gunnery at Loch Doon was behind schedule. At this time Lympne airfield was overcrowded and the billets obtainable locally were unsuitable for the needs of the RFC, so it was decided that Lympne Castle should be taken over by them. It was being used as a convalescent home for Canadian servicemen, but in fact there were few billeted at the castle and it was

Conditions at Lympne proved difficult during the winter of 1916–17. In snow mechanics and fitters worked on many types of aircraft of the period in canvas hangars. Just visible to the right is an F.E.2b, possibly one handled by No.8 (AAP).

Further evidence of the airfield's expansion during 1915–1918 are these wooden huts, many constructed by local builders, one of which being William Harbrow Ltd. based at St Mary Gray, who it is known, worked at Lympne, Detling, Bekesbourne and Throwley and Eastchurch airfields.

agreed that they should be sent elsewhere. Undoubtedly, Lympne was of importance to the RFC, with both No. 1 (Auxiliary) School of Aerial Gunnery and No. 8 Air Acceptance Park sharing the site.

The expansion of the airfield at Lympne in 1916 included the erection of Bessonneau hangars, a structure covered in canvas, technical buildings and workshops, while the officers' mess was established at Lympne Castle. The airmen's tents had been replaced by wooden huts situated on allotment sites over the road from the main airfield – not the best way of winning over the local residents in a quiet village! By late 1916, the Machine Gun School was re-formed as the School of Aerial Gunnery, Hythe. The airfield at this stage was then home to F.E.8, F.E.2b, Armstrong Whitworth F.K.8, R.E.8 and Sopwith Camel aircraft.

On 4 March 1917, an unusual aircraft visited Lympne – the Bristol M1B monoplane, developed by the company for the RFC in response to the need for properly armed fighting scouts. This aircraft, A1539, had previously been sent to France for evaluation by operational pilots, but Gen. Trenchard was not impressed with the type. It returned to England and after remaining at Lympne for two days was allotted to No. 50 Squadron at Bekesbourne for Home Defence purposes.

Daylight raids by the Germans increased and on 25 May 1917, when Lt Gathergood was again airborne in DH.5 B347 of No. 8 AAP, the German force of Gotha bombers dropped bombs on Lympne during an attack on Folkestone, causing some damage to the incomplete hangars under construction for No. 8 AAP and destroying aircraft. At the beginning of June, DH.4 B3955 left the De Havilland factory for Yeovil and was allotted to No. 8 AAP, unfortunately crashing at Lympne on arrival.

A daylight raid on London took place on 13 June 1917, flown by twenty Gothas, eighteen of which found their target. Ninety-four sorties were flown that day. At 11.05 a.m. six aircraft of No. 8 AAP took off in the search of the attacking force but no combat was reported. During this raid 162 people were killed and 432 injured, including 43 children. Following a public outcry, the War Cabinet met, as a result of which it was decided to patrol air space over both sides of the Dover Strait. Very much against his wishes, Gen. Haig was ordered to send one squadron to Calais and another was to come home from France. No. 66 Squadron went to Calais and No. 56 Squadron were moved from France to Bekesbourne, an airfield not many miles from Lympne. Pilots and ground crew were delighted to be returning home.

Accordingly, No. 56 Squadron took off from Estrée-Blanche early in the morning of 21 June 1917. Forming an arrowhead formation, sixteen S.E.5s headed for England, crossing the Channel without any problems or loss of aircraft. First stop was Lympne, where they were to await a

Specifically constructed for No. 8 Air Acceptance Park in 1917, this is the first of three pairs of Belfast Hangars, so named because of its wooden trusses supporting the roof. They were 80 feet long and situated on the south-west boundary of the airfield. All nine remained in use until 18 August 1940 when, so badly damaged by enemy bombing, they had to demolished.

A mechanic fits a Vickers gun onto the 'scarf ring' behind the rear cockpit of a DH.9, while two other airmen attend to the aircraft. This aircraft is thought to be D607 or D609, both of which were handled by No. 8 AAP in 1917.

telephone call informing aircrew that the squadron's ground crew had arrived at Bekesbourne, near Canterbury. As the S.E.5s started to land, Capt. L. M. Barlow MC lined up A4858 but bungled the landing and crashed on the airfield at Lympne, with the words of the squadron's CO, Maj. R. G. Blomfield, ringing in his ears – 'I shall sack anyone who makes a bad landing at Lympne.'

Barlow climbed from his damaged aircraft uninjured. He was a popular and experienced pilot and a valuable member of the squadron, and thus nothing was said about the incident. As the flight had gone well and had taken only one hour and five minutes, everyone except Barlow was pleased, even more so when were given a full English breakfast. At 11 a.m. the same day, the squadron took off from Lympne for their new base. Barlow was driven to Bekesbourne, and despite his indignation at crashing, was pleased to be home. Sadly he was later killed in a flying accident at Martlesham Heath.

Harwich and Felixstowe were targeted on 4 July 1917, and aircraft of No. 66 Squadron, based at Calais, landed at Lympne following a futile search for the enemy between Dunkirk and North Hinder lightship. Having been airborne for two hours, with increasingly poor flying conditions and cloud, they had to abort the search and on landing at Lympne the pilots were informed that the German aircraft had already returned to their base in Belgium. Eight sorties were flown by No. 8 AAP during an attack by Gotha bombers on London that took place on 7 July 1917. Another occurred on 12 August, when nine aircraft were airborne during a daylight raid on Southend, which was the last time the AAP unit was on Home Defence duties. Sopwith Camel F.1 B2323, having been delivered to No. 4 AAP at Lincoln intended for the Expeditionary Force, was diverted to No. 8 AAP on 20 August 1917. During the flight the pilot found himself short of fuel and with a cracked propeller. Realising he could not reach Lympne, he landed safely in fields at New Romney, and following refuelling and with a new propeller, reached Lympne without further incident.

Being the ideal location for the dispatch of aircraft to France, Lympne was also the stepping-off point for squadrons en route to the Western Front. One such was 69 (RAAF) Australian unit, which arrived at Lympne on 24 August 1917, having previously been based at South Carlton. It remained at Lympne, preparing its R.E.8s and training until 9 September, when it moved to St Omer. Originally known as 3 Squadron RAAF, to avoid confusion with the British 3 Squadron RFC, it was known to the British military as 69 Squadron RFC. No. 64 Squadron RFC, also in transit at Lympne, arrived on 14 October 1917 and flew to France the following day. The squadron had formed at Sedgeford on 1 August 1916 as a training unit with FE2bs and Farmans, but in June 1917 received

An F.E.2b serial No. B453 built by Ransome, Sims & Jeffries of Ipswich who supplied 100 aircraft of this type to the RFC. Although slow and cumbersome the FE2b proved itself in France and was a match for the German Fokker monoplane.

fighter types in preparation for operations in France. In October 1917, the squadron moved to the Western Front for fighter patrol and ground attack duties for the rest of the war. In February 1919, it returned to the UK and disbanded on 31 December 1919.

During a routine delivery flight on 25 September 1917, from No. 8 AAP Lympne to a unit of the Expeditionary Force, DH.4 A7551 flown by 2nd Lt F. G. Litchfield and 2nd Lt H. Nunn stalled the aircraft and crashed in a field at Wilmington near Dartford. Litchfield was killed instantly and Nunn injured. In August 1917, the pilot had flown RE8 A4424 from Lympne in an effort to intercept Gotha raiders.

At 9.45 a.m. on 29 September 1917, 2nd Lt C. H. Drew took off from Lympne to ferry Sopwith Camel B5153 to St Omer. He flew into heavy fog over the Channel and decided to turn back, but at that moment a rigging wire broke. He limped back to Lympne and on landing found that the wing was nearly off. When riggers checked the wing it was discovered that it had not been secured correctly; it was a miracle that the aircraft had not ditched in the sea.

Some aircraft at No. 7 (Kenley) AAP, a sister unit to that at Lympne, would fly aircraft to Lympne for eventual delivery to France. Corporal Clerk H. M. Reay with the RAC wrote:

The usual procedure was to fly aircraft to Lympne and then onto to France. Occasionally one would come down adrift en-route to the coast

An unusual visitor to Lympne a captured German Albatros D.V given British marking G56, at Lympne in 1917. A gift for the RFC, and which probably was later flown to other units for evaluation by pilots and engineers. Note the camera on a tripod to the right of the aircraft.

and the pilot had to phone in and ask us to send down a Crossley Tender to pick it up from where he had force-landed.

On 1 March 1918, No. 98 Squadron moved to Lympne under command of Maj. H. MacD. O'Malley RFC. Transport left Old Sarum on 19 March 1918, arriving on the 23rd. The following day they were moved over to France, disembarking at Le Havre, spending a night at Rouen before returning to Le Havre the next morning and remaining there for three days. On 25 March, the aircraft flew back to Lympne and, despite several accidents, the squadron had eighteen aircraft left at Lympne, the ground crews being brought back on the 28th to join the squadron at Lympne. However, on 1 April 1918, the birthday of the Royal Air Force, they moved to St Omer. Two days later, the squadron flew to Clairmarais, an airfield only a few miles away and was soon replaced by the day and night Bombing Observation School, equipped with DH.4, DH.9 and DH.9A aircraft, all single engine bombers. A new influx of observers arrived on 25 February, mostly ex-cavalry from the Lancers, Hussars and Yeomanry, and soon the squadron had eighteen aircraft complete with their guns.

By the time No. 50 Squadron (Home Defence) and No. 53 Wing arrived at Lympne in 1918, the airfield covered some 175 acres and had been

An R.E.8 came to grief on the airfield at Lympne during a test flight, the fate of the pilots unknown but it was most probably salvaged and later scrapped. Christened by the RFC in cockney rhyme, as the 'harry tate'. Used for Reconnaissance it proved unpopular with pilots and ground crew alike.

designated as a first class landing strip, its length being 3,000 feet. No. 50 Squadron, which had been based at Bekesbourne in 1918 and was converting from the S.E.5a to the Sopwith Camel fighter, used Lympne as an emergency landing ground, as did other Home Defence units. It is known from his log book that Capt. W. W. Wakefield, later to become known as Lord Wakefield of Kendal and a director of Skyways Coach Air Ltd, flew with the Sopwith Camel squadron from Lympne at this time. In fact he flew Camel F.1 E1428, although it would appear from records that he joined the Royal Naval Air Service and the first Camel he flew was No. 8809, in which he half sank on the River Medway on 19 September 1918, during tests on air bags.

It is interesting to note that an R.E.8, F3556, delivered to the RAF on 25 October 1918, survived the war. Test flown by Lt Halstead for thirty minutes, it was sent to No. 1 AAP at Coventry and later dispatched to France, arriving on 11 November 1918. As hostilities had just ceased it was sent back, still crated, and went into store at RAF Tadcaster before being transferred to RAF Cardington. The aircraft remained in its crate until its transfer to the Imperial War Museum, and it went on display at Crystal Palace during 1920. In 1974, F3556 was moved to Duxford for its first thorough restoration, which occupied most of the latter half of the 1970s. Following its second restoration, completed in 2006, the aircraft is now on display at Duxford's Airspace feature.

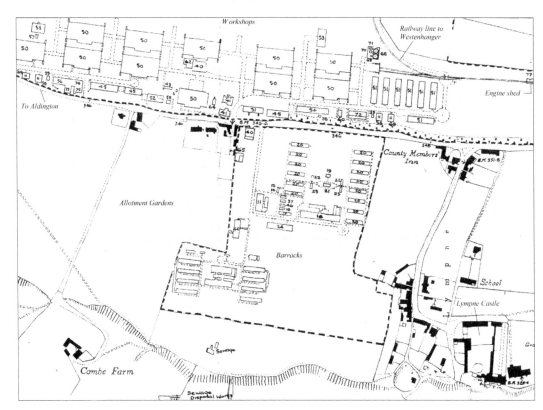

Lympne airfield in 1921, showing Main Workshops and Aircraft Repair Sheds, to the right the railway line from Westenhanger is shown as it terminates opposite the County Members public house.

With the continuing commitment of work by No. 8 AAP, the proposed closure of Lympne was delayed and plans for extending the airfield to the north-east were being considered. On 25 March 1918, twelve aircraft left Old Sarum for Lympne. During the flight one aircraft crashed and was destroyed by fire, killing the pilot 2nd Lt R. C. Bark, who died of his injuries three days later. The unfortunate passenger, a fitter, Cpl L. N. Witley, was burnt to death. Another aircraft crashed at Lympne, flown by 2nd Lt F. Smethurst. The following day, five more machines left for Lympne, and the remaining aircraft took off on the 27 March.

On 1 April 1918, eighteen aircraft left Lympne for St Omer. Of these, only one crashed, piloted by 2nd Lt E. F. Stein, his fate unknown. DH.9 D1664 was due to fly to the Expeditionary Force in France from Dover but the flight was cancelled, and D1664 was flown to Lympne, where it crashed on 13 April 1918. Chief Mechanic A. H. Reffell of Central Dispatch Pool, based at Hendon, flew DH.9 D5576 from No 218 Squadron at Dover to France via Lympne. However, on 25 May 1918, the aircraft's tailplane failed on approach to the airfield and it crashed; thankfully the pilot was not seriously injured.

Lt Henry Shaw joined No. 8 AAP at Lympne in April 1918. His main duties were that of test flying aircraft to be dispatched to France and other locations. His first flight was on 7 April when he flew an S.E.5a, C6412, on a routine test flight during which one of the engines valves broke, but he returned to Lympne and landed safely. On another occasion he was flying DH.9 D2151 to Kenley when a connection rod broke, smashing the engine. This time the engine caught fire and he made a hasty landing at Penshurst, but was uninjured. On 13 August 1918, Lt Shaw was ferrying eight passengers to Lympne in a Handley Page O/400, D9699, designed as a bomber. This particular machine had been fitted out with sixteen forward-facing seats and the internal bomb racks had been removed. Returning to Lympne, both engines stopped through lack of fuel and the large biplane struck a fence, tearing away the undercarriage and damaging the lower port wing. Despite the damage, all the passengers and the pilot got out of the aircraft safely.

As a pilot of No. 8 AAP, Lt Shaw flew many types of aircraft on test flights and ferried passengers between Lympne and Marquise, France. However, on 11 November 1918, he was given the opportunity to fly one of Germany's most successful aircraft, a Fokker biplane that had been captured in France and brought back to England. After flying around for thirty minutes and reaching a height of 4,000 feet he landed back at Lympne. The entry in his log book reads, 'My first trip in a Fokker biplane – a very fine machine.' However, this was not the only German aircraft flown by pilots of No. 8 AAP. On 16 February 1918, Lt Drew test flew a Rumpler from Lympne and was impressed by its performance. After being evaluated by pilots and engineers, some of these captured German aircraft were put on public display throughout England.

On 22 May 1918, No. 85 Squadron arrived from Hounslow, Middlesex, with its S.E.5a aircraft. Following final checks on the aircraft and refuelling, it took off the same day for Marquise in France where it joined the rest of the squadron. At about this time in 1918, the modified Handley Page O/400s were used to ferry personnel between Marquise and Lympne. The massive biplane aircraft had been originally designed as a bomber, the idea being to attack Berlin, but the war ended before they could be used in this role.

The last RFC Squadron destined for France had arrived at Lympne from Netheravon on 3 August 1918. The spectacle of the unit's Handley Page O/400 twin-engine bombers attracted a crowd of airmen as the aircraft gracefully touched down on the grass airstrip at Lympne. Their stay was brief: the following morning, with refuelling and final maintenance completed, they took off bound for Le Bourget, later moving to Xaffevillers where they operated until 17 November 1918.

Following the Armistice on 11 November 1918, Lympne's role in the First World War ended, but it remained an active airfield. As some squadrons and their aircraft returned home to an uncertain future, others remained or arrived at Lympne.

No. 108 Squadron, which arrived at Lympne on 16 February 1919, was disbanded on 3 July 1919, and No. 120 Squadron, which had been flying air mail services between Hawkinge and Maisonelle in France in the unit's DH.9 aircraft, moved to Lympne on 17 July 1919. However, as the need for such a service was infrequent by this time, mail was being handled by civilian aircraft and a detachment moved back to Hawkinge on 2 August 1919.

At RAF Hawkinge more thought had been given to the general layout of the airfield, which helped newly arrived airmen find their way around various buildings occupied by their squadron or unit. This was not so at Lympne, where the buildings were spread out and airmen often used transport to move quickly between the various buildings designated to the squadron they were attached to. In fact, newly arrived airmen often turned up at another squadron's workshops or stores. However, the spirit of co-operation between officers and other ranks overcame the problems and 120 Squadron soon settled in at Lympne.

Engaged on a new role, airmen of No. 120 Squadron were keenly interested in their work, as many hoped to remain in the forces. They were using every effort to make the experiment a success. Having been GHQ in France, they felt entirely separate from the others at Lympne – almost superior to them. At Hawkinge every officer and airman knew one another, whilst at Lympne there were many new faces and those of No. 120 Squadron resented their individuality. Rowdy pilots poured into the quiet and sedate little mess at Lympne Castle and took over, while NCOs and other ranks took over the hangars, stores and offices.

On 17 July 1919, on the first air mail flight, Lt Murphy's initiation into the new service almost cost him his life. He was carrying mails across from Lympne to Marquise, for No. 110 Squadron to fly to Cologne. Having left the English coast in poor weather, and with no sight of the French coast, he realised his compass was not working. With no land or ships visible, Murphy had no idea whether he was flying down the Channel or up into the North Sea. At last he found a ship and circled around it, firing off red rockets before coming down on the water some distance ahead of the vessel. The lower wings of his DH.9 were badly damaged and the aircraft started to sink, so he made his way to the aircraft's tail.

By the time the vessel, a Dutch tug, came alongside he had moved over to the top-plane, while his mailbags were under water. Clambering aboard

Another captured German aircraft at Lympne, a Fokker D.VII in German markings on the, an airman stands by the port wing. Being close to France Lympne would have been the ideal place for collection of such aircraft. This type contributed to the German efforts to regain control of the skies and proved a worthy opponent.

Perhaps one of the most successful fighters of the period was the Sopwith Camel, this one serial No. N6336 served at Biggin Hill, and Isle of Grain. This aircraft was possibly at Lympne in September 1917 for modification and repair and had previously been flown by Captain H. B. R. Powell.

No. 8 Aircraft Acceptance Park during 1917 was assigned large numbers of aircraft destined for France. At Lympne they were tested and refuelled, some being assembled having arrived on the airfield on the railway which operated from Westenhanger.

the tug, the sailors managed to recover eight of the nine mailbags with gaffs before DH.9 1206 sank below the waves. They were twelve miles off the Dutch coast and headed for Brunsbüttelkoog in Germany. On arrival, the captain would not let Murphy leave his boat without paying a reasonable sum of money for his services. As there was no British Consul available, the pilot wrote out a cheque which on his return to Lympne he could cancel. After two days, and with great difficulty, he finally obtained transport for himself and the remaining eight mailbags and was on his way to Cologne. Unfortunately, the German customs officials demanded 1,000 marks from the British postal services in the city; this was paid, although the sum was later recovered in a diplomatic manner.

It was often the case that pilots were unable to make the coast when crossing the Channel. On one occasion, Lt Ratten had just reached the sands at Zeebrugge. He had a high ranking officer as his passenger and on take-off had run out of sand and tipped onto the aircraft's nose. The propeller was stopped but no damage was done. However, his passenger had great problems getting out of the DH.9, cursing his luck as he climbed down. On another occasion, when returning from a postal delivery at Marquise in DH.9 9026, Lt Pearce-Gervis was alarmed at a terrific noise and vibration coming from the engine when he opened the throttle heading for the French coast again. He turned off the engine in fear of it shaking itself loose from its bearings. He was losing height rapidly and there was no chance of landing at Wissant sands, which were now visible. Seeing the tide was out, he tried to reach the sand at Gris Nez but crashed on rocks. The aircraft was a complete write-off, but fortunately the pilot was uninjured. It was felt that if wirelesses had been fitted to the DH.9s, it would have saved delays with mail delivery and possibly lives. Much to the surprise of everyone on the squadron, orders arrived to say that a maintenance section would be established at Lympne to fit all aircraft with a wireless.

In 1919, Lympne remained the control station for the 86th Wing machines en route to and from France. The airfield had expanded by then and was well established, comprising three twin hangars with sliding doors each 170 feet by 100 feet, plus ten sheds which measured 170 feet by 80 feet, and one shed 160 feet by 80 feet. A large barrack area had also been established, as well as various workshops, stores, a bath house and even a gymnasium.

On 12 August 1919, orders arrived from HQ Cologne to the effect that No. 120 Squadron were to be disbanded under GOC South Eastern Area. All air mail would be abandoned on 31 August 1919, and Nos 18 and

Pilots of No. 120 Squadron in 1919, by one of their DH.9 which they flew to France delivering mail to the Western Front. Two of the officers are already wearing the new RAF cap which was introduced following the formation of the RAF on 18 April 1918.

110 Squadrons took over the remaining days as No. 120 Squadron were needed to ferry aircraft back from France. Eventually No. 110 Squadron took on the task. Air Transport & Travel Ltd, which operated a civilian version of a DH.9A aircraft, G-EAHF, took over the mail flights to France until August 1920. It was not unusual for passengers to be flown back to Lympne for a single fare of £3.

At the end of the First World War, both Lympne and Hawkinge had become important airfields in the south-east of England. The Air Ministry was in favour of closing one site, as both were, after all, only a few miles apart and the need for the continuation of these excellent airfields had receded. However, it was finally decided that both should be kept open, and by good fortune civil aviation was permitted to use Lympne.

Following a successful stay at Amsterdam, at the first air traffic exhibition of joy-riding in August 1919, which detained Blackburn Argosy G-EAIT, operated by the North Sea Aerial Navigation Co. at the aerodrome, the aircraft took part in starting, climbing and short-landing competitions – a remarkable achievement for a large twin-engine biplane. The profits made by these flights encouraged the company to dispatch a second aircraft, G-EAIU, to Amsterdam, flown by Capt. S. J. Wooley out via Hounslow and Lympne on 28 August 1919. The exhibition organisers presented Wooley with a gold watch, despite G-EAIU coming last in the air circuit race over Holland for commercial aircraft. With a week left before the air traffic exhibition closed, Capt. Wooley, Capt. R. W. Kenworthy and Maj. Veale in G-EAKQ had amassed 1,400 hours of fare-paying passenger flights and given many free rides without incident. The three aircraft were to return to Brough. On the way, Kenworthy flew G-EAIT from Amsterdam to Lympne in three hours, and from Hounslow to Brough in two hours.

The final decision by the Air Ministry to retain Lympne airfield was clinched by the North Sea & General Transport Service Ltd, which wanted to operate Blackburn Kangaroos carrying cargo between Leeds and Amsterdam. The first operation, a charter flight for Heatons (Leeds) Ltd, took place on 5 March 1920, to beat a dock strike in the Netherlands. The crew of Blackburn Argosy G-EAKQ consisted of R. W. Kenworthy as pilot and T. Bancroft as engineer. They left Brough at 12.30 p.m. and landed at Lympne the following day at 5 p.m., arriving at Amsterdam at 10.30 the next morning. An unusual load of over 1,000 lb of ladies' raincoats and garments made of West Riding cloth was hurried through Dutch customs and onto lorries. However, faced with hostile strikers, Kenworthy had to fly his aircraft to Soesterberg Aerodrome for military protection before a return flight on 13 March. Their cargo on this occasion was 1,200 lb of German aniline dyes for the Bradford Dyers' Association. Sadly the long

A Sergeant checks mail bags being loaded into a waiting DH.9 of No.120 Squadron bound for France. The squadron although formed at Lympne, also flew services from Hawkinge to Maisoncelles in November 1918. Its original role was that of a bomber squadron.

detour to customs aerodromes in the south delayed operations and the scheme was a failure financially.

On 19 September 1919, No. 83 Squadron, which had been based at Hawkinge since 19 February 1919 acting as cadre, moved to Lympne, but was moved on to Croydon later that year, on 19 October, only to be disbanded on the last day of 1919, a casualty of disarmament. In fact, its role was night bombing and reconnaissance, flying the F.E.2b, and it had previously been based at Cerny in France before returning to England. In France the squadron took part in a raid to destroy a large naval gun that had been shelling towns in the back areas on the Arras front.

Likewise No. 102 Squadron returned from Cerny at the end of March 1919 and was also based at Lympne until July 1919 when it was disbanded. The squadron also flew the F.E.2b, acting as cadre, another term for surplus to requirements, or a group of officers or NCOs around whom a unit is formed, or training staff. Also joining the units based at Lympne at this time was No. 108 Squadron, which was to have joined forces with No. 120 Squadron. However, as it turned out, by the time their F.E.2ds arrived at Lympne, No. 120 Squadron had been sent to Hawkinge to act as a postal service to France, but returned to Lympne for the same purpose as described earlier. No. 108 Squadron were also disbanded in July 1919. However, all three squadrons were to be re-formed during the late 1930s as part of the RAF's expansion before the Second World War.

It was fortuitous that Lympne airfield was aided by Philip Albert Gustave David Sassoon, born in 1888, a descendant of two Jewish families. His mother was a de Rothschild; his father, Sir Edward Sassoon, was a close friend of King Edward VII and was a highly respected politician. Born into such a wealthy family, it was natural that he would be educated at Eton and Christ Church College, Oxford. It was his father's wish that he enter politics and the third baronet, Sir Philip Sassoon, became MP for the Hythe Division of Kent. When war came in 1914, he was a lieutenant in the East Kent Yeomanry and was private secretary to Sir Douglas Haig, the Commander-in-Chief of the British Army. It was not until March 1919 that Sir Philip was demobilised, and having inherited millions of pounds, he was a wealthy bachelor.

Despite owning properties such as Trent Park, Shorncliffe Lodge, and a shooting lodge in Scotland to name but three estates, he bought a site to the west of Lympne Castle. Under Sir Philip's direction, the architect Philip Armstrong Tilden designed his new home, Port Lympne, containing a hundred rooms, fountains, and a beautiful Moorish patio. In the spring of 1920 he invited Lloyd George to Port Lympne for the first peace conference. Being fluent in French was a great asset to the proceedings, and he soon gained not only the respect of the delegates present but also admiration for his new home.

Unfortunately, he was considered remote from the locals and felt to be sensitive and reserved, out of touch with the general public. During the 1920s and 1930s, many rich and famous people visited Port Lympne and enjoyed Sir Philip's hospitality, including the Prince of Wales and Mrs Simpson, HM Queen Mary, Noel Coward, Winston Churchill, Lord Beaverbrook, Charlie Chaplin and many others. By then, Sir Philip was the Under Secretary of State for Air and was privileged to be Honorary Air Commodore of No. 601 (County of London) Squadron RAuxAF (Royal Auxiliary Air Force).

Perhaps one of the most charismatic and controversial visitors to Lympne in the 1930s was T. E. Lawrence, better known as 'Lawrence of Arabia'. After his adventures in the Middle East, he joined the RAF in 1922, becoming a leading aircraftman (LAC) following an interview with none other than W. E. Johns, author of the Biggles books. Johns rejected his application at first, correctly believing he was joining under the false name of John Hume Ross. However, Capt. Johns was ordered to accept his application. Lawrence later wrote the book *The Mint* using his false name but writing the foreword of the book as T. E. Lawrence, the subject being

An Avro 504K registration G-AAEM, similar to Sir Philip Sassoon's Avro 504 G-AENN, both these aircraft flew from Lympne airfield.

his life at an RAF depot in 1922. In fact, he went on to be a leading light in the development of RAF air sea rescue launches. Sir Philip had made friends with LAC Shaw (the other name used by 'Lawrence of Arabia') when he was serving with No. 60 Squadron. At the time, Sir Philip was flying to India with the RAF on a survey for the Imperial Airways passenger service.

It is interesting to note that on 13 April 1920, Sir Philip Sassoon was probably the first private owner of Avro 504 G-EANN, in which he commuted regularly from his home at Lympne. His purchase of an Avro for getting about, particularly between London and Lympne, was the first of its kind. It took seventy minutes to reach Lympne by air as opposed to ninety minutes by train. Later Sir Philip was involved in the debate about the Air Ministry's outdated policies and did much to influence important changes, especially with war in Europe seeming inevitable. Towards the end of the 1930s, his visits to Port Lympne were less frequent and his final visit was in April 1939. Complaining of not feeling well, he returned to London where he died at Park Lane on 3 June 1939 and was cremated the following day. Members of No. 601 Squadron scattered his ashes in the grounds of Trent Park, his ancestral home in Hertfordshire.

Early in 1920, night landing arrangements at Lympne were in force. Every evening for two hours after sunset two searchlights were placed about fifty yards apart on the leeward side of the area most suitable for landing. The beams of light were directed upwind, illuminating the landing area and converging at a point sixty yards from a line joining the two lights. Aircraft would glide in over this line, landing as near to it as possible and in the lit area. Pilots wishing to land at Lympne later in the evening advised the Civil Aviation Traffic Office (CATO) direct of the intended time of arrival beforehand.

Sgt Maj. Sydney John Dupe had served in both the RAF and Army. On leaving the RAF in 1919 he was a carpenter, but in 1920 he was employed at Lympne by CATO. He had previously married Clara Annie Brigden, and they had four sons and three daughters. One of the girls married Arthur Geal who worked at Lympne airfield as air traffic foreman and both families lived in two cedar wood bungalows situated just inside the main gate of the airfield, No. 1A being the home of the Dupe family. Arthur Geal and his wife moved into the bungalow next door with their daughter Maisie and two sons Norman and Geoffrey. Maisie was born at the airfield in 1931. John Dupe's role at Lympne was varied, including responsibility for the airfield's security, and he appears in many photographs taken during his time at the site.

Another innovation was the introduction of radio telephony stations at Hounslow and Lympne, which by 1920 were working on a 900-metre wavelength. At the time it was thought that most of the public did not appreciate that a wireless telephone could be so efficient that aircraft crossing the Channel could be heard speaking with the receiver lying on the table at a London airfield. As a temporary and emergency measure to assist the aircraft to locate their destination after dusk, the Air Ministry arranged for vertical searchlight beams to be projected from the following airfields about dusk until all service machines arrived – Hounslow: one vertical beam; Kenley: two vertical beams; Lympne: three vertical beams arranged in a triangle.

Lympne airfield passed into the control of D. A. Davis DFC, as a civilian customs airfield under the control of the RAF. Davis controlled non-military aircraft as the civilian air traffic officer under the Controller-General of Civil Aviation. He had previously been on duty at Hounslow aerodrome. The control of traffic passing to and from overseas could be a problem, and was one that the Air Ministry had worked closely with the Home Office and HM Board of Customs and Excise to solve. It had been decided that aerodromes that could be used solely for this traffic should be limited to four and be on the coast, with the exception of the London terminal aerodrome at Hounslow. They were Lympne (continental traffic); Hadleigh in Suffolk (Dutch traffic via Harwich); New Holland in Lincolnshire (Scandinavian traffic via the Humber); and Hounslow (traffic direct to London).

Customs officials in Kent had to follow certain procedures agreed in 1919. In the event of an aircraft arriving from abroad and landing in any place other than an appointed airfield, pilots were informed that the civilian air traffic officer in charge of Lympne would in future maintain a list of all customs officials serving in the county of Kent for the information of pilots in charge of aircraft who had been compelled to land outside customs aerodromes. On application, the CATO Lympne would give the name and address of the officer nearest to the place of landing. In all cases, it was necessary to dispatch a customs officer from a government controlled civil aerodrome to the scene of the forced landing in order to clear the aircraft. The aircraft's operator paid a charge for this service.

CHAPTER 3

Development of civil aviation after the First World War; aircraft incidents; Lympne trials; Cinque Ports Flying Club and record-breaking flights

By 1921, passenger-carrying aircraft were operating between Europe and Croydon. Handley Page were very keen to market their aircraft both abroad and in the UK. To establish the viability of operating large passenger aircraft, R. H. McIntosh, who was well known for his flying exploits in bad weather, was assigned to lead a flight of two HP O/400s from Paris to Croydon. They made good time until reaching the French coast, but were caught by strong gales crossing the Channel and decided to land at Berck-sur-Mer. Capt. A. S. Wilcockson in the second aircraft landed, but after the passengers had alighted, and before anything could be done to protect the machine, the aircraft was lifted onto a wing and wrecked. McIntosh, who was about to land, saw the accident and decided to fly onto Croydon. On another windy day, Wilcockson took more than six hours to fly from Paris to Lympne, where he had to refuel. He was able to do so by contacting Lympne by wireless, enabling ground staff to be ready for refuelling. This is an example of how the airfield at Lympne was to play an important role in the development of cross-Channel flying.

Lympne contributed further to the progress of cross-Channel flights when a 'cone light' was erected at Croydon, and a neon light was installed with beacons located at Cranbrook, Tatsfield and the ELGs at Penshurst and Littlestone on Romney Marsh. Strong winds and gales caused problems for other operators such as KLM, the Dutch airline. On one occasion a Fokker F.II, flown by Robin E. Duke, took four hours to fly from Amsterdam to Lympne. As it was getting dark, Duke decided to stay overnight and continue the following day to Croydon. On landing, the wind tipped the Fokker onto its nose, causing considerable damage.

Farman F.60 Goliath F-GEAF '*Vendee*' housed in one of Lympne's hangars during a short stay at the airfield during the 1920s. Several airliners arrived at the airfield during this period, perhaps for fuel or with technical problems.

Fokker F.III, H-NABT of KLM, crashed on approach to Lympne at Pedlinge near Hythe on 18 May 1922, having taken off from Rotterdam at 3.35 p.m. The passenger, W. B. Van der Vis, was slightly injured, but the pilot, W. Warnaar, was unharmed. Arriving over the English Coast at a height of less than 100 feet above sea level, the aircraft appeared out of the gloom over Folkestone harbour. It flew along the coast to Hythe and turned inland with the intention of landing on the rifle ranges, but owing to heavy mist the pilot lost his bearings and collided with a tree while circling. The Fokker had struck the ground at an angle of 45 degrees, crashing forty yards from the tree. The front end of the fuselage and the leading edge of the main-planes were crushed but the passenger cabin and rear fuselage were intact, the starboard tailplane and elevators having been damaged by the impact with the tree. There were no mechanical failures discovered and it was concluded that the pilot had hit the tree whilst attempting to land in thick fog.

On 27 August 1923, J. J. Denneulin, a pilot employed by the French Air Union, was flying Farman Goliath F-AECB from Le Bourget to Croydon and landed at Berck-sur-Mer to pick up three additional passengers. He was concerned that weather conditions were deteriorating, and being an experienced pilot was well aware of how quickly the weather could change. Approaching the English coast, he gained height to clear the high ground at Lympne, but in doing so he detected a change in the sound of the port engine. He checked his instruments and it was clear that the engine was overheating. Being over Lympne, he decided to land at the airfield and get assistance so he could continue the flight. He was lucky. An enthusiastic mechanic checked the engine and discovered a leaking radiator. Once the repair was completed, the Goliath took off at 4.47 p.m. On reaching Maidstone, he decided to fly over Biggin Hill before descending to Croydon Airport. Without warning the starboard engine stopped. The mechanic contacted Croydon, but the aircraft crashed at East Malling Heath, killing one passenger. Of the remaining seven passengers, four were seriously injured as was the mechanic, but the pilot survived with minor injuries. Had Denneulin decided to remain at Lympne until the weather improved, the mechanics could have checked the engines thoroughly and the accident might have been prevented.

Such was the success of a glider meeting at Itford Hill in 1922 that the following year the *Daily Mail* and the Duke of Sutherland sponsored another competition, this one for motor-gliders. The Royal Aero Club drew up the rules, which stipulated a maximum engine capacity of 750 cc. Optimum performance therefore depended on a high power-to-weight

The hangars constructed during the First World War, and located close to Otterpool Lane on the West side of the airfield. An interesting view across the runway area, the railway being demolished in 1921.

ratio, and the principal prize, one of several totalling £1,500, was to go to the aircraft that flew furthest on five litres or one gallon of fuel. These conflicting aims demanded careful work on the part of the designers.

For the first meeting, twenty-seven machines were entered for the competition, which began at Lympne Aerodrome on 8 October 1923. In the event, only twelve actually appeared and these included designs from leading manufacturers of the day – Avro, De Havilland, Gloster, Short Bros, Parnall, Handley Page, Handasyde and English Electric. Nearly all the aircraft were fitted with motorcycle engines just under the maximum permissible power, except for the English Electric Wren. This long-winged monoplane kept aloft on a 398 cc ABC engine, which put out between 3 and 7 hp. Capt. Geoffrey de Havilland brought his DH.53 Humming Bird, a delightful strut-braced, low-wing design, but the most curious entrant was the Short Gnosspelius Gull, an appropriately named bird-like design whose 698 cc engine drove a pair of pusher propellers via a chain arrangement.

Gales, rain and fog plagued most of the week and prevented many of the competitors from giving their best performance. One of the Wrens flew 85.9 miles on four to five litres (one gallon) of fuel, sharing the fuel economy prize with an ANEC monoplane, which also took the £500 prize offered by Sir Charles Wakefield for maximum altitude with a climb to 4,390 metres (14,400 feet). The 750 cc Parnall Pixie was fastest, lapping

Anec II G-EBJO at the 1924 competition, was to flown by John Herbert James but as the result of several engine problems was eliminated from the trials. Later having a replacement engine and winning the Air League Challenge Cup in 1927.

at 76 mph, though the ANEC, easily the best all-round competitor, came within 2 mph of that figure.

The final day of the 1923 Lympne Trials was marred by a fatal crash. Alexis Maneyrol, the only French pilot competing on the Saturday, crashed and was killed. In the morning he had reached a height of 9,400 feet and made a landing which stood out conspicuously as the finest performance of its kind since the meeting opened. Shortly after noon he went up again in another attempt to beat the altitude record. His descent was being carefully watched by spectators in the expectation of seeing a repeat of the exhibition. Suddenly, when the aircraft was at 100 feet, the wings appeared to crumble and fold upwards and the machine fell like a stone onto the airfield. Ambulance attendants and doctors rushed over to the wreckage, but the unfortunate pilot was terribly injured and died almost immediately.

The Duke of York, who had been watching the flights, sent his equerry to convey his deepest sympathy. At the inquest Col. A. Bristow of the Royal Aero Club described the accident, stating that the collapse of the right wing of the monoplane was attributed to failure of the front main spar of the wings and that the spar broke exactly in the centre. It was also noted that the aircraft was caught in a strong wind and the accident

The rugged Blackburn Bluebird G-EBKD took part in the 1924 Trials but was plagued with engine troubles and did not qualify. However it flew in the Grosvenor Cup and entered the 1926 Trials following an engine change.

occurred when Maneyrol was making a steep turn, causing excessive strain on the wings. The East Kent Coroner returned a verdict of death by misadventure.

Overall, however, the meeting had been a success, and the spirit of the day was typified by an incident recounted by Capt. Cockerel, the pilot of a little Vickers Viget biplane. After a forced landing about six miles from the airfield, he was pushing the aircraft back with its wings folded when he stopped for refreshment at a public house. A large crowd gathered. 'When does the show start, mister?' they enquired, believing the curious-looking contraption to be a travelling Punch and Judy show.

A celebration dinner and dance was due to be held at the Imperial Hotel, Hythe, following the meeting, but on this occasion only the dinner took place, the dancing being cancelled following the tragic death of the French pilot. This decision was not popular, as it was contrary to tradition in any way to mark the death of an airman killed while flying. Everyone was bored until A. V. Roe (who established the Avro Aircraft Co.) climbed to the top of the central staircase and started dropping slow-descent parachutes he had made. He was soon joined by others and a competition started. The question of which model parachute would make the slowest descent was soon forgotten – chairs, sofas and other heavy objects were hurled to the bottom, after which the guests had to pay for the damage caused. Roe later remarked, '… and I was trying to introduce such a quiet game!'

Flown by Harold James 'Agony' Pain – an apt nick-name, in the Vickers Vagabond G-EBJF at the 1924 Trials.

Successful though many of the little motor-gliders had been, the Air Ministry realised that a twin-seater would be needed for the flying clubs which it hoped to establish around the country. Another Lympne competition was proposed, with a major prize of £3,000 put up by the Air Council. Aircraft and engines had to be of all-British design and were subject to a maximum engine capacity of 1,100 cc. This time the emphasis was on efficiency and reliability rather than outright economy. The aircraft also had to demonstrate their ability to make short take-offs and landings over barriers and to lift a load of 340 lb, not including fuel. Entries included a pair of Bristol Brownie monoplanes, a Blackburn Bluebird biplane with side-by-side seating, Sydney Camm's delightful Hawker Cygnet, the Supermarine Sparrow biplane and the Short Satellite, which was remarkable in having all-metal, stressed-skin construction. Other competitors included W. S. Shackleton's Beardmore Wee Bee monoplane, biplanes from Avro and Vickers, and a biplane Woodpigeon and monoplane Widgeon from Westland. Parnall's two-seat version of the successful Pixie, which could be flown as either a biplane or a monoplane by means of a detachable upper wing, was also entered.

The English Electric Wren, G-EBNV, flown by Walter Hunt Longton and Maurice E. A. Wright in the 1923 Light Aeroplane Trials, and the DH.53, G-EBHX, flown by Geoffrey de Havilland and H. Broad, were both later handed over to the Shuttleworth Trust Museum at Biggleswade. Miss D. Gray-Fisk was often seen flying the Wren; in fact, she later became a first officer with Skyways International, flying the HS.748. She went on to become a first officer on Dan-Air Comet airliners. On 8 December 1923, Sir Alan Cobham, flew the DH.53, better known as the Humming Bird, from Lympne to Brussels. Tragically, G-EBHX crashed during a flight test three hours before an air show at the Shuttleworth Collection on 1 July 2012, killing its experienced pilot Trevor Roche, who had flown for British Airways and during the Gulf War.

Eliminating trials held on 27-28 September 1924 reduced the fifteen entrants to eight. Engine problems beset nearly all the survivors during the week of flying and it fell to the Cherub-powered Wee Bee to take first prize. The similarly powered Bristol Brownie I and Cranwell CLA.2 were also among the winners. Although the contest had produced the first true light aeroplanes as opposed to motorised gliders, no single design had emerged that was suitable for operation by the non-professional owner or by flying clubs for instruction. A new set of rules was therefore drawn up for 1925. All restrictions on engine capacity or horsepower were abandoned in favour of a maximum engine weight of 170 lb. However, because the rules were not announced until April 1925, there was no prospect of suitable engines being built in time for the August bank holiday meeting, which

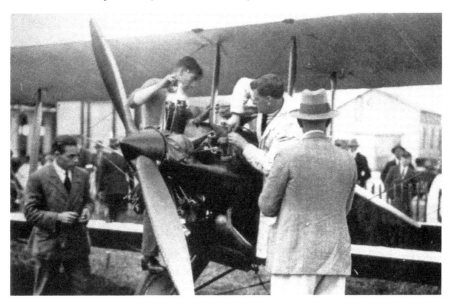

The first Avro Avian at Lympne in 1926 with H. J. L 'Bert' Hinkler, far left, looking on as mechanics of the Cinque Port Flying Club work on the engine.

was therefore confined to racing and performance measuring of existing types.

The entry for the meeting, which was held between 1 and 3 August 1925, included many competitors from previous years. On the first day Flt Lt J. S. Chick took the silver RAE Hurricane to first place in the Light Aeroplane Holiday International Handicap, beating a De Havilland Humming Bird into second place. Chick's speed over the 50-mile course was 73.41 mph. Meanwhile, Geoffrey de Havilland had built, flown and was actually delivering to aero clubs a light plane that was an ideal private owner's machine – the DH.60 Moth. Its 60 hp Cirrus engine weighing 290 lb excluded it from the official races, but Alan Cobham, flying the prototype, beat test pilot Hubert Broad in an unofficial trial during the 1925 meeting, and Capt. Broad demonstrated an SE5a fighter from the First World War, which delighted the crowds at Lympne.

On 3 May 1926, the first day of the General Strike, there was a rush on the continental routes to deliver the *Daily Mail* to Europe by air. At the time there were three Tiger Moths of the London Aeroplane Club available. By Friday 7 May, the *Daily Mail* had devised a system whereby copies of the paper which had been printed at its Paris offices were being transported on Paris–London passenger aircraft, landing at Lympne, where other aircraft waited to pick up the papers and fly them on to Birmingham. Two Club Moths, one piloted by Capt. F. G. M. Sparks and one by Mr Whitcombe, undertook this task. Bad weather forced them to land at Kenilworth and Leamington, from where the papers were distributed instead of Birmingham.

Next morning Valentine Smith, circulation manager of the Daily Mail, arranged for further aircraft to be sent to Lympne: a Moth privately owned by Mrs Eliott-Lynn, and three DH.9s of the De Havilland Company, flown by F. T. Courtney, C. D. Barnard and R. Y. Reeve. All these machines arrived at Lympne on Saturday afternoon, and R. A. Loader of the De Havilland Company went down there as transport officer for the emergency service. That same afternoon the aircraft delivered newspapers to Norwich, Brighton, Gosport and Bournemouth. In the early hours of the following morning large quantities of the *Daily Mail* reached Lympne by air from Paris, where awaiting aircraft delivered them to Brighton, Gosport, Bournemouth and Birmingham. All aircraft returned to Lympne that evening.

In the meantime the fleet increased by the addition of two Avro Avians of the Southern Aviation Co., flown by R. H. Leavy and H. Lawson. On Sunday 9 May, the fleet flew 3,500 miles, delivering many thousands of papers to Birmingham, Portsmouth, Norwich, Bournemouth and Brighton. On the same day a DH.9 from ADC Aircraft Ltd, fitted with one of the new 330 hp Nimbus engines and piloted by H. H. Perry, joined the fleet. In addition to all the locations previously mentioned, the *Daily Mail* delivered papers to Nottingham, Taunton and Oxford, and again all aircraft returned that night to Lympne. On Tuesday, still working from Lympne, they covered all the previous ground with the addition of Brooklands and Cambridge. On Wednesday, still functioning with absolute reliability despite poor weather conditions, the fleet repeated all the deliveries of the previous day, with the addition of a load to Spittlegate, for Grantham. On 14 May, the *Daily Mail* was able to deliver all its newspapers without any problems.

With Air Ministry interest waning, the *Daily Mail* again came up with £5,000 in prizes for the 1926 event, all six days of which were to involve cross-country flights taking in major seaside resorts and totalling 1,994 miles. Subject to a minimum average speed of 50 mph over any stage of the course, and a useful load of at least 340 lb, the competitors were assessed according to a formula that multiplied the load carried by the number of miles flown, and divided the result by pounds of fuel consumed.

Geoffrey de Havilland developed a lighter, five-cylinder Genet-powered Moth to enable him to take part. Avro produced the Genet-powered Avian, and Blackburn came back with its Bluebird. Apart from the ANEC IV Missel Thrush, the remainder of the thirteen entrants were built by amateurs, many of the designs being familiar from the 1924 trials, including the Cygnet, Brownie, Pixie, Woodpigeon and Satellite. The

Sir Sefton Brancker Chairman of the Royal Aero Club's Racing Committee, presents the Grosvenor Cup on the 23 June 1923 to Ft Lt W. H. Longton in Sopwith Gnu G-EAGP at Lympne. Sir Sefton, himself a pilot, qualified on 18 June 1913 and was killed in the disastrous crash of the British airship R101 near Beauvais, France on 5 October 1930.

Missel Thrush, Cranwell CLA.4, Bluebird and Satellite were eliminated during the pre-event trials, leaving nine aircraft to set off for Brighton on Sunday 12 September 1926. The two Hawker Cygnets and the Avro Avian (which was flown by Bert Hinkler) quickly emerged as clear leaders. However, on the second day the petrol tank of Hinkler's Avian developed a leak which a liberal application of soap failed to cure and another annoyingly small failure in the Avian's Genet forced him to retire.

Capt. Broad's Genet Moth was disqualified when it was discovered that a ballast weight was missing from his aircraft, having been removed by a souvenir-hunter. By the final day, George Bulman looked invincible in the Hawker Cygnet and although it was misty, he completed two laps of the Lympne–Croydon course, crossing the line to the accompaniment of hooting car horns.

Another Cygnet, entered by the Royal Aircraft Establishment Aero Club, was placed second overall, followed by the Brownie and Pixie. Bulman's Cygnet had covered nearly 2,000 miles at an average speed of 65 mph, with fuel consumption averaging 39.2 miles per gallon – figures with which few motor cars of the day could compete. The winning Wren, ANEC, Wee Bee and Cygnet quickly disappeared from the private flying scene, while the unsuccessful Avian, Bluebird, Widgeon and most notably the Moth were to become the backbone of Britain's flying clubs until the

Newspapers were often delivered to the Continent during the 1920s, by aircraft such as this three engined Fokker F.VII/3M serial number 00-AIH.

outbreak of war. The Lympne trials in the 1920s undoubtedly laid the foundations of private flying in Britain.

On 8 February 1925, a Farman Goliath crashed whilst attempting to land at Lympne. The aircraft was on a cargo flight from Paris to Croydon when an engine failed over the Channel. On landing, a wing tip caught a fence, resulting in the undercarriage being ripped off and the aircraft landed on its bottom wing. The pilot was Jean Emile Joseph Delisle, who was later to die in a crash which occurred near Lympne on 18 August 1926 when Bleriot 155 F-AIEB 'Wilbur Wright', crashed two miles south of Lympne airfield and two crew and two passengers lost their lives. Another Bleriot 155, F-AICQ, crashed near Lympne on 2 October 1926. Christened the 'Clement Ader', it was piloted by a twenty-seven-year-old Frenchman, Henri Jacques Mallet. The aircraft was on fire before it struck the ground, after which it was engulfed by flames, killing all on board. It was this aircraft that had been used to fly the remains of the unfortunate Delisle back to France a few weeks previously.

The proposed forming of an East Kent Flying Club was due to the efforts of R. Dallas Brett and H. E. Thwaites, whom the *Kentish Express* credited with the enthusiasm for the idea. After an attempt to promote it as a private company had failed through lack of support, despite the enthusiasm of the local press, two film shows and a lecture campaign, the money came in slowly. But the majority of supporters were Hythe shopkeepers who willingly bought their £1 shares without any expectation of getting

De Havilland DH.51 G-EBIM prototype seen at Lympne in 1924, first flow July 1924 and was sold to F/O G. E. F Boyes who named the aircraft '*Come To Steve*' for the Kings Cup Race.

anything out of it other than a badge entitling them to free admission to any flying meeting organised by the club at Lympne. The club was saved by the Air Ministry revoking its earlier offer of accommodation at Lympne at a nominal rent and its granting of a full subsidy to a club designed to encourage the training of reserve pilots for service in the RAF in the event of another war.

In the minutes of the inaugural meeting held at Hythe Town Hall, on 23 November 1927, Dallas Brett stressed:

> You will see, therefore, that it must never be forgotten that we exist primarily to help our country; if we can make the process enjoyable, well and good, but business first and our main business is the manufacture of pilots. In order to learn to fly at a commercial school of flying you would have to pay at least £100. We hope to teach our members for £20 per certificate, exclusive of their subscriptions to the club. This is only possible by reason of the subsidy.

In February 1928, a company was floated with an issued share capital of some £910 and plans were announced for the initial purchase of one aircraft, although this was not really thought to be adequate.

Amongst the founder members were Maj. F. W. Butler (Chairman); R. Dallas Brett (Hon. Secretary); H. E. Thwaites (Hon. Treasurer); P. D.

This aircraft De Havilland Moth G-EBQE flew with the Cinque Ports Flying Club Lympne in 1929 and was later sold to Kensington-Moir & Straker Ltd. Croydon in July 1931.

Barker (Ashford); T. M. Lewis (Postling); J. A. Somerset-Webb (Ashford); F. D. Little (Folkestone); G. E. Took (Dover); E. H. Evenden and M. S. Faraday (Canterbury), who together with Dr E. D. Whitehead Reid (Hon. Medical Officer) formed the first board of directors. To promote interest in the locality, and to gain more members, an aero show was advertised by posters and handbills around the district and arranged in Folkestone's T. A. Drill Hall in Shellons Street in March 1928, when four sample light aircraft were on display, as well as various aviation accessories. The aircraft in the display were Bert Hinkler's record-breaking Avro Avian (G-EBOV), a Blackburn Bluebird, a De Havilland Moth and a Westland Widgeon.

Better supported was a flying meeting organised by the fledgling Cinque Ports Flying Club at Lympne airfield over the weekend of 6-7 April, which attracted some thirty visiting aircraft. The crowd, estimated to be six thousand people, was the largest ever seen at Lympne. A programme of competitions, air races and joy-rides was undertaken, admission to the airport enclosure being 6*d*, programmes were 3*d* and joy-rides cost 5*s*, and the flying was undertaken continuously from mid-morning until dusk. The profits were negligible, but the press gave it enthusiastic coverage, which resulted in a few more membership subscriptions being paid. The club thus got off to a flying start and purchased its first aircraft, G-EBWC, a

De Havilland DH.60X type Moth, the doyen of pre-war training aircraft, the machine being delivered on 10 May. They also set about finding a ground engineer and a pilot instructor. Mr R. H. Wynne, an 'H', 'C' and 'D1' licensed ground engineer from the Avro Works at Manchester, was engaged in the former capacity.

On a journey from Paris to London a Goliath F.60 F-AECU 'Normandie', a biplane airliner operated by the French Air Union, crashed in fields less than two miles from Lympne airfield on 6 March 1928. Trouble began early in the flight when a partial failure of the port engine occurred at low altitude in bad weather as the aircraft crossed the coast between Hythe and Dymchurch. Seeing fields and thinking it was Lympne airfield, the pilot attempted to land but the left lower wing of the giant biplane struck the ground, causing the aircraft to swing round and crash. Fortunately there were no fatalities or injuries. The following day, when the accident investigators arrived, it was evident that the wing tip had skidded along the ground for a distance of about thirty yards before the undercarriage had collapsed sideways. The Goliath had then carried on for a further thirty to forty yards and swung round through 180 degrees before coming to rest. The conclusion was that the accident was caused by the partial failure of the port engine, resulting from the fracture of one of the engines' rocker valve arms. Owing to the skill of the pilot, Capt. R. Maury, and his mechanic, Carnet, the eight passengers were lucky to walk away from the crash just shaken.

The Cinque Ports Flying Club started flying over the weekend of 12-13 May, instruction for members being given by Capt. Neville Stack AFC of the London Aero Club as the voluntary instructor, and it was continued over the following weekend by Capts F. Lines and F. Button who arrived with the British Airships Avian G-EBWU. The club had started off with twenty-two members, none of whom were qualified pilots, and commenced regular instruction on 25 May, under Maj. I. N. C. Clarke DSC, who had undertaken the post of instructor. Ten days later, the first two members to fly solo were Mr K. Edgerson Wright (an ex-war pilot) and Mr Rydals-Brett, the Honorary Secretary.

The registration letters on the first club machine, G-EBWC, caused slight embarrassment to some of the lady members, who objected to 'WC' (Water Closet), the term used in those days for a toilet! It had therefore been arranged with the Civil Aviation Registration Board for this to be changed, but before this could be done she was taxied violently into the side of a hangar by a member on 7 July and completely wrecked. Another type of Moth was ordered as a replacement, G-EBSS 'Jeunesse', which had formerly been owned by Vicomte de Sibour and had been used by him for his 'round the world' flight. Flying instruction was resumed on 15 July.

The club machine, together with privately owned aircraft of other club members, was housed in No. 3 hangar, the furthest from the airport entrance gate. The club had its own refuelling point adjacent to its hangar when Messrs Pratts installed a petrol service station between Easter and July 1928, which the Cinque Ports Flying Club members used. One of the members, Frank Cruttenden, recalls:

> The first important event in which the club participated was the King's Cup Race around the UK on 20-21 July, when competitors had to stop at Lympne for thirty minutes to refuel. Members of the club assisted in marshalling and refuelling the machines landing at Lympne, one of the various control points around the country. Joy riding was available in the Avro G-EBZA of Messrs Skytrips of Folkestone, while at 4 p.m. a formation of five machines arrived from Bekesbourne, where Dr Whitehead Reid had been giving an aerial picnic.

The standard of tuition at Lympne may be gauged from the case of Mr S. O. Crowther, who joined the Cinque Ports Flying Club on 3 August 1928. He had commenced his flying instruction on Friday 27 July with no previous flying experience. Being unable to fly on the Saturday or

G-EBTD DH.60X Moth was owned by the CPFC from October 1935 until being impressed into RAF service, as serial No. AW153, eventually being scrapped at RAF St Athan in 1941.

Sunday, he resumed his instruction on Wednesday 1 August, and went solo on Tuesday (his third day) after only four hours and forty-five minutes' instruction. He resumed his training on Thursday and passed all his tests for his 'A1' licence on Friday after just six days with the club.

Membership of the Cinque Ports Flying Club continued to flourish right up to the outbreak of the Second World War, attracting some of the best-known aviators in light aircraft circles in the UK, including Lord Patrick Crichton-Stuart, T. B. 'Cocky' Cockburn and Tony Law, the son of Prime Minister Bonar Law. A local pilot, Harold Chater, owned and flew his Avro 504, G-EBFW, from Lympne and once hit a wire fence on take-off, which was not good for either the pilot or his machine. One youngster, Norman Geal, was given a flight in this machine, which inspired his lifelong interest in aviation:

> My first memory is from when I would have been approximately four years of age and my grandfather took me up to the flying club. Harold Chater had his old Avro 504K up there that he had just rebuilt himself, and was flying around. My grandfather had arranged for me to have a flight with Harold, which I did, with an aunt of mine as the passenger in the back seat and I sat on her lap. I can vividly remember that 504, and it was absolutely fantastic. It was the first time I had ever flown, and I shall never forget it. This aeroplane looked so big to me at the time, because the Avro 504 had a wide wingspan. Anyway, we had a good flight and the most important thing I can remember is flying from the airfield, as we took off from No. 1 hangar across towards Bill Davis' house (Berwick Manor), I can remember flying along over Westenhanger race course. I can still remember that vividly, turning off from Westenhanger and flying over Saltwood Castle, over Stone Street and remember seeing that from the air – it sticks in my mind after all these years.

About this time the flying club reached an agreement with the War Office to train some of the officers who were on courses at the guards depot at Canterbury and the Hythe School of Musketry. The subsidy thus gained by the flying club enabled them to purchase another De Havilland and Moth 1, G-EBNN, which was delivered on 22 September. At the beginning of October 1928, Maj. Clarke resigned and his place was taken by Maj. H. G. Travers DSC of Walmer. On 12 October, he was appointed as a temporary flying instructor, but his time with the club started badly.

On 13 October 1928, a member of the flying club, G. T. Skinner, took off around 5 p.m., reaching a height of about 2,000 feet to practise aerobatic manoeuvres. Skinner had previously flown nearly twelve hours under dual instruction and so flying the club's new Tiger Moth DH.60X, G-EBSS, was

Sergeant S. J. Dupe Airfield Manager at Lympne, stands by the Rolls Royce especially adapted as a Fire Engine, seated is Mr Bloomfield who occasionally drove this vehicle.

his first solo flight. Suddenly the aircraft fell into a spinning nosedive, but a sudden and violent recovery from the spin was made at a height of 800 feet. At that moment, the pilot was seen by horrified spectators to fall out of his aircraft, and not being equipped with a parachute he fell to his death. Thus the Cinque Ports Flying Club suffered its first serious accident when Skinner fell from his machine while stunting after only four hours' solo experience.

His seat belt had broken and both he and the aircraft fell on land near Selby Farm, New Romney. As his body lay on the parish boundary between Hythe and New Romney, there was some dispute as to which local authority should assume responsibility for its removal, so it was housed in a nearby shed overnight while the matter was resolved. Herbert Travers blamed the ground engineer at Lympne for the accident; nearly five years later, the engineer was caught red-handed, having been suspected of defrauding the club of petrol and other supplies, and was sacked.

The wrecked aircraft was replaced by another Tiger Moth DH.60X, G-EBRI, which had formerly belonged to the Duchess of Bedford. This machine was delivered on 16 December. The club now had its own clubroom at the eastern side of its hangar, which was first opened to members at Christmas 1928. At the end of the club's first year of operations, it showed a profit of over £96 and had trained fifteen pilots and instructed some forty-two others. Maj. F. W. Butler and Dr E. D. Whitehead Reid had resigned from the board.

Easter 1929 saw a repeat of what was to become an established annual event and a highlight of every subsequent year for the club. An International Air Rally was held over the weekend, with some fifty light aircraft on view, coming from aero clubs in Germany, Holland and Austria as well as the UK. A programme of flying displays, competitions and a Cinque Ports Handicap Race over thirty-seven miles were the order of the day. Sydney St Barbe wrote 'RONUK' (a popular brand of floor polish) in smoke over local towns while flying from the aerodrome in the modified SE5a he used for sky-writing. However, public attendance at this event was rather disappointing.

On the day before this weekend, Moth G-EBNN had come to grief in a field at Newingreen while Maj. Travers was flying with his wife:

Hermia's [Mrs Travers'] account was the one which stuck in my mind for a good many years. She had expected the machine to blow up at any moment and spent an unpleasant time trying to lift the machine off him, sniffing all the while for the smell of petrol. At the time she had thought him more seriously injured than in fact he was, as he was pouring blood from his mouth and face.

She could not get the machine clear, partly because she had broken her wrist when the Moth hit the ground and it was not functioning properly. Eventually she ran for help but others who had seen G-EBNN come down were there to help and he was freed by the time she returned. Travers recorded in his log-book: '27 March DH.60 G-EBNN. Lympne local. Ten minutes pupil H. E. M. T. turns and landings, soon after second take-off motor cut out, aircraft badly damaged in subsequent forced landing from 150/200 ft while avoiding cattle. Sustained loss of two front teeth and a cut lip.'

On 21 May, another Moth was purchased, G-EBPM, and it arrived resplendent with gold nose and lettering on the silver-doped machine, while half the fuselage was in black and white checks. Nigel Geal remembered the new aircraft with pride:

Club colour schemes used at the beginning of the club on the Moths – the Cirrus-engined Moths, not the Gypsy-engined ones, and the zigzag stripes which you can see on G-AAKN. The main-planes were silver but the actual fuselage was painted white, the lines were orange at the top and blue at the bottom, and the registration letters were in black. Then the colour scheme was changed; I can't remember what year it was, but then the whole of the aircraft was silver and the top deck of the fuselage half way down was royal blue and then underneath that there was a red zigzag just like a lightning strike. You can see this on the photo of Tiger

Moth G-ADWG, where the registration letters were blue on that as well. All except on the Aeronca, and that was a peculiar scheme all together. I've got an idea that it was in dark blue and red. Major Travers resigned from his post of Chief Flying Instructor to take up a similar post with the London Aero Club and Mr K. K. Brown took over from him on 24 April 1929. Mr Brown, who was always known as K. K., was one of the finest pre-World War Two pilots and well liked by everybody, having spent five years in the Royal Air Force at Hawkinge and two years with the joy-riding firm of Skytrips. He had also flown with Sir Alan Cobham's National Aviation Day flying circus.

Another who remembered K. K. Brown very well was Norman Geal:

As a boy I got to know all of the staff. From the age of seven, I was running around the flying club doing odd jobs and one man that I considered my hero was K. K. Brown and he was the chief instructor. He was a marvellous man, and he had a lovely little dog called Bonzo who came up every morning to the hangar in the car and would jump out, and I'd have the dog all day practically, running around the place. One thing I remember is that K. K. Brown gave me a cricket bat when I was young but I'm sad to say I wish I had it now, because on the blade of the bat I had all the autographs of various people that had been flying through Lympne, such as the record breakers. K. J. K. Brown signed it, then Jean Batten, Amy Johnson, Jim Mollison, Major Sevensky, Charlie Roscoe, Bert Hinkler, Gabriel Paterson, Bill Davis, Duncan Davis, Leslie Cliff, who was an instructor at the flying club and he and his wife were either in the Olympics or the Empire Games ice skating as they were the British champions. I also managed to get the autograph of Sir Jack Hobbs who happened to be at Lympne one day.

So successful had the arrangements been the previous year, and so great the popularity of the event, that this exercise was repeated on 5 and 6 July 1929, when Lympne was again chosen as a control point on the first day of the King's Cup Race, an event which Frank Cruttenden recalls:

The first competitor arrived at 12.30 p.m. and although a gale was blowing and the aircraft had to be held down while being refuelled, all the competing machines were checked through the controls in an hour and a half. The only mishap was to Mr Ashworth's Avian which tipped onto its nose and broke the propeller. The R.A.F at Hawkinge supplied some helpers for the refuelling and a Hucks Starter (motorised propeller swinger) for the heavier machines.

By July 1929, the club membership had topped the hundred mark and included pilots and trainees from London, Southampton, Hastings, Esher, Feltham, Tidworth, Dublin, Auckland, Kenya, India and China, as well as from all parts of Kent. On 25 August, Dr Furlong, a member from Dublin, put up a fine performance, passing all the tests for his 'A' licence after going solo in that afternoon. By October of that year the membership had grown so much that the clubroom in the corner of the hangar had to be extended to cope with the increased numbers. This lounge was also remembered by the youngsters of those who were employed at Lympne airport for other reasons, as Norman Geal recalls:

> There used to be a party every Christmas in the Flying Club lounge, and the children, my brother and myself, and my young sister all attended these parties there with my grandfather and grandma and all the club members. They were really big parties, every Christmas, and when I was about seven or eight years old I was presented with a Frog flying model aeroplane by Mrs Ann Davis. As the No. 2 hangar was always empty at that time as it wasn't being used, I was soon off to fly my new Frog aeroplane in this hangar because it had a lovely smooth floor surface for take-off.

During the week ending 28 September, the club put up an astonishing record of fifty hours' flying with just two machines in six days. J. Bowring, aged sixteen, went solo that week, but had to return to school before he could take the tests for his 'A1' licence. At the beginning of October, two club members – Mr G. F. E. Storey, the first pupil to gain his 'A' licence, and Mr H. E. Thwaites, the Club Treasurer – carried out an eight-day tour of Germany and Holland. After taking off from Lympne into a gale, they took some forty-five minutes to cross the Channel, but the tour was completed successfully and on time, despite the poor weather conditions.

On 27 February 1930, the club's latest acquisition, G-EBWC, was crashed in a field at Smarden near Ashford by a club member flying with a passenger, fortunately without injury to either. It was replaced by another Tiger Moth DH.60X, G-EBQE.

At the end of the second year's operation the club secretary could report a good year's work, without any major mishaps and a record number of pilots licences having been obtained by members, bettered only by the National Flying Services School at Hanworth in Middlesex. On 2 May 1930, Miss Grace Aitken of Horley became the first lady pupil to fly solo at Lympne, followed on 5 May by Mr Maxwell-Williams, a sixteen-year-old who had passed all his tests for his 'A' licence and thus became the youngest member to qualify at Lympne. Shortly after this a third machine, a Mk II Moth, G-EBSA, was added to the Cinque Ports Flying Club fleet (G-EBRI and G-EBQE still being in commission), which was delivered on 23 May. On the 29th, Miss Aitken passed all her tests for her 'A1' licence. The July Landing Competition was won by Mr K. H. F. Waller with Miss Aitken second, but competitions for August and September were cancelled due to lack of entries, the whole series being suspended until May 1931.

In August 1930, the club suffered its second fatality, when Nigel Cohen, one of its most enthusiastic members, was killed in his own De Havilland Moth when it crashed at Newingreen after a wing broke off in a steep dive. At the beginning of September the Air Ministry lifted its ban on foreign nationals joining the subsidised clubs, and six or seven joined up at Lympne almost immediately. Dallas Brett wrote:

On 14 November Mr Siang Tai Sun, our popular Chinese member, passed all his tests for his A1 licence. In view of the fact that Mr Sun's knowledge of English is strictly limited, while Mr K. K. Brown's knowledge of Chinese is non-existent, this performance fully demonstrated the latter's remarkable gifts as an instructor.

Armstrong Whitworth Argosy I registration G-EB0Z of Imperial Airways at Lympne during 1926. This type of aircraft was eventually replaced by the company in 1933 by Handley Page H.P.42s in 1933.

By the end of the year, the club decided to acquire some more up-to-date aircraft in the form of DH.60G Gipsy-engined Moths G-EBTD, G-AAFS and G-AAKM, which were fitted with wing slots for safer flying, replacing G-EBQE, G-EBRI and G-EBSA. Members were particularly reluctant to part with G-EBRI, the aircraft having flown some 1,072 hours while on instruction, this being the equivalent of some 8,000 miles. It had not given any trouble during the two years that the club had flown it, and the club had gained a no-claims bonus from its insurers. Another decision taken was that the clubroom should be moved to the western side of the hangar, where an attractive oak-panelled bar, club lounge and some much-needed changing rooms for members were constructed.

At the end of its third year of operations the membership had risen to 151, of whom no fewer that 68 were qualified pilots, and the club had a balance of £1,500 to spend on new equipment. No Easter flying meeting and display was held the following year, due to the Royal Auxiliary Air Force holding a summer camp at the airport. However, the RAuxAF pilots mounted an impromptu flying display for the club members who were waiting to welcome home Miss Amy Johnson from India, but the airliner in which she was travelling had been refuelled in France and flew past the airfield over the North Downs, escorted part of the way by some flying club machines.

The club was now, however, getting into financial difficulties because of the reduction of the government subsidy to flying clubs during 1931 and it was decided to approach Brooklands Group based in Surrey. In January 1932, the Cinque Ports Flying Club now joined other flying clubs in the group based at Brooklands, Sywell in Northamptonshire and the South Coast Flying Club at Shoreham in Sussex, and members' subscriptions now covered the landing fees and membership at the three other clubs. Inter-club visits with the London Aero Club and the Brooklands School of Flying were a feature of the next summer season. Mr W. E. Davis, brother of Capt. Duncan Davis AFC, the group's managing director, became manager of the Cinque Ports Flying Club, and was ably supported by his attractive wife Ann. The club secretary listed in 1932 was Lt Cdr T. S. B. Gubbins RN (Retd) who was one of the club's original founder members.

On 8 January 1932, Gipsy Moth DH.60G G-AAKM was deleted from the club's register after it landed on the roof of a house at Iden in Sussex and finished up in the garden. April brought the reintroduction of some government subsidy and in the years following, the Cinque Ports Flying Club continued to make great strides under its new owners. By the next year the club was also advertising training for the 'B' (night flying) licence as well as the 'A' flying licence. The cost to pupils of obtaining the latter was estimated to be between £20 and £30. For those wishing to maintain

Traffic Staff at Lympne airfield. Maisie's father Arthur Geal extreme right, third from left is Mr Bloomfield, who drove the fire tender, and Sgt. S. J. Dupe third from right.

their own machines, training for ground engineers' licences was available, while the cost of owning and maintaining their own aircraft would compare with the cost of purchase and maintenance of a medium or large motor car.

Among those who worked at the Cinque Ports Flying Club at this time was Norman Geal, who did not even have to apply for his post. He recalls:

> Reminiscences of Bill Davis are something very personal to me as he was such a great family friend. Everything about Bill and Ann Davis was just aviation and they worked solidly for the causes of aviation, and especially in the civil flying club side of it. Bill Davis was a man who took an interest in everything and we apprentices all thought the world of him because he was really down to earth, wanted to know, wanted to do, wanted you to do, everything. We would ask him everything.
>
> That's how I first became an apprentice; I had only just left school, but I wasn't working there yet, but they had taken me on as a boy doing odd jobs, and I was actually giving the old Hendy Hobo G-AAIG a bit of a clean-up. Bill Davis walked up to me as I was cleaning the old Hobo and said, 'Your Grandpa tells me that you're leaving school shortly.' 'Yes, sir, that's right,' I replied. 'Well, you'll be starting here on Monday!' and that was that.

Naturally it didn't even enter my head, my father's head, or Mr Bill Davis' head that I would do anything else when I left school. I didn't ask for the job, he just said, 'Well, you're coming here' so that was how I started my apprenticeship with the Cinque Ports Flying Club, and later Cinque Ports Aviation. I had a number of little aeroplanes that I had to look after, as I was a very junior apprentice. I used to end up with Club Gipsies [Gipsy Moths] and a number of little planes like that.

The Luton Minor was a horrible little thing, but was among the planes I was allocated. I never managed to get my hands on G-AEXF the Mew Gull of Alex Henshaw that would have been the crowning glory if I'd got that one. There was an old WW1 Bristol F2B Fighter [probably K. K. Brown's G-ABYT] there in the hangar – it didn't fly much, just occasionally.

The Avro Aircraft Company sold several Avro 626 single-engine biplanes to the Egyptian Army Air Force during the 1930s for survey work and anti-hashish patrols over the Sinai Desert. Egyptian pilots were given a familiarisation course at Lympne before a formation flight began on 18 November 1933, but two crashed in fog in France. Their stay at Lympne created much interest, and they were certainly an unusual sight on the airfield. All these aircraft had been modified and fitted with an Armstrong Siddeley Cheetah V, similar to the engines fitted to the Avro Anson, much used by the RAF.

During the years preceding the outbreak of the Second World War, the Cinque Ports Flying Club became known both nationally and internationally as one of the most popular flying clubs in the country, where a warm welcome was guaranteed whether you were Amy Johnson, Geoffrey de Havilland, Jim Mollison, or an ordinary flying club enthusiast. As well as the regular flying displays, international air rallies, and the annual air races they also took part in 'extra-mural' activities, which started in 1929 with a 'bombing the baby' item on the air display programme, involving an Austin 7 car, when one flour bag landed in the driver's lap! On another occasion, K. K. Brown flew over the Venetian Fete on the Royal Military Canal at Hythe and dropped bags of flour on the spectators. This flour bombing seems to have become a feature of the displays, as one programme included the bombing of a mock-up Chinese junk on the airfield, and even social events were not exempt from this activity, as Mrs C. Brotherston recalls:

My mother and father were married in Lympne Church, where several of my forebears are also buried. It was the custom of the Cinque Ports Flying Club aircraft to bombard any members or employees on their wedding day, with flour bags. This also happened to my mother and father and, I believe, to my sister.

Maisie Dupe and her cousin John Henriet remember Sir Philip Sassoon and the parties he arranged for families of the flying club and local children at Christmas. Ann Davis, the wife of the club's chairman, is remembered for her kindness to the children and they thought how glamorous she looked. HRH Edward, Prince of Wales and Mrs Simpson were also guests of Sir Philip. During their stay Sgt Dupe was contacted by Sir Philip at Lympne Place, asking if he could provide ball boys for a tennis party he was arranging for them. So Maisie's two brothers and John Henriet's two uncles were recruited for the task. On returning home from the tennis, the three children told the family that they had been sworn to secrecy regarding the identity of the guests – no doubt necessary to prevent the press descending on Lympne. They were called upon several times to assist at the tennis party. One of the boys was R. F. C. 'Reggie' Dupe, who was killed during the Second World War. His father, Sgt Dupe, had served in the Royal Flying Corps, so it was no surprise when Reggie joined the RAF. It seemed natural that with the initials of RFC he should enlist in the RAF.

At Reggie Dupe's passing out parade following flying training, the VIP attending was none other than Sir Philip Sassoon, who recognised Reggie as he inspected the parade, saying: 'Hello, Reggie, I'll tell your father I've seen you!' This apparently threw the RAF top brass into a bit of a panic,

Handley Page H.P.42 G-AAXD '*Horatius*' of Imperial airways called into Lympne for refuelling in 1937. Aircraft of Imperial Airlines frequently landed at Lympne *en route* to France.

but it does show that Sir Philip was genuinely concerned about people from Lympne. It must have been wonderful for the children to be present when pilots such as Amy Johnson and Jean Batten flew into or from Lympne on their epic flights. Often Maisie was able to climb up into KLM aircraft when they were taxied into the hangar to stay overnight or were being maintained by staff at the airfield.

In the *Daily Express* of 21 May 1932 a regular columnist, Denis Dunn, known as the flying reporter, published a small report as follows:

> Lydia left-banked steadily, levelled off and thumped gracefully onto Lympne grassland. The prop skittered to a stop and across the aerodrome marched an impressive figure. A ruby-red-faced Sgt Dupe appeared at the cabin window and said: 'Have you flown from France?' – 'No, from Broadstairs, Mr Dupe!' I replied. He was tall and broad, and a replica of Bairnsfather's Old Bill. He radiated jollity and good cheer. I might remark that civilian pilots and children at night-time are taught to remember Mr Dupe in their prayers. He is the hero of a thousand pilots, he looks after Lympne, and when the nights are dark and rainy, and weary novices on B certificate tests land, Mr Dupe is always there with a kindly tip about guiding lights and wind vagaries.

The caricature of Old Bill appeared in magazines, postcards and reports at the time of the First World War and typified the spirit of an old-timer in the British Army with a dry sense of humour. The illustrator was Bruce Bairnsfather. As for Lydia, it is assumed this was the name of the flying reporter's aircraft.

The Cinque Ports Flying Club now undertook the maintenance of its own aircraft, using the portion of No. 3 hangar nearest to the airfield, with the formation in 1936 of Cinque Ports Aviation Ltd for this purpose, as is recalled by the former company secretary, T. W. Osbourne:

> The company was an offshoot of the flying club, primarily to look after the club's aircraft, but later undertook outside work. It had been started by Bill Davis, his wife Ann and Tony Duport, with a capital of 100 shares of £100. It never made any profits but the directors did OK. When Bill Davis was killed in the crash of Monospar G-AEJV in 1938, I was asked to take over as company secretary, even though I was in hospital recovering from influenza at the time. The works manager was J. R. Currie, who was building his wood and fabric-covered 'Wot' assisted by the students of the College of Aeronautical Engineering where Currie was a lecturer.

One of those who worked for Cinque Ports Aviation was Ronald Giles who, as a sixteen-year-old apprentice in the covered component section, was involved in fabric covering, doping and spray painting.

> I remember making up the wing ribs for the Currie 'Wot' on a wooden jig and gluing the joints, then assembling them onto the spars. The fabric covers were machined together to make up the length and seams went back to front when sewn on with blanket stitch on the trailing edge with strong linen thread and a curved needle, then sewn through and over the ribs every four inches. Doping was done in the Paint and Dope Shop, which was like an asbestos garage with double doors, the dope being supplied by Berger Paints. We had to drink a pint of milk a day to counteract the effects of the fumes, and you certainly needed it after working in a confined space breathing in those fumes. The last aircraft I re-covered and painted was an Avro biplane which was of metal construction and the fuselage was painted red, the fabric was a bag which laced up on the underside.
>
> Charter flights could be arranged and a club machine and pilot to fly where you will could be hired at very reasonable rates. Members could hangar their aircraft at the club for a charge of 1s 6d per night, while a monthly subscription of 30s was available to those who were only in the neighbourhood for a short time. For the amusement of members, various flying competitions, club dinners and dances and displays formed part of the annual programme. All of the above, with a brief guide to 'how to learn to fly', was included in the club's 1934 handbook, *Aviation at the Cinque Ports Flying Club*.

As the years progressed, so did the variety of aircraft to be seen in the flying club's hangar, both instructional machines and private owners' aircraft. De Havilland Moths of various types predominated, club machines being G-EBTD, G-AAKP and G-ABOG. The club now also flew the Leopard Moth G-ACPG (actually owned by Mrs Ann Davis), which was used as the club 'hack', ferrying instructors and members to other flying club rallies and aeronautical garden parties which were popular in those days. For example, during April 1939 it was used for flights to Ostend, Calais, Le Touquet and Paris. Two weeks later it was chartered by the press to photograph the passage through the Strait of Dover of six German destroyers.

Another regular member of the club's fleet was Puss Moth G-AAZO. This machine distinguished itself for making forced landings at places as varied as Nethercourt Farm, Ramsgate, and at Swingfield near Dover, and colliding with the cooling pond near No. 3 hangar. This was used in conjunction with the airfield's own power station which generated electricity for the First World War RFC camp, as there was no connection to an outside power supply until 1940. On one occasion the aircraft had to be rebuilt after hitting the telephone wires that ran along the Aldington Road boundary while landing, and turning turtle on the airfield.

Individual owners hangared their aircraft at Lympne, including a wide variety of light aircraft ranging from the diminutive motorised glider, the American designed Aeronca C-3 G-AEFT, the De Havilland Moth Major G-ACHH owned by Tony Duport, and the little Hendy Hobo G-AGIG that had been modified for air racing for Lord Patrick Crichton-Stuart, the B.A. (British Aircraft) Swallow G-ADLT owned by works manager D. C. Palmer, the Cirrus Moth G-EBVD owned by Dr Turner, and David Llewellyn's Mew Gull G-AEXL.

Another offshoot of the club's activities was in connection with the College of Aeronautical Engineering, part of Brooklands Group, and was affiliated with the Automobile Engineering Training College, based in Chelsea. Apprentices from this college, including both mechanics and draughtsmen, came to Lympne to finish their last year of training with practical work for six months in the hangars at Lympne. As already alluded to, one flying club member even designed and built his own aircraft. John Currie, a lecturer at the College of Aeronautical Engineering (CAE), decided to adapt the design of the De Havilland Moth to a single-seater aerobatic machine, incorporating some of his own ideas. The trainee draughtsmen from the CAE assisted with the detailed design work, and the apprentice mechanics assisted with its construction. Much speculation was generated by the project and its progress was watched with interest by club members and instructors, who received various enquiries as to what it was to be called. Finally, in desperation, Currie chose the name 'Wot' for his brainchild, two of which were completed at Lympne. The prototype, G-AFCG, was first flown in 1937, followed by G-AFDS in the following year. Both prototypes, as well as some partly completed Wots, were destroyed when Lympne was bombed in August 1940. Norman Geal remembers the Currie Wot's first flight:

This was after we had gone into the business of servicing aircraft and then we come to the part of the story when we built the Currie Wots. They were fantastic little aeroplanes, beautiful machines, but the first one wasn't so nice because everything was square on it and we apprentices didn't like that as it didn't look right. So then we started rounding things off, such as the wing tips, the rudder and fin, trying to give it a little better shape as on the first one all these things had been squared off.

Frank Cruttenden vividly remembered this period at Lympne:

> We had the little two-cylinder J.A.P. engine [salvaged from the Aeronca
> G-AEFT after it crashed]. The man who actually tested the Wot when it
> flew (and I'm positive of this) was K. K. Brown. We were all lined up on
> the tarmac outside to see the take-off. John Currie didn't fly it for quite
> some time; I think he wanted to make sure that it would fly before he
> went up in it. But K. K. Brown flew it quite often, and David Llewellyn
> flew it as well. It was all painted up in the club's colours and it looked
> very nice. They were both lost when the hangar roof fell in after the
> bombing of August 1940.
>
> Another innovation was developed at Lympne, and although it was
> not directly connected with the Cinque Ports Flying Club, it would have
> been of great benefit to all flying club members. This was a lightweight
> radio receiver of only some 7 lb weight, which was small enough to
> be carried in an attaché case. It was developed by Mr Carmichael, the
> inventor of the micro-ray, who tested this device at Lympne when it
> proved satisfactory for use in light aircraft. However, soon afterwards
> Mr Carmichael died, and when enquiries were made of his widow
> about his invention, it was found that she had sold all her late husband's
> paraphernalia to the local rag and bone man – as junk!

In June 1937, club secretary B. C. Palmer inaugurated a scheme to
encourage the training of youngsters who showed aptitude for flying
training but could not afford to pay for their own flying instruction:

> It was at that time when I realised that war with Germany would come
> sooner or later, and that we should need more pilots than the flying clubs or
> the RAF could train under existing arrangements – club flying instruction
> was still quite expensive [£20 for a pilot's licence, plus a minimum of
> £4 10s for three hours' solo flying per year to keep it up to date].
>
> So in June 1937 I donated £100 to the Cinque Ports Flying Club to
> encourage the training of boys who had shown promise as pilots after
> a trial flying lesson at the club and had written an essay on why they
> were interested in becoming pilots. Then, the six trainees who had
> been successful had only to pay £2 2s per week over forty weeks to
> complete their flying training. We had so many applications that later
> we had to limit candidates to those who lived within 15 miles of Hythe.
> In November 1937 one lad, George Uden, went solo after only 1 hour
> 15 minutes' dual instruction under David Llewellyn. However, we had
> to bring our Youth of Britain Flying Training Association scheme to an
> end when a similar air league scheme known as the Civil Air Guard was

started in 1938. Although the Air League never acknowledged it, I am sure that they pinched our idea as their own!

The Cinque Ports Flying Club started its own branch of the new Civil Air Guard and was immediately successful; within the next nine months over 100 pupils were being trained at Lympne. To cope with the increased demand for instruction, the club had to increase its fleet of aircraft, and took this opportunity to acquire some more modern types. Firstly the twin-seater B.A. Swallow, both Pobjoy radial engined G-ADSF and Cirrus Minor in-line-engined G-AELI, G-AEVC and G-AEYV versions. One of these Swallows, G-AEVC, distinguished itself by taking off on its own, as Norman Geal recalls:

> One of our apprentices was starting it up by himself, and had set the throttle a little too far open while he swung the propeller to start the engine. Before he could scramble into the cockpit it started to taxi forward.

R. Brotherston, who worked at Lympne, remembers:

> There is an odd thing that happened during those days at Lympne. A Klemm aeroplane [the B.A. Swallow was based on the Klemm design] once took off all on its own. It was chased by another flying club aeroplane but the Klemm flew to Folkestone where it circled and then flew on to Hawkinge aerodrome, where it landed itself unharmed.

The B.A. Swallows were followed by some more De Havilland biplanes in the following year when the club acquired a couple of DH.82 Tiger Moths, G-ACGE and G-ADWG, the latter arriving resplendent in a red and white chequerboard pattern colour scheme it had sported when flown by Geoffrey Tyson with Sir Alan Cobham's flying circus. However, as Norman Geal recalls, Cobham's flying circus did not stage an event at Lympne:

> I don't remember the Cobham Flying Circus ever performing at Lympne, but I think they did call in to refuel occasionally. But the old Tiger Moth G-ADWG, she was with Alan Cobham [then with C. W. A. Scott's British Hospitals Air Pageants] when it was painted in red and white squares as in the picture, a horrible-looking colour scheme, but then it was painted into club colours. Then it looked like a real aeroplane, not all that nonsense of checkers. The international air rallies continued to be held up to 1937, but that year the influence of Nazi Germany was seen when the contingent from that country arrived with swastikas emblazoned on

their machines and one report was circulating that whenever German civilian machines arrived for a rally they already had fittings for a machine gun!

So far as the German aircraft visiting the international rallies with machine-gun mountings in the cockpits, I can remember something being said about this, but I didn't see it myself. Anyway they were far too light and small to have had anything like that [they may have been wooden dummy guns]. At one international air rally the Messerschmitt Me 108 came over. That was quite an excitement to see before the Bf 109 had been developed; it was a nice little aeroplane. But again it wasn't a military type as it had a little cabin to hold three people but was quite neat though.

The following year the planned international rally was cancelled after the German contingent wrote to say that they would probably not be allowed to attend that year. This was at the time of the Munich Crisis, in September 1938, and more weightier matters were exercising the minds of the members of the Cinque Ports Flying Club. They were also doing something else to help preparations for the coming war. Norman Geal continues his account of events:

Another memory that comes into my mind is that in 1938 the Flying Club had purchased a Short Scion twin Pobjoy engined, high wing, cabin monoplane, and that was a nice aeroplane. They had a contract with the Army people who were doing their training with searchlights. It must have been the Royal Artillery or suchlike [probably the Royal Engineers T. A.] and we used to fly at night and I used to get in on that, naturally. If there was any chance of me flying I'd have a go at it. So whenever I could jump aboard the Scion when she was going on one of these exercises, I'd go with them.

We used to fly along the coast at various heights, from Lympne via Hythe, to Folkestone, Dover, and Capel-le-Ferne was one of the turning points. We started off at say 3,000 feet and then increase each run by 1,000 feet so we eventually finished off at about 8,000 or 9,000 feet. The searchlights would try and pick you up, and they did pick us up occasionally. If we were a bit worried about these searchlights [dazzling the pilot] we carried a Very pistol which we used to fire and then the searchlights would be switched off. We used to go for two-and-a-half to three hours at a time and it was quite a stretch when you think of it. We didn't do anything much, apart from just sitting there and eating pickled eggs which Mrs Davis had got Jock Warner [the club steward] to cook for us when went on night flights. They were delicious.

William Eric Davis was born at Birkenhead, Cheshire, on 25 August 1903. Early in 1932, he was secretary and manager of the Cinque Ports Flying Club, but had not yet learned to fly. However, it was not long before he commenced flying lessons and was taught by the club's senior instructor K. K. Brown. On 1 April 1932, Bill obtained his Royal Aero Club Aviators Certificate at the club, flying a DH.60G Gipsy Moth.

At 4 pm on 12 March 1938, after an enjoyable tea with friends, Bill suggested that he took them for a local flight in his Monospar G-AEJV. On take-off the aircraft climbed perfectly up to about 200 feet and he then prepared to do a right-hand turn. It was, however, flying very slowly and suddenly it got into a spin at the end of the turn. He struggled to recover from the spin but did not have the altitude to pull out. The aircraft disappeared beyond the airfield's boundary and twenty seconds later smoke and flames could be seen. A witness said that as the aircraft flew over him, he heard one of the engines cut out and that the port engine was racing.

The inferno was all-consuming and everyone on board perished, including Bill Davis. Flying with him were Mrs Gertrude Mohr, a German citizen living in London, Mr Raymond, A. J. Henru, an architect, and his sister, Miss Yvonne M. M. Henru, both from London. At an inquest held the following Monday, Capt. F. S. Wilkins of the Air Ministry Accident Investigation Branch stated that he had examined the wreckage and found the main petrol cock closed, cutting off the petrol supply from the engine, and that in his opinion it had been inadvertently turned off by the pilot. He considered that the cock handle was unsatisfactory, the pilot having mistaken the long end of the handle for the short end. It was apparent from previous accidents of this type of aircraft that the starboard engine would often cut out after the aircraft had climbed to about 250-300 feet, followed by the port engine. Both engines were stripped down but no defects were found. It would seem that although the aircraft type was sound, the petrol cock was a poor design and would have to be replaced.

The chief ground engineer at Lympne, John R. Currie, had prepared the machine for flying and said that when he was finished the cock was fully on. Norman F. Newbury, a ground engineer, had warmed up both engines on Bill Davis's instructions. At 5.15 p.m. he examined the cock and it was on. He helped him into the aircraft and, as far as he knew, the cock was still on.

At the flying club hangar the following Tuesday, from where the cortège started, flags were flown at half-mast and members of 21 Squadron RAF were paraded, all ground staff and workmen of the Cinque Ports Aviation attending. As the coffin of Bill Davis was carried to the cemetery at Lympne church by mechanics of the Cinque Ports Flying Club (wearing white

Bill Davis is seated far left with Ann Davis, enjoying the company of friends and members of the Cinque Ports Flying Club during the 1938 Folkestone Aero Trophy race. The aircraft on the right is G-AEFT Aeronca C-3. General Aircraft ST-25 Monospar Universal G-AEJV is in the background, and was a wedding present for his wife, and the aircraft in which Bill Davis died.

overalls), aircraft of No. 500 (County of Kent) Squadron based at RAF Manston flew overhead in tribute. Bill will always be associated with the flying club and Lympne airfield. His resting place at St Stephen's Church is easily distinguishable by the marble grave. Bill's widow Ann took up the reins of the flying club, supported by Tony Duport and the remainder of the staff.

In July 1938, the Civil Air Guard was formed, based on an idea put forward by Capt. Harold Balfour MP, Under Secretary of State for Air, and the Cinque Ports Flying Club participated in their programme. It was a civilian organisation operated by flying clubs around the country, who would run a separate Civil Air Guard section within the club. As part of the scheme, the Air Ministry provided a subsidy to participating flying clubs, with the aim of giving flying training to members of the public. It was expected that pilots would achieve an 'A' standard licence after thirteen hours' dual and four hours' solo flying. Many RAF pilots of the Second World War were former members of the Civil Air Guard, including those who trained at Lympne.

On 21 September 1938, the Chief Flying Instructor (CFI) of the club, David Llewellyn, was killed along with Lt J. B. Kitson of the Royal Horse Guards, flying B.A. Swallow G-AELI when it crashed into a field behind

The County Members public house on Aldington Road. Norman Geal was at the spot when it happened:

> David Llewellyn, of course, we all knew him very well and the day that he crashed I had got off the bus and I was walking from the County Members pub towards the aerodrome when this B.A. Swallow came over; it didn't stall or anything, it just went straight in as the engine had cut. Because I was anxious when I saw this happening, I ran across into the field, and other people as well, and Mr Kitson was still alive when we got over to the aircraft but he died shortly afterwards. David Llewellyn was killed instantly as he was in the front of the Swallow and it had gone in nose first, and the engine was pushed right back into the front cockpit. It really shook me up at the time.

Llewellyn had made almost a complete circuit of the airfield and was preparing to come round again when the B.A. Swallow stalled and dived into the ground. A serving officer with the RAFR, he was the son of Sir William Llewellyn. J. B. Kitson, a nephew of Lord Strathcona and Mount Royal, was on a course at the Small Arms School at Hythe and had several instructional flights with the Cinque Ports Flying Club.

In 1935, with Doris Jillian Wyndham, Llewellyn broke Amy Johnson's Cape to England record by eighteen hours and forty-eight minutes, completing the distance over six and a half days. During 1937, he flew both ways on the Cape–London route, attempting to break records, but engine trouble and unfavourable weather prevented him from doing so. Amy Johnson subsequently recaptured the record. In the autumn of 1937, Llewellyn was appointed chief instructor at Lympne, where he had put many young RAF officers through their elementary flying training. He competed in an air race at Lympne with a broken rib in July the following year. It was the result of a remarkable accident a few hours before, when he was flying at 200 mph. The wind had ripped off the entire roof of the aircraft's cabin and part of the wreckage caught in the tail; he only regained control after falling 700 feet. He was thrown about in the cabin and, besides breaking a rib, injured an arm.

Llewellyn's attempt to fly to the Cape and back was an example of his determination. His plans were formed at the end of the unfortunate Portsmouth to Johannesburg race. Although the temptation to stake everything on a dash against unfavourable weather was often strong, he announced last-minute postponements so often that he must have despaired of ever taking off. As a director and flying instructor at Hanworth Air Park he was well known in Home Counties aviation long before his epic flights. He was planning a record flight to the island of

Cinque Ports Flying Club apprentices at Lympne in 1938. J. R. Currie, seated third left, lectured at the College of Aeronautical Engineering, Chelsea. Seated fourth and fifth front row are the clubs directors Bill Davis and Tony Duport.

Mauritius with Miss Frances Planel to take place in October 1938 and had been training a large number of members of the Civil Air Guard.

In July that year, Sandy Johnstone, later Air Vice Marshal Johnstone CB, DFC, had taken the opportunity to do some flying with the Cinque Ports Flying Club, while attending the annual training period with No. 602 (Glasgow) Squadron at RAF Hawkinge. He liked the friendly atmosphere at Lympne, which was a focal point for many civilian pilots, and it did not seem to matter whether you were Jim Mollison, Geoffrey de Havilland, Amy Johnson, a member of the RAF or the public. Having a drink at the club's bar, and chatting to David Llewellyn, Johnstone told him about his efforts to gain his 'B' licence and how he needed to take the night flying test. In response he was told, 'Get yourself made a temporary member here, and I will give you one of our kites to use.' Without hesitation, Johnstone took up the offer and made an application for the cross-country flight, whenever conditions were suitable for the test. This meant waiting for a period of no moon. The route would be flown at a height of 2,000 feet from Croydon Airport to Lympne on a full black night. Arrangements were made for the attempt to be scrutinised at both airfields and the student turned up at Lympne that morning to collect the aircraft from Llewellyn. He was told that no suitable aircraft was available but managed to provide an ageing Gipsy Moth I, which was wheeled out of a hangar. On seeing the worried expression on Johnstone's face, Llewellyn remarked, 'Don't worry, it should just about get you there and back,, a statement which the young pilot did not care to hear.

The aircraft to be used was dark red in colour and had an inverted engine, which obscured the pilot's vision. In the 1930s, pilots generally did not wear parachutes when flying a club aircraft in order to discourage panicking pilots from abandoning their aircraft at the first sign of trouble. This made the seating lower than that of an RAF machine. When he climbed into the cockpit he could hardly see, peeping over the side of the fuselage. Not to be deterred, he flew the Moth to Croydon in daylight. To fly back to Lympne by night he had to wait until 11.30 p.m. so had time for a meal and a visit to the cinema. When he arrived back at Croydon it had become foggy, but he was told by Flight Control that the fog was only local and they would telephone Lympne to ask what conditions were like there. Having reassured him that the weather there was fine, Johnstone arranged a time for take-off.

The scrutineer was waiting by the Moth with an ordinary barograph (a self-recording barometer) tucked under his arm. 'Where do you want me to put this?' he asked. 'What do you mean?' replied Johnstone, not knowing why he would need this piece of equipment. 'Well, you must take it with you as it's set to zero, and it will confirm that you have flown at 2,000 feet.'

Johnstone had planned to sneak down to Dover and follow the headlights of traffic to Lympne, but the examiner by this time had put the instrument in a locker near the cockpit. As there was no wireless in the aircraft, he had to wait for the green light from the flare-path controller before take-off, and he climbed away in the gloom. To his relief, the weather was clear and it was not long before he reached a beacon at Bethersden,
near Ashford and a second at Merle, near Tonbridge, and before long he saw the flashing beacon on the roof of the hangar at Lympne, flashing the Morse letter A.

Owing to poor vision created by the inverted engine, he had to turn the aircraft from side to side, but eventually approached Lympne. Seeing the flare-path had been lit, he came in to land but was alarmed to see people waving, so he opened up and went round again. He put down, wondering what was wrong, and bounced but came to rest. In fact, the crowd had been people from the club waving their drink glasses at him. Once he had climbed out of the Moth and whilst having a refreshing drink, Llewellyn showed him the barograph, which recorded his altitude as being erratic with up and down zigzag lines, but never flying lower than 2,000 feet he had qualified for a commercial pilot's licence.

The apprentices at Cinque Ports Aviation were encouraged to join the Civil Air Guard, and Ron Giles was among those who took this opportunity to gain their wings:

> I took lessons as a member of the Civil Air Guard at 2*s* 6*d* a time, and as my wages were only 10*s* per week, I had to take twenty minutes or half-hour flying lessons during my own lunch break. My first flight was on 5 September 1938 with Tom Hackney [who had taken over as CFI] as my instructor, in Swallow G-AEYW, and I made my first solo flight in Swallow G-ADSF on 31 October. As the Swallow was a monoplane, I progressed to Gipsy Moth I G-ABOG and on 7 February 1939 finally took my A1 licence test flight in Swallow DSF. As well as the flying tests, we had to answer questions on air navigation, landing regulations, lighting of airfields and safety procedures. We were only asked one or two; it was similar to the Highway Code questions for a driving licence. My Civil Air Guard number was 629.

Everyone at the flying club was devastated when they received the news that K. K. Brown, who had previously been the CFI at Lympne, had been involved in a mid-air collision. At the time of the accident, on 21 July 1939, he was chief instructor with the Kent Flying Club based at Bekesbourne,

The Bristol Fighter owned by K. K. Brown a CPFC instructor, and registered for civilian use as G-ABYT, in the club's hangar at Lympne following a heavy landing. This aircraft had previously flown with No. 25 Squadron RAF at Hawkinge.

but on this particular day he had taken off from Lympne on a map-reading exercise with D. W. A. Pragnell who was flying Gipsy Moth G-ABJZ of the Kent Flying Club.

Between Dover and Dymchurch their aircraft was struck from above and behind by Hawker Hind K5418, flown by Plt Off. D. C. Lewis of the Royal Air Force Volunteer Reserve. Both aircraft crashed to the ground, disintegrating on impact, and Lewis was killed instantly. The Moth landed separately from its engine, which was carried 200 yards beyond the wreckage. The Hind lost its tail and its pilot landed about twenty yards from his aircraft, while the tail fell in a cornfield adjoining Beeches Wood at Tilmanstone, about fifty yards away from the Gipsy Moth. Brown had been born in Australia in 1901 and joined the RAF in 1922, before going to Lympne in 1929. Chief instructor of the Nottingham Aero Club, he was a very competent pilot and instructor and was sadly missed when he moved to the Kent Flying Club. The incident was even more tragic, as he had no control over the circumstances of the crash – he was not flying the Gipsy Moth at the time of the accident.

Police Constable Waite of Studdale inspects the remains of DH Gypsy Moth G-ABJZ following a collision with Hawker Hind K5418 of the Oxford University Air Squadron, at Beeches Wood, Tilmanstone on 21 July 1939. K. K. Brown CPFC, D. W. A. Pragnal and D. Curig Lewis were killed.

When war was declared on 3 September 1939, activities at Lympne continued as normal. The airfield was particularly busy that day, not only with civilian aircraft movements, as at the time Lympne was host to RAuxAF aircraft. Norman Geal has vivid memories of that warm Sunday, as the inevitable news everyone feared broke:

> When war was declared I was actually up at the club and I was sitting in Ann Davis's big American Packard. It was a lovely thing, and the only car that I can remember at that time which had a radio in the car. I was sitting in the car with Ann Davis and, I think, Tom Hackney, and we three sat there and listened to war being declared on that Sunday morning. In the afternoon of that Sunday, I think it was 601 Squadron who were there with their Gladiators, and then some great big cans of green and brown distemper and brushes arrived and we camouflaged all their aircraft on the RAF side. Then we did our own aircraft, some of the Moths but not all of them, because there wasn't enough room in the hangar. We flew them, including CPG, into some woods at the back of the airport over towards Aldington. I think the land belonged to Coldharbour Farm and when we landed we put these aircraft into the spaces between the trees after folding the wings, or the ones which could be folded, and pushed them back amongst the trees, and then camouflaged them with the distemper as well. So that was those aircraft off the field and camouflaged in case the Germans tried to take photographs of the airfield. We spent nights up there because we were loaned the flying club's van in which we had makeshift beds on mattresses in the back. We would sleep there and they would bring us food in the morning from the club. It was really exciting at the time.

With the onset of war, private aircraft owners could collect their machines from Lympne, and some flying club aircraft were evacuated to Sywell for the duration, but the heyday of the Cinque Ports Flying Club had now drawn to a close. The airport at Lympne was to be used for the more serious task of helping defend the shores of Kent from an invader across the narrow waters of the English Channel.

CHAPTER 4

Royal Auxiliary Air Force summer camps; RAF development of the airfield; its survival in the 1920s and 1930s alongside civil aviation events

In 1924, the Marine Aircraft Experimental Establishment was moved from the Isle of Grain to Felixstowe in Suffolk, closing down the airfield on the Isle of Grain. The following year, Short Brothers, based at Rochester, found themselves without a suitable site for testing land-planes. They were able to secure hangar space at Lympne, but owing to its distance from Rochester, this discouraged the company from undertaking new land-based projects. However, as the Grosvenor Cup air race was held at Lympne, they maintained a foothold. Shorts had been developing a new aircraft for the role of Army co-operation and following a year at Martlesham Heath, Springbok J7295 returned to Rochester to be modified for its proposed role, re-emerging as the Chamois S.3b. It was flown to Lympne on 27 February by John L. Parker, test pilot at Shorts. On 14 and 29 March, Parker flew from Lympne, climbing to 15,500 feet in thirty-eight minutes, later returning to Martlesham Heath for further evaluation, but the aircraft was not adopted for squadrons.

On 1 January 1927, new regulations came into effect which meant that aircraft with ten or more passengers would have to carry a radio operator in addition to the pilot. In February it was reported that a Notice to Airmen had been issued, stating that aircraft coming from the Continent in conditions of poor visibility in which the radio was not functioning correctly should land at Lympne where repair facilities were available. In April it was reported that a new wireless station was being built at Lympne, and in May it was notified that the night light was again in operation at Lympne.

In July, a new system was introduced for civil aircraft flying in bad visibility between Lympne and Croydon. They were not to follow the normal Lympne–Edenbridge–Caterham–Croydon route but instead follow one of three notified alternative routes. Aircraft were to be notified by radio whenever such conditions were declared to be in effect, or whenever the weather had improved. This was aimed at preventing mid-air collisions between civil aircraft and those operated by the RAF. In December, a Notice to Airmen informed pilots that in foggy weather the position of Lympne would be indicated by flares fired from the ground. Colour was to be at the discretion of the civilian air traffic officer. The notification was quickly amended to state that the firing of red flares would be reserved to indicate that an aircraft was being instructed not to land at the airfield in question.

In a memorandum written in 1919, Sir Hugh Trenchard made it clear that a reserve air force should be formed on a territorial basis, and in 1922 a Bill was drafted. However, due to apathy and opposition to the proposal, it did not become law until 1924. Eventually twenty-one Royal Auxiliary Air Force squadrons were formed. Perhaps one of the most famous, formed at RAF Northolt on 14 October 1925, was No. 601 (County of London) Squadron. Its first CO, Lord Edward Grosvenor, was himself a pilot in the RNAS during the First World War and it was not long before the squadron were dubbed 'The Millionaires Mob'. He had, in 1923, created the Grosvenor Challenge Cup at Lympne, and was passionate about the idea of the RAuxAF. Although not the first, No. 601 Squadron can claim it was their CO who played an important role in its creation. Both Nos 600 and 601 Squadrons held summer camps at Lympne. In fact, the first annual training camp was held at Lympne in August 1926. Later COs of No. 601 Squadron were Loel Guinness, Nigel Norman and Sir Dermot Boyle.

In the summer of 1927, No. 601 Squadron arrived again at the airfield with both DH.9As and Avro 504s. At the time, only four pilots had any service apart from Grosvenor and two regulars. The squadron were camped on the airfield, convenient for the owner of Port Lympne, Sir Philip Sassoon, who later took over from Grosvenor as the squadron's CO and served as the Under Secretary of State for Air from 1924-29 and 1931-37. Grosvenor, an admirer of the French Foreign Legion, had christened No. 601 Squadron his legionaries and the name stuck. The squadron could not have had a better ally in Sassoon, who entertained the officers so well that summer camps at Lympne became known as the summer outing of White's Club, a reference to the elite club in London.

Pilots delighted in pushing their flying exploits to the brink. In one competitive performance, an exploit in which a spotted handkerchief was tied to a stick in the front cockpit of an Avro 504K trainer, the pilot flew the aircraft in the rear cockpit and after a circuit of the airfield would land with the handkerchief in his pocket. Occasionally this was

The aptly named '*Millionares Club*', pilots No. 601 Squadron enjoying Summer Camp at Lympne in the 1930s. One of many well-known guests of Sir Philip Sassoon was the actor and author Noel Coward, seated far right in civvies.

abandoned and the pilot would land the aircraft seated in the front cockpit instead.

No. 600 (City of London) Squadron used Lympne for a summer camp in 1927, the advanced party arriving from Hendon on 2 August to finalise arrangements for the squadron's arrival on the 6th. A convoy of vehicles set off for Lympne with equipment and personnel, some members travelling by rail. The first flight of aircraft to arrive were Avro 504s, followed by two flights of DH.9s. The young pilots had experienced fog and rain en route but arrived safely, having used the Southern Railway line as a guide. However, Plt Off. Hacket, who had learnt to fly in 1926 and was at the controls of Avro 504K F9776, landed in trees in a garden at Crowborough but fortunately was uninjured. Three other aircraft force-landed but, unlike F9776, were not damaged.

The DH.9s arrived at the airfield, but Plt Off. Vaisey hit a ridge on approach, losing his undercarriage. Having climbed out of his aircraft, he walked away happy that he had made what was termed a perfect belly landing. Unfortunately, owing to the continuing poor weather, flying was limited and during such pauses the squadron diarist Jenyns recorded his thoughts:

Being an old wartime airfield, Lympne is a familiar name to many of us, recalling memories of those days when we used to put in there during the war before leaving for the last "opping orf ground' in England to proceed overseas. Many changes have taken place at this station since those days. The old hangars have been pulled down and fresh ones put up at the south-west side of the aerodrome. The aerodrome is equipped with red lights and lighthouses for guidance at night of various airliners that may have to call in for petrol or other necessaries. From the aerodrome situated on top of a plateau, one has a fine view of the coast as far as Dungeness to the west and eastwards to Hythe, Folkestone and Dover and inland the wooded countryside of Kent. Such were our surroundings and a great place to camp even in wet weather!

The exploits of the RAuxAF always attracted attention from the press, and the British public also showed much interest in their activities. Maj. Turner of *The Daily Telegraph* described in one report how airmen were instructed in parachute jumping:

These city clerks showed no fear when they took up their position on the wings of aircraft and waited for the pilot to give the signal to go after he had reached a height of 1,000 feet. Twenty parachute descents were successfully made.

On another occasion, Fairey Foxes from Andover landed at Lympne to fly Sir Philip Sassoon to Manston and back, during which the squadron diarist recorded an amusing incident:

This machine and its pilot had earlier in the day endeavoured to reach RAF Tangmere but was forced to return to Lympne owing to the weather. While having tea, a machine suddenly shot out of the mist over the airfield and everyone ran out to see who it was. It turned out to be one of our own auxiliary air force pilots back from Tangmere on a cross-country flight.

During the summer camp week, Avro 504Ks of No. 600 Squadron visited RAF Manston, invited by No. 605 (County of Warwick) Squadron enjoying their summer camp at the famous airfield. On the return flight they hit poor weather flying out to sea, but they all landed back at Lympne without incident. The following day, aircraft of No. 605 Squadron flew into Lympne for a few hours – a good opportunity for pilots to exchange ideas and experiences.

A sports day was organised for 17 August 1927 in which officers, NCOs and other ranks, including some of their wives, joined in events such as a wheelbarrow race, a 100-yard handicap blindfold chariot race, tug of war and high jump. This proved a great success and was talked about for a long time. At the end of the week, the annual inspection took place, Air Cdre Felton Holt CMG, DSO being accompanied by AOC RAuxAF John Hearson CB, CBE, DSO and Air Cdre Gerrard CMG, DSO. However, the most enjoyable event was when No. 601 Squadron managed to set fire to their own mess tent, an unfortunate accident. On 21 August, both squadrons returned home to RAF Hendon, but not before a great party had been held, attended by Sir Philip Sassoon and enjoyed by all. As the night wore on, surf riding in baths towed around the airfield by cars took place.

The following year, both squadrons returned to Lympne for summer camp between 4 and 19 August, many wives and families taking holidays at Hythe, Folkestone and Sandgate. The press once again attended, *The Times* writing that the experiment of creating territorial airmen was justified and that the recruits who came from such diverse backgrounds were receiving the best of instructional flying and training – a sentiment that would be echoed when war came again in 1939. As if to prove the effectiveness of their training, a mock air raid on the Air Ministry in London was planned during the 1928 air defence exercises. At 6 p.m. on 14 August, 300 aircraft representing the enemy attacked the Air Ministry. Although intercepted over London, they did manage to stage a dummy bombing raid on the seat of the Air Ministry.

In 1929, the night flying flight arrived from RAF Biggin Hill on brief detachment, with two Hawker Horsley biplanes and an Avro Bison aircraft, N9967, which had already been detached to Lympne between 1923 and 1928 to assist in the development of acoustical manoeuvres. Some of the concave structures can still be found today at Denge Marsh.

Flt Lts G. W. Higgs and D. H. Humphreys had taken off from Lympne at 10 p.m. on 8 August 1924 to participate in one such exercise, flying Vickers Vimy aircraft F9176 and F8642. Unfortunately, due to a misunderstanding, the aircraft flown by Humphreys took off too soon after the first Vimy. Having flown across the Channel and turned back, both should have been within range of the discs (sound detectors). The readings were collated at Lympne and some sounds were detected at 10.37 p.m., while the second did likewise three minutes later. The scientific team at Lympne calculated the course of the sound source as 320 degrees, with a ground speed of 57 mph at a height of 5,500 feet. They phoned through their findings to the prediction centre at Biggin Hill where personnel were in communication with local searchlights and had been directed to switch on at the predicted angle and time to illuminate the aircraft. Nobody on the ground could tell if the sounds were from one Vimy or from different aircraft, and both Higgs and Humphreys reported that they had not seen each other until shortly before landing back at Lympne. On another flight from Lympne, Humphreys (accompanied by either Higgs or Flt Lt T. S. Horry) was closest to being picked up by searchlights, but only because he had switched on his navigation lights.

These early experiments with acoustic discs and upright discs, although not a great success, did contribute to some degree to the Army's improvement of sound locators in the 1930s. But with the invention and development of radar, which played a major role in Britain's home defence when war came, perhaps the engineers and scientists were not given the credit they deserved.

With the Cinque Ports Flying Club already at home at Lympne, the visit of the night flying flight was indeed short-lived, and it was eight years before the RAF showed any further interest in the airfield.

Often at summer camps, pilots would take off from Lympne in private aircraft and land in fields close to their favourite pub, in particular Botolphs Bridge Inn on Romney Marsh, which can be visited to this day. An incident often recalled about this hostelry involved Plt Off. Roger

LAC John Hume Ross (better known as Lawrence of Arabia—T. E. Lawrence) at Lympne in the early 1930s, stands by one of his beloved Brough Superior SS100 motorbikes registration GW2275, the motorbike on which he was killed. He died of his injuries on 19 May 1935. Apart from the first one he owned which he christened Boa short for Boanerges, he had seven others of the same type, each named after King George, the first being George I the last George VII.

Bushell of No. 601 Squadron. The young pilot had taken off in Max Aitken's privately owned Aeronca G-ADZZ from Lympne on a mission to the pub, hoping to land in a field already occupied by other aircraft. On landing, he swerved to avoid killing a sheep and crashed through a hedge. The remains of the aircraft stopped not twenty yards from the pub, destroying a road sign. Bushell, fortunately uninjured, managed to remove himself from the wreck and apologised to Aitken, and it was not long before a crowd of spectators gathered, Bushell taking it upon himself to auction the remains of the machine to those gathered at the scene. A bid of £5 was made by Ann Davis, who later wrote the following rhyme based on the aircraft's civil registration:

G-one is Max's aeroplane,
A-rtful Roger is to blame,
D-own at Botolphs Bridge one night,
Z-ero was his cruising height,
Z-oomed too low – out went the light.

The road sign became a treasured possession of the squadron, proudly displayed at their HQ. Bushell was later captured during the war and sent to Stalag Luft III, the infamous German PoW camp for prisoners who persistently tried to escape. Sadly, he was one of fifty prisoners murdered after the mass escape depicted in the film *The Great Escape* in which he was played by Richard Attenborough.

Another favourite pastime was the rabbit hunt. As night fell, rabbits were caught in the glare of headlights as revellers drove their cars around the airfield. It was said that on one occasion 200 rabbits were let loose in the bar of the Cinque Ports Flying Club.

It was said that to become an officer with No. 601 Squadron you had to have been at Eton and a student at Oxbridge. Craven Goring Hohler, the son of Edwin Theobald Hohler and Agnes Venetia Hohler (née Goring) from The Court Lodge at Stansted in Kent, was educated at Eton and King's College Cambridge before eventually becoming a solicitor. Before the war, in the early 1930s, he joined the RAuxAF as a junior officer in the squadron. The 1930s was an exciting time to be a pilot and being in the Auxiliary Air Force as a young man-about-town was as good as it got. In 1937, Hohler was made squadron leader of No. 500 (County of Kent) Squadron, another RAuxAF squadron, serving in that post until the start of the war, overseeing their move to Detling and their conversion to the Avro Anson.

In October 1939, Wg Cdr Hohler took command of No. 148 Squadron at their base at Stradishall in Suffolk. The whole squadron left Britain for

Seated in a Hawker Hart of No. 601 (City of London) Squadron Royal Auxiliary Air Force (RAuxAF), Craven Hohler with Sir Philip Sassoon prepare for take-off at Lympne. Note the winged sword on the fin, the Squadron's distinctive symbol.

Aircraft of 601 (County of London) Squadron RAuxAF lined up close to one of the hangars at Lympne. Nearest is Avro 504N serial No. J9420 and behind a Westland Wapiti.

Egypt, flying in long hops via Gibraltar over unfriendly seas to reach their stopover in Malta. A very experienced wing commander, he was flying first pilot in a crew of six in a Vickers-Armstrong Wellington, T2894, which took off from Luqa airfield at 9.01 p.m. on 28 November and set course for the Middle East. His last sighting was by his comrades covering an incoming convoy that at the time was under attack from an Italian bomber force. During this mêlée, Hohler and his crew were lost at sea. Their estimated time of arrival in Egypt came and went, and they were therefore presumed missing on Thursday 28 November. His service is commemorated and recorded on the Air Forces Memorial at Runnymede in Surrey.

On 27 October 1936, a terrific gale struck the airfield at Abbotsinch and carried away the hangars in which No. 21 (Bomber) Squadron housed their Hawker Hind biplanes, damaging all the aircraft. All but two were repaired and in some cases new parts were fitted. The following day an advance party of airmen arrived at Lympne from Nos 21 and 34 Squadrons to open up the site as a temporary home for No. 1 (Bomber) Group comprising both 21(B) and 34(B) Squadrons. Over the next four weeks, some fourteen trucks arrived with stores from RAF Kidbrooke.

Instructed to proceed to Lympne, the aircraft were flown in on 3 November 1936, by Plt Offs McCudden and McLeod, and Sgts Soivder, Tucker and Hastle. The ground party left for Lympne by special train on the 4th. Wg Cdr Baker DSO, MC, AFC took over command of Lympne from Flt Lt Wright who was acting CO. Temporary accommodation was available for both airmen and officers, without much time to recover from the move, and the remainder of November was spent unpacking and settling into their new home.

On 8 December, Wg Cdr W. A. C. Morgan MC took over command of the station from Baker. The squadron were to undertake training, but it was soon apparent that they had not been provided with bomb hooks or wireless sets, which delayed exercises, and bad weather added to the squadron's frustration. However, with Christmas approaching, morale was raised when personnel were sent home on leave on Christmas Eve. In the New Year of 1937 poor weather continued to delay training, but despite this, bombing practice was carried out at Otmoor on 18-30 January. These operations took place from Upper Heyford. On 27 January, three new Hawker Hinds were taken on charge from the manufacturers, followed by another received at the beginning of February.

On 24 February 1937, some publicity was generated when Hawker Hind K5388 of No. 21 Squadron crashed in poor visibility into a row of cottages at Ticehurst, Sussex. Fortunately, the crew was not seriously injured, nor the startled inhabitants! Further bombing exercises were

An impressive line-up of a few of 601 (County of London) Squadron's aircraft, the nearest being Hawker Hart and three Avro 504N's. The young pilots at summer camp in 1937 were not aware that in a few years' time many of them would be fighting for their lives.

Believed to be Avro Tutor T1 serial K3426 of Oxford University Squadron, following a mid-air collision with K3447 at Lympne on 23 June 1937.

Empire Air Day at Lympne 1939 attracted many aircraft. Arriving from Bicester was a Boulton Paul Overstrand serial K4553 of No.101 Squadron. This type was later replaced by the Bristol Blenheim.

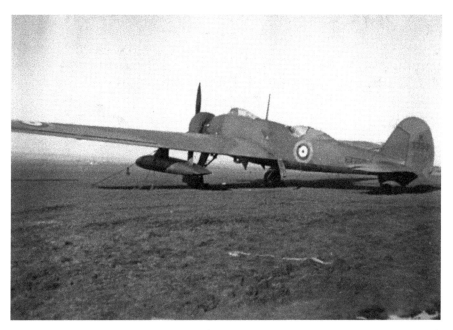

Vickers Wellesley K7759 of 207 Squadron at Lympne in 1937. This type of aircraft was in use with many squadrons but was replaced with Wellington, Whitley and Hampden bombers.

carried out, flying from Abingdon, and another new Hind arrived, bringing the unit's strength up to fourteen serviceable machines. On 3 April, Sir Philip Sassoon, Under Secretary of State for Air, visited the station, accompanied by the AOC No. 1 (Bomber) Group, Air Cdre S. W. Smith CBE. Sir Philip inspected the squadron's aircraft and spent some time talking to the pilots and airmen, which was followed by a demonstration of box formation flying.

During the afternoon of 4 June, 400 members of the Institute of Gas Engineers visited the station under the auspices of the Director of Folkestone Gas, Light and Coke Co. They were shown over the technical departments of the station and many of them went up for 5s flights with the Cinque Ports Flying Club. Nos 21 and 34(B) Squadrons gave a demonstration of formation flying, and a lone fighter aircraft of No. 25(F) Squadron at Hawkinge gave a demonstration of aerobatics. The CO attending the luncheon in Folkestone given by the Gas, Light and Coke Co. also took tea with them at the Lympne Castle Country Club.

On 1 July 1937, HRH The Duke of Kent arrived at 2.08 p.m. and was met by Brig. R. H. Willan DSO, MC, ADC, commanding Shorncliffe Garrison and the station commander for a while, and then left for Hendon at 4.16 p.m. The duke's pilot was Wg Cdr Fielden. The aircraft, Airspeed Envoy III G-AEXX of the King's Flight, was re-registered after war service as L7270. On this occasion, the duke was not accompanied by the duchess and was on his way to attend a Trooping the Colour ceremony and the presentation of a silver bugle to the Royal West Kent Regiment at Shorncliffe Barracks in Folkestone. They were met by Lt Col. W. V. Palmer, commanding 2 Battalion the Royal West Kent Regiment, and Wg Cdr Morgan MC, and returned to Hendon at 4.40 p.m.

The squadron flew to Upper Heyford on 20 May in two flights of five aircraft to take part in a mass flight formation practice for an RAF display. Lympne hosted an air display for Empire Day on 29 May 1937 in co-operation with No. 34(B) Squadron, under the direction of Sqn Ldr H. P. V. Battle CO 34 Squadron. Sir Philip Sassoon, Air Chief Marshal Sir Cyril L. N. Newall KCB, CMG, CBE and Air Cdre Smith visited the station during the afternoon.

Shortly after the arrival of the VIP party, two aircraft of No. 21 Squadron were involved in a mid-air collision whilst taking part in box formation flying. Hawker Hind K6684 collided with K4638 near the airfield at Lympne, but fortunately both pilots survived. The Cinque Ports Flying Club was not excluded, putting on a static display of civilian aircraft and a parachute descent from a Tiger Moth. Two Fairey aircraft of No. 25 Squadron based at nearby RAF Hawkinge put on a display of synchronised aerobatics. Profits raised from the show amounted to

During a Night Flying Exercise in 1936, this Hawker Hind of 21 Squadron crashed on landing at Lympne. This is an interesting scene, with hangars in the background and ground-staff debating on what could be salvaged.

On 1 July 1937 RAF Lympne was honoured when HRH the Duke of Kent visited the airfield *en route* to Shorncliffe Garrison, Folkestone.

A fascinating aerial view of Lympne of '*Kent's Garden Airfield*'—taken at the height of its pre-war use in the 1930s at an International Air Rally. As well as many privately owned aircraft there are also RAF biplanes present.

A view looking across the airfield from Otterpool Lane towards hangars and wooden huts, the object close to the fence is most probably a landing beacon.

£73 14s 3d and it was attended by no fewer than 1,733 people.

Between 12 and 14 July 1937, a flight of six aircraft had been detached to RAF Biggin Hill. Their task was to carry out experimental exercises of a secret nature with Fighter Command. The following month the squadron were involved in No. 2(B) Group tactical exercises, operating by day and night, carrying out bombing exercises at Otmoor from RAF Upper Heyford. On 16 August, Plt Off. R. D. C. Gibson was appointed adjutant to the squadron.

During the first two weeks of August, the London Infantry Brigade Territorials were camped opposite the station at Otterpool Lane. Parties of soldiers were escorted round the camp and shown the various technical departments, a few officers being taken up for flights to see their own troops carrying out exercises. The commanding officer assisted in flying these officers. At the beginning of December, units based at Lympne took part in the Bomber Command tactical exercise.

Certain personnel of No. 12(B) Squadron were attached to the station to complete 72(B) Wing. The squadrons taking part were Nos 21(B), 34(B) and 12(B). On 12 August 1938, Air Cdre Smith again visited Lympne in the company of the station commander. They drove to Littlestone landing ground on Romney Marsh to view a demonstration of a landing given by an aircraft of No. 34 Squadron and to determine whether the airfield was suitable as a satellite to Lympne. The landing ground at Littlestone had been opened on 1 August 1917 when No. 3 (Auxiliary) School of Air Gunnery was formed at Littlestone/New Romney. The airfield, better known as Jesson Aerodrome, was used for civil flying during the 1930s. On landing at the airfield, pilots had to report to Lympne for customs purposes. Littlestone was closed before the Second World War and reverted to farmland.

Following bombing exercises at the beginning of September, No. 21 Squadron moved for two weeks to Armament Training Camp at Woodford, Dorset, returning to Lympne in the first week of October. Much to everyone's relief, the squadron stood down for their annual leave – a period of much needed rest. On return, further tactical and normal service training resumed until February, when the squadron moved to West Freugh for the month to the Armament Training Camp. Unfortunately, five aircraft were damaged during a sudden squall but were repaired without delay, as all machines were needed for navigational training for all the squadron's pilots.

On 28 May 1938, a mass flight demonstration and practice flying took place at Abingdon and Cranfield in preparation for the Empire Day air display that was held at Lympne. Both Nos 21 and 34 Squadrons took part, but some of the programme was cancelled due to poor weather.

Handley Page Heyford III bomber serial K5183 of 102 Squadron visiting Lympne in 1937. This aircraft crashed at Honnington on 16 December 1937 where the squadron was based. This unit had previously served at Lympne in 1919.

Supermarine Walrus Mk.1 serial L2191 of 712 (FAA) Squadron parked during visit to Lympne by Naval Personnel for a meeting. The Walrus was used extensively by the Fleet Air Arm and with Air Sea Rescue flights. Perhaps one of the best known of these was 277 Squadron which was based at RAF Hawkinge.

Hawker Hind K4645 of 21 (Bomber) Squadron served with the unit at Lympne in 1937 and also flew with 34 (Bomber) Squadron based there. It was often the case that aircraft were transferred from one unit to another on the same airfield.

However, despite this, there was a good attendance and the public showed great interest in ground exhibitions provided in the hangars. Following annual leave in June, aircraft were provided by No. 21 Squadron for Observer Corps calibration exercises.

Shortly after, No. 34(B) Squadron moved from Lympne to Upper Heyford, on 11 July 1938; thus No. 21(B) Squadron was the only one located at RAF Lympne. CO Sqn Ldr P. Murgatroyd retired at his own request in July and Flt Lt A. R. Sarel took over as squadron commander temporarily until Sqn Ldr I. T. Keans was posted as CO on 28 July 1938. With the expansion of the RAF, No. 21 Squadron dispatched twelve aircraft to RAF Waddington to take part in Home Defence exercises.

It was now No. 21 Squadron's time to move, so on 15 August 1938 they journeyed by train to RAF Eastchurch, Isle of Sheppey. Two aircraft were to remain at Lympne, later being allotted to maintenance storage units. Eventually the squadron were re-equipped with fifteen Bristol Blenheim aircraft. No. 34(B) were moved to Upper Heyford on 11 November 1938, and were also re-equipped with Blenheim Mk 1 aircraft. The School of Clerks, Accounting, was formed at Lympne on 17 October 1938, and in the same month RAF Lympne was transferred from Bomber Command to RAF Training Command. Despite Christmas, the likelihood of war

In 1932 Britain was selling aircraft to other air forces, in this case two Bristol Bulldogs have called into Lympne *en route* to join the Swedish Air Force in 1932. The RAF received Bulldogs in May 1929 until replaced by the Gloster Gladiator in 1937.

A Hawker Hind of 21 (B) Squadron parked outside one of the hangars at Lympne in 1937. Note the bomb racks mounted on the underside of the lower wings.

with Germany was on everybody's mind, none more so than pilots and airmen of the RAF returning home from leave in 1938. It was to be the last peacetime Christmas for six years.

The inhabitants of Sellindge were used to the aviation events and flying activities at Lympne, the village being situated not far from the airfield. However, on 1 June 1938, a Fokker aircraft with the civil registration OO-AIL, owned by the Belgian airline Sabena, crashed on Springfield House. Piloted by Pierre Genis, with wireless operator Paul Pevenage, it had become lost in a thunderstorm, having taken off from Croydon bound for Brussels during late afternoon. It was rumoured that the aircraft was one of three of this type that in addition to carrying passengers also transported gold bullion.

Making an approach to Lympne, the aircraft's undercarriage struck the chimney of Springfield House which at the time was occupied by a Mrs Pope, who remarked that they had just finished spring cleaning the house! The Fokker then hit telegraph wires alongside the road and cartwheeled across the small grass paddock before finally crashing into the rear of a chapel, coming to rest with its tail portion across the chapel boundary fence and just clear of some buildings. Debris from the machine and slates and bricks from the house were strewn all over the road and paddock,

Flying over the Kent countryside is Hawker Hart K3031, the black and red pattern on the fuselage side are the distinctive markings adopted by the squadron and appeared once again on their Meteor F8's of the 1950's.

and electricity power lines were also severed, cutting off the local supply. Springfield House was severely damaged; the ceiling fell in on two upper rooms and a greenhouse at the rear of the property was smashed by falling debris. A car parked outside the house also suffered damage.

The crash happened at 5.15 p.m. when people were enjoying tea after attending an event at the chapel. Everyone thought they had been struck by lightning. On going outside, the Revd A. S. Higson saw the occupants of the aircraft stepping out uninjured and offered them shelter and a strong cup of tea. Petrol burst from the aircraft tanks, but there was no explosion or fire, and it was extremely fortunate that nobody was killed. The following day a team arrived to remove the remains of the aircraft.

CHAPTER 5

Continuation of civil aviation alongside RAF occupation; Lympne's activities prior to the Second World War; epic record-breaking flights of the 1930s

Despite the aftermath of the First World War, during the 1920s and 1930s much design and development of new aircraft continued, with many new types taking to the skies. Civil aviation thrived. Aviators such as Amy Johnson caught the nation's imagination and inspired many more to take up flying. With this background, Lympne airfield gained popularity and must rank as a truly significant airfield, both in terms of civil aviation and RAF activities, their paths crossing.

An early event at Lympne was the Grosvenor Challenge Cup, which took place on 23 June 1923, a new award for air racing, which Lord Edward Grosvenor had instigated for British aircraft with engines of not more than 150 hp and flown by British pilots. The first contest was a race over a handicap course of 404 miles from Lympne to Croydon, Birmingham and Bristol, returning via Croydon to Lympne. First out of the nine starters was Flt Lt W. H. Longton in a Sopwith Gnu, G-EAGP, in 4 hours 38 minutes 6 seconds at 87.6 mph. Second was F. P. Raynham in Avro 504K G-EAMZ at 96 mph, and third came H. J. L. Hinkler in Avro 543 Baby G-EAUM. Dr E. D. Whitehead Reid in his SE5a G-EBCA had to retire at Birmingham. Sqn Ldr F. L. Robinson retired from the competition when his Boulton Paul PR.9 G-EAWS developed engine problems. The event was marred when Maj. E. L. Foot was killed when the 140 hp Bristol Lucifer M.1D G-EAVP he was flying crashed at Chertsey in Surrey – a sad ending to the popular event.

The *Daily Mail,* a keen supporter of British aviation for nearly twenty years, offered £1,000 as the main prize for its Motor Glider Competition, which took place at Lympne on 8 October 1923 over a period of one week. The Air League Challenge Cup, held at Lympne on 1 October

1924, was flown over a course of 100 miles, the contestants being from Nos 25, 32 and 56 Squadrons. Those of 25 Squadron at RAF Hawkinge were Flt Lts W. E. Mann, E. B. Mason and C. R. Keary, the latter winning in 59 minutes 7.4 seconds at an average speed of 100.2 mph. Three days later, the Grosvenor Cup was again held at Lympne, with nine out of the ten entries completing the 100-mile course. Bert Hinkler took first place in a Bristol Cherub I Avro 562 Avis, G-EBKP, at 65.87 mph for eight laps of the 12.5-mile course. Flt Lt S. H. Gaskell was second in a 32 hp Cherub III Westland Woodpigeon I, G-EBJV, and third was T. W. Campbell in a Cherub I Bristol Type 91 Brownie, G-EBJM, christened 'Jim'.

The following year, 1925, racing took place over a period from 1 to 3 August 1925 at Lympne by the Royal Aero Club, including the Light Aeroplane Holiday International Handicap over fifty miles on day one with fourteen contestants. Flt Lt J. S. Chick was in first place, flying Cherub III RAE Hurricane G-EBHS at a speed of 73.41 mph. In second place was Wg Cdr W. S. Douglas in DH.53 G-EBHX at 67 mph, and third place was taken by H. J. L. Hinkler in his Avis, G-EBKP, at 64.7 mph. The International Scratch Speed Race over fifty miles for two-seat aircraft, also on 1 August, was won by Capt. A. N. Kingwill at 32 hp with his Cherub Beardmore W.B. XXIV Wee Bee I, G-EBJJ, at 66.49 mph, with Flt Lt P. W. S. Bulman second at 65.95 mph in the Hawker Cygnet G-EBMB, these being the only two starters.

The other event held that day was the fifty-mile International Scratch Speed Race for single-seat aircraft. There were four starters, and Flt Lt Nicholas Comper was first in the 32 hp Cherub Cranwell CLA.3 parasol monoplane G-EBMC at 81.89 mph. Capt. F. T. Courtney was second in Parnall Pixie II G-EBKM and J. H. James came third in the ANEC Mk IA G-EBIL. The following day five races were held at Lympne, each over a 10.5-mile course with variations in the laps stipulated. In the first event, over two laps, Alan Cobham was first in Tiger Moth G-EBKT at 81.95 mph; the second event, of one lap, was won by Sqn Ldr R. A. de Haga Haig in Parnall Pixie III G-EBKK at 60.06 mph; the third was won by Capt. Hubert Broad in Tiger Moth G-EBKU at 74.75 mph, who also won the fourth event, of two laps, but flying the DH.54 G-EBKI at 103.40 mph; and the fifth was won by Flt Lt Chick in the Hurricane G-EBHS at 72.16 mph.

The weather was fine on 3 August and three events took place. Various types of aircraft competed in the first, which was a 100-mile international handicap without restrictions. Flt Lt Bulman took first place in Cygnet G-EBMB at a speed of 75.48 mph, second was C. T. Holmes flying Bristol Type 83 Trainer G-EBGD, and Cyril Uwins was third in a Brownie I, G-EBJM. Alan Cobham crashed on the last lap, making a forced landing in Tiger Moth G-EBKU but was uninjured. Chick won the Grosvenor Challenge Cup in G-EBHS at 81.19 mph, Uwins was second in G-EBJM and Comper third in CLA.3 G-EBMC out of twelve starters. The final race of the three-day event was the four-lap first private owners' race. First place was taken by Chick at 81.55 mph in G-EBHS, second was Dr Whitehead Reid with G-EBCA, and Comper was in third place in G-EBMC.

In June 1926, Charles Lindbergh arrived at Kenley, returning from his triumphant solo flight across the Atlantic. Intending to stay just for lunch, he was prevented from flying on to Paris by poor weather conditions. The following day he continued his flight, escorted by two Gloster Gamecocks and landing at Lympne. Although it was only a brief stay, he had time to talk to people and sign a few autographs, and it was indeed an honour for those present to meet such a famous aviator. Eventually he left the group of onlookers and well-wishers and continued his flight to Paris on his tour of lectures and interviews.

On 17 September 1926, not long after the light aeroplane trials that year, the stewards' handicap race took place at Lympne, over a twenty-five mile course. The event had been organised for those aircraft that did not qualify in the light aerospace trials. The winner was Flt Lt Comper in Cranwell CLA.4A G-EBPC at a speed of 70.85 mph. Other aircraft

Fokker F.VIIa G-EBTS named *Princess Benim* at Lympne in the 1930s. This aircraft was flown by 'The Flying Duchess' the Duchess of Bedford and Captain Barnes on their record breaking flight from India to England on 19 August 1929.

were Blackburn G-EBKD, ANEC IV Missel Thrush G-EBPI, Avro 562 Avis G-EBKP and Supermarine Sparrow II G-EBJP.

The following day, the last of the light aeroplane competitions, three races were held. The first was the fifty-mile Lympne Open Handicap for a prize of £100, which was won by Flt Lt Chick flying Hawker Cygnet G-EBJH, competing against fifteen other entrants including the Avro 562 Avis G-EBKP, Parnall Pixie III G-EBKK, Cranwell CLA.4A G-EBPC, Short Satellite G-EBJU, Brownie I G-EBJM, Cygnet G-EBB, Short Mussel I G-EBMJ, RAE Hurricane G-EBHS, SE5a G-EBCA, Avro 581 Avian G-EBOV, two Moths including G-EBMO, Scooter G-EACZ, SE5a G-EBPA and SE5a G-EBPD.

Also taking place was the Society of Motor Manufactures and Traders' 100-mile handicap race for a prize of 200 guineas, open to aircraft that completed 50 per cent of the light aeroplane competition course. Bert Hinkler took first place in Avro 581 Avian G-EBOV at 90 mph, ahead of Cyril Uwins' Brownie II G-EBJK, Hubert Broad in his 75 hp Genet DH.60 Moth G-EBOU, and a Hawker Cygnet. However, the main event on 18 September at Lympne was the seventy-five-mile handicap for the Grosvenor Challenge Cup and £100 prize over six laps of a twelve-and-a-half-mile triangular course. Some twenty-six aircraft entered the race, which W. H. Longton won at a speed of 84.95 mph in his Blackburn Bluebird I G EBKD.

The RAF was keen on record attempts, and Flt Lt Robert L. Ragg rose to the challenge on 23 August 1927 to break the long-distance record for light aircraft. Taking off from Lympne in a 30 hp ABC Scorpion Hawker Cygnet G-EBJH of the RAE Aero Club, he was attempting to fly to North Africa. This was an ambitious flight that ended shortly after take-off when a down current forced the single-seater into a row of telegraph wires, Ragg escaping uninjured.

At the beginning of September, Lt Richard Reid Bentley, who had flown with the South African Air Force as a flying instructor, bought an 85 hp Cirrus II DH.60 Moth G-EBSO from the De Havilland Company at Stag Lane, Edgware, and planned to fly it back to Cape Town. Recently engaged to Miss Dorys Oldfield of Pretoria, Bentley named the aircraft 'Dorys'. He took off from Lympne at 10.30 a.m. on 1 September, attempting the first solo flight of a light aircraft between England and South Africa in fourteen days. Following delays, he reached Cape Town after flying 7,250 miles in twenty-eight days, which was the fastest recorded time that year.

In 1928, Fokker F.VIIa, G-EBTS, was sold to Air Communications Ltd and a flight was planned to India, returning to England in eight days. The aircraft, piloted by Charles Douglas Barnard and Flt Lt Eric Herbert Alliott accompanied by the sixty-two-year-old Mary, Duchess of Bedford as a passenger, they had taken off from Lympne on 10 June. They were delayed by a faulty engine at Bushire, Persia, after a 48 hour flight, but Karachi was reached on 22 August after a new Jupiter VI engine was fitted and they took off from Karachi on 2 September, returning to Croydon on 6 September 1928.

Amy Johnson started her first flying lessons on 15 September 1928 at Stag Lane. Weather conditions were not the best for such a venture, but she was too impatient to wait for spring. Under the tuition of Capt. Matthews she made little progress, her next instructor being Capt. James Valentine Baker, who had a bullet lodged in his spine from the time he served in Gallipoli. This had not prevented him from learning to fly, and he was later awarded the Military Cross for having reputedly shot down fifteen Germans. Baker was an excellent instructor, and eventually he pronounced that Amy was ready to go solo, but heavy fog delayed the flight. He was then offered a job at Heston Aerodrome, so Amy was again placed in the hands of Matthews, who during a critical stage in her lessons became ill, delaying her chance to qualify. Maj. Herbert Gardner Travis then took over. Before joining Stag Lane he had been a temporary instructor with the Cinque Ports Flying Club at Lympne. It was Travis who was flying the club's new Moth 60X, G-EBSS, when his pupil G. T. Skinner was killed, as mentioned in Chapter 3.

In another incident at Lympne in March 1929, Travers was giving his wife a flying lesson when at 150 feet the Moth's engine cut out and they were forced to land in the nearest field. The aircraft flipped over and Travers was trapped under the wreckage, with petrol leaking from the fuel tank. It was the ground engineer's job to check there was enough fuel for the flight, but it was the pilot's responsibility to check the supply before take-off. A dispute ensued, leading to his resignation from the club. He was an intimidating man, and was at least a foot taller than his star pupil Amy, but he was a good instructor and a great character. He always flew in an old duffel coat and wore his lucky flying helmet – and was always puffing away on his favourite pipe. With his skill and her determination, Amy finally qualified and went solo on 9 June 1929, but by this time she was again under the tuition of Matthews. Travers also gave flying lessons to Francis Chichester and Jean Batten.

Amy's first solo flight to Australia was an attempt to beat Bert Hinkler's record of sixteen days. She took off from Croydon on 5 May 1930 in a DH Gipsy Moth, G-AAAH, named 'Jason', her family's business trade mark, and landed at Darwin on 24 May after a flight of 11,000 miles, the first woman to fly alone to Australia. Another attempt on the long-distance record flight to New Zealand had taken place at Lympne on 24 April 1929. The pilot was Frank Mase, flying his 95 hp Cirrus III Simmonds Spartan

ZK-AAP, which was painted black as its name, 'The All Black', suggests, in honour of the New Zealand rugby team. Mase reached Roanne in France, where on taking off to resume his flight, the aircraft was damaged and the attempt abandoned.

During the Easter meeting in 1929, organised by the Cinque Ports Flying Club, R. G. Cazalet won several cups. His daughter Gillian later flew a Tiger Moth in the National Air Races in 1960 and won the Ladies Handicap at Thruxton in the same year. She went on to be a senior first officer with Skyways International, flying HS.748s, only the second woman to do so. The King's Cup of 1929 was held at Heston, beginning at 8 a.m. on 5 July. Out of the sixty original entrants there were only forty-one starters. The course covered a distance of 589.5 miles from Heston to Henlow, Norwich, Hadleigh, Hornchurch, Lympne, Hamble, Bristol and Blackpool. The race was won by Flt Lt Richard 'Batchy' Atcherley, accompanied by Flt Lt G. H. Stainforth as navigator at 150 mph. In second place was Lt L. G. Richardson at 100.2 mph, and third was W. L. Hope at 91 mph.

An attempt on Bert Hinkler's solo flight from England to Australia took place from Lympne on 23 March 1930 by C. P. Patterson, a businessman from New Zealand in a DH.60G Gipsy Moth, G-AALM. It had been the intention to leave Lympne on 15 February, with arrival at Port Darwin scheduled for the 27th. Following damage to the aircraft at Lizy-sur-Ourcq, thirty-five miles north-east of Paris, he ended the flight. However, a second attempt was made from Croydon in April 1930, but Patterson crashed after hitting a tree in fog and the Gipsy Moth caught fire, the pilot managing to escape uninjured.

At about the same time, the Aga Khan offered £500 to the first Indian pilot to fly solo between England and India, and it was not long before an intrepid pilot took up the challenge. Manmohan Singh, an Indian student at Bristol University, left Stag Lane on 11 January 1930 in a DH.60G Gipsy Moth called 'Miss India', but following several forced landings the aircraft was flown back to Lympne from Le Bourget on 25 January. The same day he tried again, this time from Lympne, reaching Cosenza in Calabria where he crashed on 3 February.

On 10 April 1930, Fokker F.VIIa G-EBTS, 'The Spider', left Woodford after an overhaul and a respray of the silver fuselage and blue registration, for its take-off from Lympne bound for the Cape. The pilot, C. D. Barnard, and relief pilot, R. Little, were in good company, with the Duchess of Bedford as passenger. However, she was allowed to take over the controls for short periods. The record was achieved when they landed at Cape Town on 19 April after a distance of 9,000 miles, flown in 100 hours, returning to Croydon on the 30th.

Attempts on Hinkler's England–Australia record-breaking flight were numerous. One such flight was undertaken by E. L. Hook and J. Matthews who took off from Lympne on 20 June 1930 in Gipsy Moth DH.60M G-AAWV. Their aircraft was unusual as it had a metal fuselage. Sadly, they crashed after making good time at Tomas in Burma on 3 July. Matthews was found alive and rescued, but Hook was found dead on the day the Moth crashed in jungle.

C. D. Barnard, mentioned above, left Lympne bound for Malta in his DH.80A Puss Moth G-AAXW on 31 July 1930. His destination was reached in thirteen hours, Barnard returning to England and landing at Croydon on 1 August after a flight of fourteen and a half hours. These were the first flights to be made non-stop between England and Malta, lasting a total of twenty-seven and a half hours over 2,800 miles.

A 27 year old Scot, Oscar Garden, who later learned to fly during 1930, was domiciled in New Zealand as a commercial pilot, and was the next pilot to emulate Hinkler's epic flight from England to Australia. Garden had learnt to fly in 1930 and was a commercial pilot. On 17 October that year he took off from Lympne in his DH.60G Gipsy Moth G-AASA 'Kia Ora', previously owned by Gordon Selfridge, and landed eighteen days later at Wyndham in Western Australia on 4 November. He did not, however, set a new record time for the flight.

On 17 January 1931, Breguet 280T F-AIVU crashed whilst attempting to land at Lympne. The aircraft caught the boundary fence and crashed onto the airfield, damaging the forward fuselage and undercarriage. Running late because of strong northwesterly winds, light on fuel and with light fading, the pilot decided to land at Lympne to make use of ground lights. The mechanic was the only person injured and the passengers later continued their journey by rail. The pilot again crashed when flying Breguet 280T F-AJNS two days later at Smarden but was again uninjured – apart from his pride.

Amy Johnson returned to Lympne airfield on 28 July 1931, when she took off in a Puss Moth at 12.35 a.m. on a beautiful moonlit night, accompanied by Jack Humphreys in 'Jason II' to attempt the record on a flight from England to Japan. There were no extra tanks fitted, as they wanted to show how a normal light aircraft could fly, but as a result they had to refuel four times a day. The attempt was successful, notching up another record flight for Amy. However, she had to abandon her flight from Stag Lane to Peking via Warsaw and Siberia on yet another record attempt in her DH.60G Gipsy Moth G-ABDV 'Jason III' due to dangerous weather in Poland and suffered several forced landings. The aircraft therefore needed repairing, and she eventually flew back to England, arriving at Lympne on 11 February 1931, after travelling by train to

Moscow and enjoying a winter sports break in Switzerland. On the same day that Amy arrived back at Lympne, Tommy Rose started out for the Cape from Lympne at dawn. His aircraft was G-ABIE, an Avro Avian that had been fitted with an extra fuel tank. On the return trip in May he had to abandon his attempt thirty miles south of Luxor, with sand in the engine.

The record time for the flight from England to Australia was also in the sights of a twenty-eight-year-old Englishman called Charles William Anderson Scott. His flight began at Lympne at 4.55 a.m. on 1 April 1931 in his silver 120 hp Gipsy Moth II DH.60M, G-ABHY. He arrived at Port Darwin at 5.40 p.m. on 10 April. The new record holder completed the flight in nine days, four hours and eleven minutes, covering 10,358 miles at an average speed of 100 mph. Scott's return flight to England from Australia in the Gipsy Moth which had been registered VH-UQA, departed Wyndham on 26 May 1931. He arrived at Lympne at 7 p.m. on 5 June after a flight of 10,570 miles in ten days, thirteen hours and twenty-five minutes. On landing, Scott recalled, 'As my wheels touched the ground I felt like bursting into tears. I arrived punctually as a train.' The new record beat the time of the famous aviator Kingsford Smith by two days. Scott's flying escapades make interesting reading in *Scott's Book*, written by him and published in 1934.

Seated in the rear cockpit of his DH.60M registration VH-UQA is C. W. A. Scott who arrived back at Lympne on 5 June 1931. His flight from Wyndham, Australia to England, beat Kingsford Smith's time by two days. Amy Johnson is seated in the front seat.

Scott and Kingsford Smith shared a competitive rivalry, and an unusual custom had developed in the Cinque Ports Flying Club. They would both toss coins, usually pennies, with stamps adhered to them, in such a way they that they stuck to the asbestos ceiling. Scott's stamp was 1½d and Kingsford Smith, in a bid to outdo his rival, used a *2d* stamp. Having stuck their stamps to the ceiling it was then necessary for the thrower to climb up by any means available to him to sign his name across the stamp. The tile bearing the stamps and signatures of both pilots came into the possession of Ann Attree (née Davis), having rescued them from the rubble of the clubhouse in 1940.

Following the successful attempt to fly from England to Berlin in one day by J. R. Chaplin and T. N. Stack in Vickers 146 Vivid G-EBPY on 8 April 1931, they took off from Lympne on 2 May 1931 at 4.22 a.m., landing in Istanbul at 9 p.m. after a flight of 1,660 miles, setting another record. However, they did have problems with the aircraft's Lion engine, which delayed the return to Heston on 4 May.

On 28 July 1931, Amy Johnson again tackled the flight from England to Japan. Flying conditions were perfect. With her was C. H. G. S. Humphreys, who had been a member of the London Aeroplane Club, as they took off from Lympne at 1.27 a.m. in Puss Moth G-AAZV 'Jason II'. They were hoping to make Tokyo in the record time of seven days and they reached their destination on 6 August, after seventy-five flying hours. They took off on the return flight on 24 August, but had to return to Osaka due to bad weather, eventually leaving on the 28th and reaching Lympne on 9 September after seventeen days, having again been delayed by poor weather.

Yet another record-breaking attempt took place on 27 October 1931, when two brothers – Flt Lt Leslie S. Hamilton and Kenneth A. Hamilton – took off from Lympne at 12.30 a.m. Their aircraft was a Gipsy III-engined Puss Moth G-AAXW that C. D. Barnard had used for his flight to Malta in 1930. Their flight ended with a forced landing in Tullin, near Vienna, and the aircraft was brought back to England for a later attempt.

The Comper Swift, G-ABRE, flown by C. Arthur Butler, took off from Lympne bound for Australia at 5.17 a.m. on 31 October 1931. This aircraft was a long-range version, and took off with an all-up weight of 1,160 lb, arriving at Darwin in nine days, two hours and twenty-nine minutes, covering 10,425 miles and beating C. W. A. Scott's time by 102 minutes.

One of the lesser known female pilots of the 1930s was Miss Peggy Salaman. At the age of twenty-one she was accompanied by A. Gordon Store, assistant instructor at the London Aeroplane Club in 1930-31, in an attempt on the record flight from England to Cape Town. They took off from Lympne at 11 p.m. in a navy blue Puss Moth, G-ABEH, named 'Good Hope'. All went well and the triumphant duo arrived at Maitland Airport on 5 November after a flight of 7,050 miles in a time of sixty-four hours, a new record. For his attempt on the England to South Africa record, Jim Mollison flew his Gipsy Moth VH-UFT from Lympne on 6 November 1931. He had to return due to thick fog, but set off again from Lympne at 3 a.m. on 13 November, crashing in Egypt after suffering engine failure, the aircraft overturning on landing and ending the attempt.

After a four-month break, Flt Lt Leslie Hamilton prepared his Puss Moth G-AAXW for a second attempt on the England–Australia record. His companion was Flt Lt R. K. Coupland, and they took off from Lympne on 19 February 1932. The flight ended when the aircraft crashed into a hillside in fog at Ruvo di Puglia in Italy, slightly injuring both of them. Lady J. Chaytor, who lived at Witton Castle, left Lympne with R. T. Richards to try for the England–Australia record in DH.60G Gipsy Moth G-ABSD, but their dream was dashed and the flight abandoned en route. However, it was time for C. W. A. Scott to regain the England–Australia record, this time in DH.60M Gipsy Moth VH-UQA, originally registered G-ACOA. He left Lympne at 5.05 a.m. on 19 April 1932 and did indeed succeed, beating Arthur Butler by a staggering five hours and forty-two minutes. Meanwhile at Lympne, the Folkestone Trophy Race had been organised for 25 August and, with twenty confirmed entries, promised to be an exciting event for all concerned. It was won by Comper Swift G-ABWH of the British Air Navigation Co. of Heston, flown by A. J. Styran, reaching a speed of 141 mph.

Following an invitation in June 1932 from Sir Philip Sassoon to Douglas Bader to spend a few days convalescing at Lympne, Bader turned up on a Saturday afternoon in his MG with a friend, Peter Ross. Lying beside the swimming pool at Lympne Place, seeing Hawker Demons taking off and climbing away, Bader remarked, 'I wish I was up there again.' Turning to Sir Philip, he added, 'I'm sure I could fly perfectly well.' His host replied, 'We have an Avro 504 on the aerodrome. Would you like to have a shot at it?' Nigel Norman, the CO of No. 601 Squadron, was persuaded by Sir Philip to allow Bader to fly. The following morning Bader walked over to the aircraft and climbed into the cockpit without any problem. He was back in an aircraft at last! Declining an offer to let Ross, who was flying as passenger, start the engine, Bader taxied out on the grass stretching down to Romney Marsh, opened the throttle and took off. As ever, he had his own ideas and flew to Kenley where he had not been since his horrific accident. This was an unofficial flight, and when one of the flight commanders at Lympne asked the sergeant in charge of the Avro where it was, he replied, 'Dunno, sir. Some bloke with no legs took it away.' A subsequent medical examination proved Bader fit for active service, but in April 1933 he received notification that the RAF had decided to reverse the decision on the grounds that this situation was not covered by King's Regulations. He later returned to flying with the RAF – and a legend was born.

At Lympne airfield at 6.37 a.m. on 14 November 1932, a mobile floodlighting truck illuminated the small gathering of well-wishers, local dignitaries and the Countess Courtney who, despite the cold, had turned out to see Amy Johnson set off on another record attempt, this time to Cape Town, flying her new DH.80A Puss Moth G-ACAB 'Desert Cloud'. She arrived at her destination on 18 November after a flight of 6,200 miles which took ten hours and twenty-six minutes. As if this was not enough, she added the return flight to England in record time, landing at Croydon on 18 December.

William Courtney who wrote extensively on civil aviation in the 1920s and '30s, flew to Lympne with Jim Mollison to see Amy take off from Lympne. He wrote:

In the cold grey darkness of pre-dawn the little Puss Moth, which had been filled overnight ready for its great adventure and which was christened Desert Cloud, was wheeled out of the big hangars at Lympne. Captain Jeffs, who was in charge of control at the time, had the mobile flood-lighting truck moved into position. The flood-lights were turned on to bathe the ground in soft white light. The blood-red boundary lights still twinkled in the dark sky. Kathleen, Countess of Drogheda, who was a friend of them both and who had come down with us, their secretary, Miss Pickering, together with the Mayor and Mayoress of Hythe, Councillor and Mrs George Few, all turned out to bid Amy goodbye.

After a brief warming of the engine, during which the exhaust gases from her new 130 hp Gipsy Major engine flashed blue and red, she bid us all goodbye, calmly went over last-minute details herself to be satisfied that all was in order, and taxied to the take-off point. Captain Jeffs and Sergeant Major Dupe had unobtrusively brought the ambulance out of the hangar. It was parked with engine running at a convenient point in case its grim services were required. Her machine carried 120 gallons of petrol in the wing tanks and a special cylindrical tank fitted behind her in the cabin. Amy took off, climbing to a height of 1,500 feet. She turned on the course heading for the Channel and France. Jim Mollison had also taken off, escorting her for part of the way until the French coast came into view, when she waved her final goodbye and [he] returned to Lympne.

On 15 January 1933, an attempt on Amy Johnson's record time for the flight from England to South Africa was made by Lady Bailey, who set off from Croydon in a DH.80A Puss Moth, G-AAYA. Later she was reported missing, but was located on 19 January south-west of Babau, 300 miles from the River Niger, having landed and drifted off course. Lady Bailey abandoned her attempt, returning to England and landing at Lympne on 14 February. Jim Mollison, who had married Amy Johnson, wanted to attempt the flight from England to Australia in three-and-a-half days, the same flight Bert Hinkler attempted, ending in his death (his body and the wreckage of his aircraft were not found until 28 April 1933; he had crashed on 7 April in the Apennines in Italy). Amy had arrived at Lympne to see Jim take off on 7 January 1933, when Hinkler was still missing.

Spurred on by his wife's success, Jim Mollison took off from Lympne in Puss Moth G-ABXY, 'The Hearts Content', on his flight to Brazil on 14 February. His was the first solo flight to South America and he was the first pilot to fly solo across both North and South America, also having completed the first solo flight across the Atlantic from east to west. Enter Jean Batten, a twenty-three-year-old New Zealander, who had learned to fly in England in 1929 with the London Aeroplane Club at Stag Lane. Having qualified, she set off from Lympne in her second-hand DH.60M Gipsy Moth, G-AALG, once owned by HRH The Prince of Wales, *en route* to New Zealand on 9 April 1933. Reaching Karachi, she force-landed and was injured after a connecting rod broke. Sadly, the flight had to be abandoned.

Geoffrey Arlington was greatly influenced by his uncle, Patrick Hamilton, who had learnt to fly in 1911, but was later killed flying with the RFC in September 1912 and was buried at Hythe. Educated at Blundell's School in Devon, Geoffrey became very keen on all things mechanical, gaining his pilot's 'A' licence at Lympne in 1933 before leaving school:

> By a quite extraordinary coincidence, my uncle, Captain Patrick Hamilton, had flown for the last flight of his life behind a rotary engine, and I flew on the first flight of my life behind a rotary engine, fitted to an Avro 504K. The aircraft had come down in a field near the school at Tiverton to give joy-rides and my mother happened to be visiting me, so we both went up for a flight over the school. I can remember the blipping of the engine and the lovely smell of castor oil and holding on very tight as there were no seat belts. I also remember vividly the very steep angle of descent but it was all over too quickly. The recent crash of the R101 was forgotten in the excitement.
>
> When I was seventeen, I found that I had saved enough money to learn to fly, so during the Easter holidays of 1933 I went to stay with

my aunt at Hythe in Kent and joined the Cinque Ports Flying Club. K. K. Brown was the instructor, and a very good one too. Calm but firm in the air, he immediately gave one confidence as his quiet voice came through the Gosport speaking tubes with which the Gipsy Moths were all fitted in those days. What a wonderful area to learn to fly in. Lympne was a grass field, and on taking off to the south as one generally did, the moment the aeroplane had climbed above the line of trees at the end of the aerodrome, the most wonderful view unfolded. You could see to Dungeness across the marshes, the coastline from Folkestone to Rye, the military canal starting at Hythe and twisting and turning to Rye, where a small puff of smoke indicated that the miniature train was on its way across Romney Marsh between Hythe and Dymchurch, and even, if one looked across the water, France could often be seen.

It was wonderful to have control of this aircraft which answered to one's slightest touch, much as a well-trained horse. I was flying now all over the area my uncle knew so well. He used to land his Deperdussin on Folkestone racecourse and give exhibition flights. He must have known the surge of lift as the wind swept up the slope from the marshes below Lympne. Each instructional flight was thirty minutes and each day, weather permitting, I flew three times. After seven and a half hours' instruction my instructor was teaching me how to get out of a spin and then a few more landings in rather strong winds, then we taxied in to the clubhouse front. My instructor got out and quietly said, 'Right, off you go. Just do one circuit and landing. You will find it will climb much quicker without me' – and he walked away.

So this was the big moment. I taxied out carefully, turned into the wind for take-off, made certain that no other aeroplanes were landing, adjusted the cheese-cutter or elevator trim, and slowly opened the throttle. The Gipsy Moth DH.60X G EBKT fairly leapt off the ground and we crossed the boundary at twice the normal height. I throttled back the engine a little and did a gentle turn to the left, not completely at right angles but heading up slightly into the wind so my actual track over the ground would be at right angles to my line of take-off. Not too bad, for we had done it in practice many times before: round again down wind, turn again. Now was the time to judge things correctly for a final turn in to land. I am higher than usual so I will cut the motor now and glide. A final gliding turn into the wind and a quick glance at the air speed indicator out on the wing to see it was about 55 mph.

I was still a bit higher than I wanted to be. (I had not yet been taught how to lose height by side-slipping.) I will make it well into the aerodrome. I start to flatten out the glide now and keep looking well ahead. Back more on the stick, more, more, more, now right back in my

tummy. The aeroplane hung, stalled for a second or so, and then there
was a bump, just one, which meant it had been a three point landing,
albeit a heavy one. Having taxied back to K. K. Brown, who had been
watching my first solo, he told me to carry on and do another three
circuits and landings which I then did. In the afternoon I put in a further
hour's solo flying, consisting of two half-hour periods.

Then the next day, 4 May, as I had to go back to school that night, I
flew solo for a further two and a quarter hours and passed my tests for
my pilot's 'A' licence, so I was able to return to school with part of my
ambition accomplished. When the summer holidays eventually arrived
(how slowly that seemed to pass!) I joined my mother who was staying
at Bitterne, Southampton, and immediately joined the Hampshire
Aeroplane Club to start really learning to fly. I was instructed in cross-
country flights. Maps, from early childhood, have always interested me,
so map reading, applying deviation, variation and allowing for wind
were no trouble, and I was soon left alone to go whither I wanted. The
first cross-country I did was to visit my old Cinque Ports Flying Club at
Lympne. This was a flight of 105 miles and I made certain I did not veer
off my track the slightest degree. It was excellent practice for a beginner,
as the visibility was very poor, so that I had to fly by compass and map,
for we had no directional giro to make course-keeping easy. Having had
tea with Ann Davis, who, with her husband, W. E. Davis, owned the club,
I climbed into the Moth and came back all along the south coast for the
fun of it, and for the beauty of the scenery.

I had now done a total of forty hours' solo and dual, and I was
approved to carry passengers, so I took up my brother Rupert, who was
in the Navy, stationed at Portsmouth, as my first passenger, and flew him
round the Solent and Isle of Wight for an hour. My mother, who was also
a pilot, took another club aircraft and we played about, formating on
each other. It was one of those glorious summer days, when the yachts
were becalmed in little groups, obviously racing and trying to make the
best use of each cat's paw that ruffled the surface of the water. We dived
down to look at them and then climbed away, revelling in our freedom
of movement, and eventually back to Southampton. I was gaining
experience and confidence all the time. I had finished with my public
school and this was my last holiday before I started at De Havilland's
Aeronautical Technical School at Manor Road, Hatfield.

It is worth pointing out that the DH.60 Gipsy Moth in which Arlington
had learnt to fly was G EBKT, the first prototype built by De Havilland
at Stag Lane, on 22 February 1925. In this aircraft, Alan Cobham later
flew from Croydon to Zurich and back in a day, a distance of 1,000 miles.

Arlington was later to remark that had he known this aircraft was famous, he would have treated it more carefully. Did the Cinque Ports Flying Club know of its history? If so, why did Brown not let the student pilot know?

On 11 April 1933, Capt. W. N. Lancaster tried to better Amy Mollison's time from England to the Cape, setting off from Lympne at 5.38 a.m. in his Avian V, G-ABLK, which had belonged to Kingsford Smith. On reaching Reggan in Algeria he disappeared into oblivion, a mystery which remained unsolved until February 1962, when by chance a French Army patrol found the aircraft and the pilot's remains 170 miles from Reggan – a sad end to a brave pilot.

During the Wakefield Cup Race, an event held during the Lympne International Air Rally on the weekend of 22-23 July 1933, Wg Cdr H. M. Probyn flew the first production aircraft of the Miles M.2 Hawk, G-ACHJ. There were ten starters and Probyn finished in first place at a speed of 115.5 mph. The following month, on 26 August, there were seventeen entries, and Flt Lt D. V. Ivan's Bristol F.2B Fighter G-EBIO, a Mew Gull, DH Moths, Swifts, an Avian, a Cadet and a Puss Moth all competed for the trophy, which was won by K. H. F. Waller at a speed of 103 mph.

Sir Charles Kingsford Smith took off from Lympne for Australia at 5.28 a.m. on 4 October 1933, on a solo flight, flying Gipsy Major Percival Gull Four G-ACJV, 'Miss Southern Cross'. He arrived on the 11th, after seven days, four hours and forty-four minutes, landing at Wyndham, 10,000 miles from Lympne – a new record for Kingsford Smith. Spartan Air Lines' Spartan Cruiser II G-ACDW, named 'Faithful City', had arrived at Lympne from Heston on 10 October for an attempt on the Australian record. The aircraft was piloted by P. W. Lynch-Blosse, the chief pilot of Spartan Air Lines, accompanied by Lord Apsley, Capt. W. P. Crawford Green and a mechanic. The twin-engined monoplane landed at Wyndham on 27 October, flying on to Sydney on the 30th. It arrived back at St Osyth, Clacton, Essex, on 26 December, having flown 32,000 miles in seven weeks.

England to Australia had been selected for the MacRobertson Race in celebration of the centenary of the State of Victoria, sponsored by the Australian chocolate millionaire Sir Macpherson Robertson. A £500 gold cup and cash prizes totalling £15,000 were on offer. On 22 March 1934, in preparation for their entry, Bernard Rubin and his companion K. H. F. Waller took off from Lympne in DH.85 Leopard Moth G-ACLX to survey the planned route. They did so successfully, reaching Darwin on 6 April after a flight of fifteen days. They left for England on the 23rd, arriving at Lympne on 1 May in a record time of eight days and twelve hours.

One of the first contestants in the MacRobertson Race was H. L. Brook in Puss Moth G-ABXY. He took off from Lympne at the crack of dawn on 28 March. Brook's aircraft, 'The Hearts Content', had previously been flown by Jim Mollison and was a reliable and well-maintained aircraft, but unfortunately, after only a few hours' flying, ice formed on the wings as the Moth reached 12,000 feet, causing the aircraft to crash. The flight was abandoned due to fog and snow at Mont Lozère near Génolhac.

Jean Batten returned to Lympne on 22 April for a second attempt on the England–Australia record, flying the DH.60M Moth G-AARB. She landed near Rome as she was running out of fuel, slightly damaging the Moth, then returned home to Lympne for repairs, preparing for a third attempt on 8 May 1934. It was a successful bid for the record; she landed at Darwin on the 23rd after a flight of fourteen days, twenty-two hours and thirty minutes over 10,000 miles, beating Amy Mollison's record by over four days.

The 1930s was indeed the decade of the record-breaker, but other aviation events already established at Lympne continued. The Folkestone Aero Trophy was held on 1-2 September 1934 over three laps, a total of fifty miles, with ten finalists. The event was won by J. G. Brown at a speed of 101.25 mph in DH.60 Moth G-AAMU. The Wakefield Cup Race was won by the same aircraft, piloted by G. B. Fellowes at a speed of 100.5 mph. Other aircraft competing included Leopard Moth G-ACOO, Hendy 302A G-AAVT, Swift G-ABWW flown by Alex Henshaw, the Spitfire test pilot, M.2 Hawks G-ACIZ and G-ACTO and the British Klemm BK1 Eagle G-ACRG.

In October 1934, an unusual machine, the Avro-built Cierva C.30A Autogiro, G-ACVX, piloted by Mrs Victor Bruce, took off for Cape Town on the longest autogiro flight attempted. Sadly, G-ACVX was damaged in France and returned to England for repair, as Mrs Bruce was hoping to make a second attempt.

The Cinque Ports Flying Club members and visitors were in for a treat on 2 November, when the DH Comet Racer G-ACSR 'Reine Astrid' arrived at Lympne on its return flight from Australia. Owen Cathcart-Jones and Ken Waller had secured fourth place in the MacRobertson Race in four days, twelve hours, thirteen minutes and thirty seconds, taking off from Melbourne on 26 October 1934 in an attempt at the out-and-back flight. The return flight had taken thirteen and a half days. H. L. Brook was successful in the MacRobertson Race of 1935, taking the record for the fastest solo flight. One reason for his success was the decision to increase the fuel tankage fitted to his M.3 Falcon, G-ACTM. The aircraft took off from Darwin on 24 March on the flight to England, landing at Lympne at 3.55 p.m. on the 31st, the return trip taking seven days, nineteen hours and fifty minutes.

The Flying Flea captured the imagination of the budding pilots of the 1930s, as it was fairly simple to construct. Its celebrated designer, the

The designer of the popular Flying Flea or Interceptor 'Pou-du-Ciel', flew his own aircraft into Lympne on 30 August 1936 during his tour of the UK. The Flea was popular as it could be constructed economically at the owner's home if necessary.

Frenchman Henri Mignet, had first published his book *The Flying Flea* in 1934 and it was translated into English the following year. The first British Flea made its maiden flight on 25 July 1935, ending up in a cabbage patch. The *Daily Express* by then had decided to sponsor the Flea, providing its owner with cash to rebuild it. Shortly afterwards, the newspaper invited Mignet to England in order to show the public how to build the aircraft, but on 12 August, when he reached Calais, his Flea ended up on its nose with a wrecked engine. The next day he had fitted a motorcycle engine, tying a deflated cycle inner tube around his waist, just in case, and took off for the English coast. The *Daily Express* chartered an airliner that met him mid-Channel and escorted him to Lympne, where he was greeted by an enthusiastic crowd. There then followed a south coast tour sponsored by *The Daily Telegraph*.

International air rallies organised by the Cinque Ports Flying Club were held at Lympne over a weekend in August 1934 and 1935 with the permission of the Air Ministry. At the event held on 24-25 August 1935, the club invited pilots from France, Belgium, Holland, Germany, Czechoslovakia, Austria and other countries to visit Lympne and the neighbouring towns as their guests. Many of these countries were represented in the Cinque Ports Wakefield Cup Race. The meeting was only possible through the generosity of Viscount Wakefield of Hythe, Mr J. P. T. Evans of C. T. Bowering & Co., the British Aircraft Manufacturing

Co. and others who gave donations towards the expenses and prize money for the race, while the members of the flying club had subscribed to a formidable guarantee fund to cover the cost of running such an event. Everyone at the club, including their friends and families, worked hard to ensure the air rally was a success and that Lympne provided an excellent venue to promote various aircraft manufacturers' latest machines.

Sir Philip Sassoon attended the rally, primarily to welcome visitors to Lympne airfield, and in his capacity as Under Secretary of State for Air was an excellent ambassador for British aviation. In fine weather, the first event to take place commenced at 11.45 a.m. and ended at 12.30 p.m. This was a sealed time arrival competition, which meant that whichever aircraft landed nearest to the sealed time would be the winner. Joy-riding began at 12.30 p.m. and continued throughout the day, apart from intervals to allow other events to take place.

The afternoon opened with a demonstration arranged by the distributors R. K. Dundas Ltd including an AS.6 Envoy, a commercial twin-engine monoplane built by Airspeed Ltd, of which Sir Alan Cobham was one of the original directors. The Envoy, with a retractable undercarriage and seating capacity for six or eight passengers, could fly at 192 mph and was

Damaged on landing at Lympne during 21 Squadron's service at the airfield, K6686 was repaired and was still flying in 1938. Warrant Officer E. P. Dupont a mechanic helped maintain this aircraft and took this photograph, which is signed on the back by him and the other three airmen who worked on this aircraft. The pilot and gunner were not seriously injured.

followed by a Monospar, similar to the winner of the 1934 King's Cup Race, a twin-engine light aeroplane with seating for four, including the pilot, and manufactured by General Aircraft Ltd at Hanworth Air Park. Other aircraft taking part in the display were the B.A. Eagle, Miles Falcon and Percival Gull.

Hythe Motorcycle Club gave an impressive demonstration of their handling skills and performed a mock rescue of a British prisoner in China on the Yangtze River. For this, a large junk had been constructed from which the captive was helped to escape. An aircraft of great interest to the public was the autogiro piloted by Capt. R. Brie, the chief test pilot of Cierva. Flights were available at a cost of 10*s*. At 3.30 p.m. an impressive aerobatic display was given by George Lowdell in a Hawker Tomtit owned and used by Wolseley Motors (Lowdell was Wolseley's chief test pilot). It was said that the small aircraft's performance was as impressive as that of an RAF fighter of the period. During this event L. H. T. Cliff, the flying club's assistant instructor, gave a fine demonstration of flight and simple aerobatics, with the chief instructor, K. K. Brown, acting as the pupil. Cliff endeavoured to show how these manoeuvres should be carried out, while Brown showed how they should not be carried out.

Heats were then flown for the Wakefield Cup, held on 28 August, under the competition rules of the Royal Aero Club and the regulations of the FAI. So many entries were received for this race, which was rapidly growing in popularity, that it had been necessary to have two heats in order to eliminate some of the entrants. After take-off, the machines' first turning point was to be north-east of Lympne, then round Summer House Hill, turning left and proceeding to a pylon in a field at Hastingleigh near Wye and left again to a pylon east of Aldington church, returning to Lympne, making a right-hand turn round a flag in the field west of the airfield, a left-hand turn round a circle in the middle of the airfield and on to Summer House Hill. Three circuits were necessary to complete the course and the third time across Lympne to the finish.

Ten entrants, the first five finishers in each heat, competed in the final over a course of three laps totalling fifty miles. A Belgian, Guy Hansez, in Renault Six Caudron Simoun F-ANCE won at a speed of 177.5 mph, Flt Lt A. E. Clouston in Desoutter I G-ABMW was second at 113 mph, and Flt Lt R. Duncanson in Hendy 281 Hobo G-AAIG was third at 103.5 mph. Other aircraft included London Film Productions' Falcon III Bristol Type 96A Fighter Mk IV G-ADJR, flown by Nigel Tangye, Hendy 302A G-AAVT and B.A. Eagle 2 G-ADJO.

Another display over the weekend included a demonstration by a BAC II of the Channel Gliding Club piloted by C. M. C. Turner and a Hawker Hart flown by George Bulman, a test pilot for the Hawker Aircraft Co.

Typical 1930s artwork—the 1935 programme for the International Air Rally. A popular event and perhaps one of the last such shows in England before the war.

Bill Fairlie, the chief tester of GQ Parachute Co., thrilled the crowds with a parachute drop as a finale to the International Air Rally at Lympne. Joy-riding continued until sunset, at a cost of 5s. The aircraft flown were a DH Dragon Rapide, a DH three-seater Leopard Moth, a DH two-seater Gipsy I Moth, an Avro 504 three-seater, and last but not least the autogiro. The charge for joy-riding in the autogiro was from 10s.

The Folkestone Aero Trophy was contested over a three-mile lap on 14 September 1935. The winner was L. Lipton in DH.60G III Moth G-ABVW, followed closely by J. B. Wilson in prototype BK1 Eagle G-ACRG. Kingsford Smith took off from Lympne, bound for Melbourne at 8 p.m. on 6 November in Lockheed Altair 8D 'Lady Southern Cross' G-ADUS, previously VH-USB. Sadly, this was his last flight. He disappeared and nothing further was known until nearly two years later when part of the undercarriage was washed up near Aye Island off the coast of Burma on 1 June 1937. On 11 November, another record flight, of six days, twelve hours and seventeen minutes, was achieved by a Parnall Heck on a trip from Cape Town to Lympne.

By late 1935, Jean Batten had replaced her Moth with a Gipsy Percival Gull Six, G-ADPR, named 'Jean'. She achieved a new record from England to South America, leaving Lympne at 6.30 a.m. on 11 November on the first leg of her 5,000-mile journey and landing at Thies in Senegal after a thirty-six hour flight, only to find that her fuel supplies had gone to Dakar by mistake. Fuel was eventually found and G-ADPR took off for Brazil, landing on 13 November. The total time was two days, thirteen hours and fifteen minutes, nearly twenty-four hours less than the best time for the flight by Jim Mollison, thus setting a new record. Jean Batten had become the first woman pilot to make the crossing.

Miles M.3B Falcon Six G-ADLC, the winner of the 1935 King's Cup, was flown from Lympne on 7 January 1936 on the England–South Africa solo record-breaking attempt by Tommy Rose. When ice formed on the aircraft, Rose put down at Abbeville but the Falcon was damaged when landing in the dark. Following repairs, he attempted the flight again from Lympne in G-ADLC on 9 February, returning to Croydon on 9 March and securing a record, beating the existing time by five hours and twenty minutes.

On 7 February 1936, Flt Lt David Llewellyn's next record-breaking attempt to South Africa set off from Lympne, flying a JAP Aeronca C-3, G-AEAC, and arriving at Johannesburg after twenty-three days on 1 March. Two months later, H. L. Brook, flying Praga B Baby G-ADXL, took off from Lympne on 6 May 1936 with Cape Town as his destination. He arrived after sixteen days, four hours and thirty minutes, landing on 22 May after a flight totalling 135 hours.

The weather was a problem for contestants eager to fly in the Folkestone Trophy Race held on 1 August 1936, which was over three laps each consisting of fifty-eight miles. The winner was R. R. Grubb at a speed of 84.75 mph flying Aeronca C-3 G-ADYR. There were ten entrants and among those who completed the course were Lord Patrick Crichton-Stuart in Hobo G-AAIG and E. W. Percival flying Mew Gull G-AEKL. This Wakefield Trophy Race was again held at Lympne on 29-30 August 1936, and eleven finalists took part in the second day over an eighteen-mile triangular course. The first place was taken by an American racing pilot, James Haizlip, who reached a speed of 145 mph in his Cessna C-34 Airmaster.

Lord Crichton-Stuart also competed in this race, flying G-AAIG into eighth place. Amongst others flying that day was R. J. Waight in (DH Technical School) TK.2 G-ADNO, with an average speed of 170 mph. This aircraft had shortened exhaust stubs, lengthened spats and a curved windscreen, increasing its loaded weight. On 31 July, the 1937 Folkestone Aero Trophy Race at Lympne was flown by nineteen entrants, with Alex Henshaw coming in first in his white Mew Gull, G-AEXF, at a speed of 210 mph. In second place was A. J. S. Morris in Hobo G-AAIG at 126 mph; Geoffrey de Havilland in TK.2 G-ADNO came in eighth.

Lympne International Rally was held for the fifth time on 28-29 September 1937. The main event was the Cinque Ports Wakefield Cup Race, with sixteen competitors flying on the first day over three laps of sixteen and a half miles each. The following day, the same course and laps were flown, being won by Herr Clausen at 120.75 mph in Klemm Kl 35 D-EHNE, with B. Karlis in VEF I-12 YL-ABG at 141 mph in second place. Alex Henshaw finished in fourth place in G-AEXF.

Geoffrey Arlington was flying a Dart Kitten, G-AEXT, having been asked by Dart Aircraft Ltd of Dunstable to join the company as sales manager and demonstration pilot. There were ten machines in the final, with Arlington taking off first as his was the slowest aircraft in the race. He had a twenty-five minute, twenty-eight second start on Alex Henshaw in his Mew Gull. The course was flown over three circuits of about twenty miles per circuit, and the whole race could be seen from Lympne.

The handicappers had done a wonderful job, for all the competitors arrived together over the airfield. The Mew Gull passed the Dart Kitten before it reached the airfield, five other aircraft overtaking the Kitten between the boundary and the finish line, so Arlington finished in seventh place. Geoffrey de Havilland, flying DH TK.2 G-ADNO, ended in eighth place, only one second behind Arlington. The following day the Dart Kitten flew to West Malling to be demonstrated to the West Malling Aero Club on behalf of Dart Aircraft Ltd.

John Henriet with his father Cecil Henriet at Lympne in 1937 during one of many visits to the Dupe family living on the airfield. The machine Avro C30A Autogiro G-ACWH, also flew with the RAF serial DR623, later being registered G-AHLE and restored in 1946.

Florence Mary Morris-Davies of the Cinque Ports Flying Club standing by her BA Swallow Mk.2 registration G-AEMD. This aircraft was eventually scrapped in December 1946.

Of course not all female aviators became famous, but many were influenced by the flying heroines of the 1930s. One such lady was Florence Mary Morris-Davies, born in London on 17 September 1881, who was the eldest daughter of Sir Robert Garnett Head. On 17 July 1922, Florence married Meyrick Morris-Davies, a mining engineer, and they later lived in Peking, Ceylon and India. In 1936, she became fascinated with aviation and decided to learn to fly with the Cinque Ports Flying Club, qualifying on 6 July. Later she decided to purchase her own aircraft, a B.A. Swallow Mk 2, G-AEMD, which she kept at Lympne. By this time her family lived at Guestling in Sussex and she bought a small flat near Lympne so that she could fly regularly.

Florence took off from Lympne airfield with a friend in 1937 to embark on a European trip, which gave her the opportunity to take part in the Magyar pilots' picnic in Hungary, involving many parties and much flying. She entered the air race and won the Magyar Trophy. As the war clouds gathered over Europe, the Air Ministry notified her that her beloved Swallow would be pressed into service with the RAF if war was declared. In fact, this did not happen, although many civil aircraft were handed over to the RAF. Florence died on 3 July 1979 at the age of ninety-seven. Her aviation memorabilia is proudly displayed at the Romney Marsh Wartime Collection in Brenzett.

Jean Batten hit the headlines again on 18 October 1937 when she took off from Darwin at 9.30 p.m. in Gull Six G-ADPR, landing at Lympne at 3.45 p.m. on 24 October after a flight of five days, eighteen hours and fifteen minutes, beating the record held by H. F. Broadbent. A large crowd gathered at the airfield as she landed, the crowd pressing forward, some shouting 'Good old Jean!' Her limbs were so crammed that she had to be helped out of the cockpit and was carried into the captain's office by an RAF sergeant and Sgt Maj. S. J. Dupe, the aerodrome officer, who placed a guard on her aircraft. Jean did not stay long as was soon taking off again for Croydon. In an attempt to regain his record, Broadbent took off from Lympne for Australia in Vega Gull G-AFEH, at 3 a.m. on 12 March 1938. He made a forced landing at Flores Island in the Soemba Strait, Dutch East Indies. Apart from damaging the propeller on landing, he was physically exhausted and had to abandon the attempt.

By 1938, Lympne had become the alternative airfield for Imperial Airways, and on one occasion in November that year Handley Page HP.42 G-AXXC 'Heracles' was flying between Croydon and Paris. Force-landing at Lympne, its undercarriage was damaged and the aircraft remained at the airfield until it was repaired. It was company policy to avoid adverse publicity, so the company's name on the aircraft was blacked out before the passengers disembarked at Lympne as a precaution to confound

Harold Broadbent on arrival back from Australia in 1937, being filmed by Gaumont Newsreel, the film was shown to the public the following week. Such news and film was of great interest to the public who followed the exploits of these flying heroes.

This Fairey Hendon serial K5094 of No. 38 Squadron attracted much attention by RAF personnel and is being refuelled at Lympne in 1937. Note the airman seated astride a towed fuel bowser who appears to be checking the amount of fuel available for this giant. Just visible on the engine cowling is painted: 'Keep clear of the air-screw' (propeller). The squadron was based at RAF Mildenhall, and was on a training flight.

newspaper photographers, eager to take a few shots of the situation. The aircraft was repaired and successfully returned to Croydon, and disgruntled passengers were transported back to London.

On 30 July 1938, the final for the Folkestone Air Race at Lympne consisted of eight competitors, the race being won by Hugh Buckingham at a speed of 123.25 mph in a Hornet Moth, G-ADMT, closely followed by G. Samuelson flying a Swift. Third was Geoffrey de Havilland in his TK.2 G-ADNO followed by Bill Humble in Miles Sparrowhawk G-ACTE. A. J. S. Morris was last in Hobo G-AAIG. Flt Lt Llewellyn also completed the course successfully.

The final Folkestone Aero Trophy Race before the outbreak of war was held at Lympne on a beautiful summer's day, 5 August 1939, and was the last major air race in the UK until the end of the Second World War. The 1930s had been a successful decade for air racing, with many major new records set by an elite group of both male and female pioneering aviators, and Lympne was witness to these epic flights, earning its place in aviation history.

During the 1930s, Geoff Jordan was often taken by his father to air shows at Lympne. Here he stands close to a line-up of Hawker Fury Mk.1s of 25 Squadron, who were based at Hawkinge. The nearest, K2041 had previously flown with No.1 Squadron.

CHAPTER 6

Temporary use as a Royal Navy Shore Base; war is declared and the RAF returns to Lympne; attacks by the Luftwaffe; Dunkirk and the Battle of Britain; events of 1941

Plans to expand Lympne had been prepared earlier, in September 1938, with a curtailed scheme costing £20,750 to enlarge the airfield, in spite of the fact that the Accident Investigation Board considered that Lympne would still be an unsuitable base for Fairey Battle aircraft to operate from. It was felt that the surface of the airfield could be brought to the required standard in twelve months at a cost of £27,000, because Lympne was the most advanced landing ground (ALG) in England at the time and was ideal for use by aircraft operating against European targets, assuming that Belgium remained neutral. However, it was also thought that not being on the line of approach by the enemy to bomb London gave Lympne the advantage over other Kent airfields earmarked for Fairey Battle operations.

By the completion of the twelve-month period it was hoped that the RAF would have thirty medium bomber squadrons, many of which would operate from Kent if European bases were not available, and that Lympne would be of immense value as an ALG for heavy bomber squadrons. It was decided to improve the site at Lympne as early as possible, leaving the demolition of buildings until the effect of the airfield expansion became clear. Amongst other concerns were the trees on the southern boundary, but this problem could be dealt with at a later date. However, obstruction lights would be erected as soon as work began.

As a direct result of the renewed threat of war, Lympne airfield was transferred from No. 22 Group RAF on Saturday 1 July 1939, and commissioned by the Fleet Air Arm (FAA) as HMS *Buzzard*. It was reduced to a care and maintenance base until 25 September, but reopened as HMS *Daedalus II* under the control of Lee-on-Solent. Lympne became an FAA Training Establishment for aircrew, airframe fitters and apprentices,

Miles M.2H Hawk Major G-ADAB would appear to have over-shot the airfield on landing, coming to a halt in fields off Otterpool Lane. On the extreme left is a boy's pedal car. This aircraft was scrapped in December 1947.

although no aircraft were based at Lympne. Aircraft such as Blackburn Shark III K8899 were used for training.

Blackburn Skua IIs of No. 800 (FAA) Squadron were detached from Worthy Down, arriving at Lympne on 9 July. They were joined by Skua IIs and Blackburn Roc aircraft of No. 803 (FAA) Squadron at Ford, joining HMS *Ark Royal* later in the month. HMS *Buzzard* was promptly reported as having being sunk by German propaganda broadcaster William Joyce, Lord Haw-Haw, not realising that it was a shore establishment. All civilian flying was banned from September 1939, and the club's aircraft were now gathered together in the hangar ready for dispersal to less vulnerable airfields. Many were flown to Sywell, but some remained locked in No. 2 hangar.

Maisie Dupe's younger uncle, Sgt Plt Reginald Dupe was based with No. 97 Squadron. He was killed on active service on 10 February 1940, flying Whitley bomber K7255, and was buried at St Stephen's Church, Lympne. He had taken advantage of living at Lympne where he learned to fly with the Cinque Ports Flying Club, qualifying on 21 June 1934 in a DH.60G Gipsy Moth. At the time he was employed as a petrol salesman, but when at Lympne he could be found climbing in and out of the parked aircraft. Maisie's eldest brother worked for the Cinque Ports Flying Club.

John Henriet, the grandson of Clara Dupe, enjoyed visiting his cousins at Lympne airfield, spending many hours watching the flying and chatting to the pilots and ground crew, who were happy to talk to the young

Madeline Dupe with Maisie and John Henriet outside the Gate House, which was later painted white and was purpose-built for Sergeant S. J. Dupe Airfield Manager.

children living at the airfield. Maisie recalls that during one bombing raid at Lympne, a family canary kept in a cage was so shaken by the explosions that it lost most of its feathers. On another occasion, one of the young sailors with HMS *Buzzard* joined those in an air-raid shelter. He was in shock as he had witnessed the death of his chum, both of whom were on guard duty at the time. Needless to say, Maisie was terrified.

At the beginning of May 1940, the Air Ministry decreed that to meet its operational requirements at Lympne the naval establishment would have to move to another location. Preliminary arrangements had been made with the engineer officer in charge at Lympne to transfer naval personnel to a site at Newcastle, and Chatham Dockyard was to be responsible for the transfer of electrical installation to their new home. Arrangements were made with the Southern Railway to transport all personnel and equipment, with the exception of a small party, to leave Lympne by 23 May 1940, thus returning control of the airfield to the RAF.

No. 59 Squadron's Blenheims were withdrawn from Poix on 19 May. The following day, Lysander L4773 flown by Plt Off. Pennington and LAC Erskine force-landed on the beach near Calais, the first day of operations by No. 26 Squadron from Lympne. Both crew members were uninjured but were captured and taken as PoWs. The following day, Lysander L4793 was attacked by Bf 109s during a tactical reconnaissance sortie over Arras,

Maisie Conway (née Geal) talking to Able Seaman Gerald Alman who often chatted to the children living on the airfield, at the time Gerald was on Guard Duty.

Cambrai and Amiens. Both Plt Off. Dexter and LAC Webb were reported as unhurt, and their aircraft, despite damage to its tail and rudder, landed safely at Lympne. It was later repaired and returned to service.

Also in May, three Blenheims of No. 18 Squadron, one of which was almost unserviceable, returned to Lympne from France, piloted by Sqn Ldr Rogers and Flt Lts Langebear and Rees. Ground crews followed by boat via Boulogne; vehicles proceeded to Cherbourg for embarkation. From Lympne the remaining Blenheims flew to Watton, Norfolk. Within twenty-four hours of leaving France the squadron were again flying operational sorties. During the morning of 21 May, Plt Off. Light took off for a reconnaissance of the Douai-Arras-Amiens-Abbeville area but failed to return. Later the same day, three of the squadron's aircraft joined up with No. 82 Squadron to bomb armoured columns on the Abbeville–Boulogne road. One of these was lost, shot down by 'friendly fire'. During the Battle of France, Gloster Gladiators of Nos 607 and 615 Squadrons often landed at Lympne for refuelling on operations patrolling Dunkirk. Although they were no match for the Luftwaffe's Bf 109s, the ageing Gladiators put up a tremendous fight against the odds during May 1940.

Returning to Lympne on 21 May from Arras, following an attack by Bf 109s, Lysander L4793 of No. 16 Squadron landed with a badly damaged rudder. Both crew members, Plt Off. Dexter and LAC Webb, were uninjured. It was decided that the Blenheims of both Nos 53 and 59 Squadrons were to return to the South East, the Air Component HQ to Hawkinge and their aircraft to Lympne, from where they could undertake reconnaissance flights. Personnel and equipment were to go to Boulogne and Cherbourg, but both units left Lympne on 22 May. During the same day, Flt Lt G. H. D. Evans and the crew of a Blenheim of No. 59 Squadron returned to Lympne, having been damaged by a bird strike. The crew were unhurt, although alarmed at the amount of damage caused.

On 23 May 1940, No. 51 (Army Co-operation) Wing arrived at Lympne, previously having been working with the Army in France, and comprised aircraft and men from Nos 16 and 26 Squadrons under the command of Wg Cdr A. H. Flower CBE. Apart from flying duties, medical officers and personnel of Wing headquarters of the two squadrons were pooled to maintain central sick quarters, Flt Lt Walsh of No. 26 Squadron being appointed senior medical officer.

All ranks of this unit had to become conversant with the location of all shelter trenches at Lympne in order that they might be reached with a minimum of delay in the event of air raids. Blackout precautions had to be maintained, ensuring all doors and windows were covered at night. All ranks were told to keep a vigilant lookout for enemy agents or landing aircraft. If such an intrusion was to happen, the suspect was to

In March 1937 'B' Flight No.1 (F) Squadron was detached to reactivate 72 Squadron, the first unit to receive Gloster Gladiators, this news was not popular, as pilots and airmen did not wish to leave No.1 Squadron, especially as they were to re-equip with the Hurricane Mk. I. Although not based at Lympne, their Gladiators visited Lympne during this period. No.1 Squadron was later based at Lympne in 1943.

Despite the ever-present threat of bombing at Lympne during the early years of the Second World War, Maisie Conway (née Geal) found time to play with her brother Geoffrey and friend John Henriet. One of the air raid shelters, which was prepared in 1937, is visible just beyond the garden fence, in which parents and children would take cover in during raids.

be immediately arrested and taken for interrogation. Other duties carried out by the Wing included duty pilot, cypher officer, orderly officer, main guard, crash and fire picket party. Of great concern at Lympne, as with all airfields, was the threat of sabotage, and it was even suggested that saboteurs could land aircraft at Lympne bearing RAF or Allied markings, with the pilot wearing an RAF uniform. This was no joke, and warrant officers would be issued with five rounds. At night all those warned were instructed to be at constant readiness.

In the lead-up to Operation Dynamo, the evacuation of Dunkirk, orders were received by No. 26 Squadron to proceed to Lympne on 19 May 1940, and squadron transport moved to Cherbourg. Lysander aircraft operated by the unit took off at 2.10 a.m., vehicles leaving at 2.45 a.m. Plt Off. Clegg and volunteers flew one aircraft to Lympne without a parachute or air gunner owing to a shortage of crew. Fortunately they landed without incident, the remaining nineteen Lysanders arriving unhindered by the enemy.

Between 19 and 22 May, Lysanders of Nos 16 and 26 Squadrons were used for 'back violet' missions in support of the remaining British troops following the Battle of France. The next day, Blenheim Mk 1 aircraft of No. 59 Squadron were assigned to deliver 1,000 lb of anti-personnel parachute bombs to Hawkinge from Andover; these were later flown to Lympne for Lysanders of No. 26 Squadron to use.

By 19 May, Blenheims of No. 57 Squadron had been evacuated from Crécy, later moving on to Wyton on 22 May to regroup. The remaining aircraft joined them at Lympne later the same day and were moved on to Andover. However, both squadrons were soon returned to action, operating from their new bases. Blenheim L9266 of No. 59 Squadron was attacked by Spitfires during a bombing sortie on Boulogne on the 22nd, operating from Lympne. It crash-landed near Fricourt. The crew, Flt Lt F. Bird and Sgt C. Brinn survived, but sadly AC2 G. Coles was killed. That same day, the road convoy embarked on SS *Duke of Argyll* at Cherbourg and arrived at Southampton at 7.30 p.m., where officers and airmen joined a train for Folkestone, with transport arriving at Lympne three days later.

Armstrong Whitworth must rank as one of the Britain's successful aircraft manufacturers, and by 1 September 1939 the company had eleven Ensign aircraft, a four-engine, high-wing type built specially for Imperial Airways. With war almost certain, the South East was closed to civil aircraft movements, so they were moved from Croydon to Whitchurch Airport, Bristol. The Ensigns were delivered into the hands of Imperial Airways at the same time as the company merged with British Airways on 1 April 1940 to form BOAC. Some of these aircraft were impressed into service by the RAF for liaison duties, but the remainder kept their civilian status.

On 23 May, Capt. S. T. B. Cripps, the pilot of Ensign G-ADTA 'Euryalus', had taken off in formation for France from Croydon with a full load of supplies to the beleaguered forces and refugees. They flew to RAF Hawkinge to rendezvous with their fighter escort. As the civil formation circled overhead, twelve Hurricanes took off, led by Capt. G. R. Buxton in 'Empyrean' G-ADSY. The convoy set course for Merville, the strangely assorted formation arriving over the airfield approximately eighty minutes later and, while their escort remained aloft, the eight aircraft landed and parked themselves at intervals on the west side of the site. After twenty minutes, while the crews were busy unloading, Bf 109s appeared high over the airfield and engaged the Hurricanes in a hectic dogfight. With their ammunition exhausted, the Hurricanes were leaving for home when suddenly three Bf 109s swept low across the airfield, spraying the parked aircraft with machine-gun fire.

Capt. Cripps decided to fly as low as possible on the return flight, in order to cheat severe anti-aircraft fire from enemy motorised units. Just before reaching the coast, large quantities of oil began to pour from the port inner Tiger engine, oil pressure dropped and the engine had to be throttled back, leaving the Ensign flying on its two outer Tigers. Cripps decided to make an immediate landing at Lympne, the exact location of which he knew. On landing, the starboard undercarriage was not fully down, causing the wing to scrape the ground and the aircraft to go through a fence as no braking was attempted. It crashed to a halt, but fortunately there were no fatalities or serious injuries to those on board. 'Euryalus' was flown to RAF Hamble in June, but it was decided to cannibalise her to repair G-ADSU 'Euterpe', which had been damaged in an accident at Bonnington on 15 December 1939. 'Euryalus' was officially written off on 15 November 1941 and scrapped in September the following year.

A Blenheim of No. 57 Squadron, operating from Hawkinge on 24 May, crash-landed at Lympne with badly damaged hydraulics. Following an attack by Bf 110s, Plt Off. W. Hutchings was wounded in the arm, Sgt Whitlam and Cpl A. Daley being uninjured. The following day Hutchings was involved in another incident, when Me 110s attacked his Blenheim, P9243, returning from a sortie over Amiens. Despite an arm injury, he successfully crash-landed his aircraft on the airfield without injury to his crew, Sgt J. Alexander and LAC D. Goffe.

By the time they arrived at Lympne, the Lysanders of No. 26 Squadron had already been on reconnaissance flights and operations bombing the Calais area. During the war there were cases of mistaken identity, which sometimes proved fatal for the victims of so-called 'blue on blue' incidents. One such occurred on 26 May 1940, involving Lysander Mk II P9127 flown by Flt Lt Malan of No. 16 Squadron. Eight Lysanders of this unit were on tactical reconnaissance operations between Cap Gris Nez and the Belgian/Dutch border. Three Spitfires of No. 74 Squadron were also on patrol at the time and mistook P9127 for a Henschel Hs 126. Lining up on their unfortunate prey, Plt Offs Cobden and Stephen and Flt Sgt Mayne attacked, severely damaging the Lysander. Despite this, Malan was able to bring his damaged aircraft back over the Channel, crash-landing at Lympne at 7.45 a.m., but tragically the wireless air gunner, AC1 H. G. Littlewood, had been shot and killed. Plt Off. Hall was uninjured. Littlewood is buried alongside many of his fellow airmen, all victims of war, in the cemetery at Hawkinge near Folkestone.

Like the Lysander, the Hs 126 was a high-wing aircraft, so it is easy to understand why such a mistake could be made. It was not uncommon for Lysanders to be misidentified in this way, and No. 74 Squadron claimed to have shot another down three days prior to this incident, on 23 May. However, there seems to be no evidence in official records to suggest that this was another Lysander.

On 27 May, Lysander P1685 of No. 16 Squadron was hit by anti-aircraft fire during a supply drop over Calais, crashing at Lympne at 5.45 a.m. Flt Lt G. R. Shepley and Cpl Jones were both wounded and their aircraft was a write-off. In addition, Lysander L4782 of No. 26 Squadron was shot down during an armed recce, crashing at Sangatte. Plt Off. H. D. Dixon and LAC D. McL. Nimmo were killed. The same day, No. 613 Squadron, operating from Lympne, attacked gun positions at Calais and lost one Hector, K8116, when it crashed in fog at Shakespeare Cliff, Dover. Plt Off. Jenkyns was seriously injured and LAC R. V. Brown died later of his injuries. Next day, No. 16 Squadron lost another crew, when Lysander P1720 was hit by ground fire at Longuenesse, killing Flt Lt W. R. Clapham and Sgt Brown. Later that day, seven aircraft dropped supplies to British troops in Calais. Plt Offs Howarth, Dixon and Deas, and LACs McLoughlin, Bolton and Nibio were reported missing.

The late Sir Peter Bristow, who had served with No. 26 Squadron, recalled his memory of Lympne in an extract from a document held at the RAF Museum, Hendon:

My posting was to 26 Squadron. The squadron had emerged from France relatively unscathed. Like all the Lysander squadrons in France it was a completely mobile self-contained unit. It had arrived in England with all its transport and equipment and most of its aircraft intact. I was ordered to report at Lympne. Familiar territory, and just over the airfield boundary lived one of my wife's favourite aunts, where Joey had spent part of the autumn of 1939 working in the canteen they ran for the local troops. We drove from Salisbury in our ancient Ford 10. All that map-

Westland Lysander L4773 of 26 Squadron Lympne on the beach at Calais on 20 May 1940, being scrutinized by the enemy. P/O Pennington and LAC Erskine were captured and taken prisoners of war.

reading training, plus familiarity with the south of England, got us safely to Lympne in spite of the removal of all road signs so that the invading Germans should not find their way as easily as they had in France and Belgium. I duly reported on 30 May.

I was allocated to 'A' flight, one of the three flights of six aircraft of which the squadron was composed. There were accommodation problems because I had no camp kit. So everyone was delighted that I should sleep out. I found that the 'A' flight office was what had been the bar of my own flying club. Flight Lieutenant Vaughan, our highly efficient regular equipment officer, later to train as a bomber pilot, issued me with flying gear. I was told that we were one of the squadrons which had just dropped supplies to the Calais garrison. In fact, though we did not know it, after they had been overrun. I was allocated an aircraft and Sergeant Malthouse, one of the regulars as air-gunner, and told to report to the Air Officer in charge at 5 a.m. next day where I would be briefed for a sortie over Dunkirk.

It turned out to be an exquisite early summer morning. We took off from Lympne at 4.50 am. There were a number of wrecked aircraft around the airfield at Hawkinge when we landed, including burned-out Lysanders. Reporting to the Air Intelligence Office, I was told to photograph, from 5,000 feet, the line of the river inland from Nieuport from which guns were shelling what was left of the Dunkirk perimeter. The camera was installed and loaded, and off we went. In mid-Channel the scene was reminiscent of Henley Regatta, with hundreds of assorted ships and small craft on a calm sea. As we reached the Belgian coast, a summer morning, fog obliterated the whole scene. Photographing the river line was out. We flew back to Hawkinge, and parked close to the ALO's [Air Liaison Officer] hut. We saw two beautiful light blue Spitfires which had not been there earlier. We were told they were from PRU, the brand-new photo reconnaissance unit.

We were told they were also to photograph the river line inland from Nieuport from which guns were shelling what was left of the perimeter. We were told to fly back to Lympne. We were stood down till next day. When we got back, there was a French air force squadron of Dewoitine fighters on the airfield. In the next day or two, as the curtain came down on the Dunkirk evacuation, some of our aircraft were detached to France to operate over the German advance towards the Somme. They did not come back, nor did the Dewoitines. Badger Aitken of 'B' flight and I were given the job sorting out anything private which the missing Lysander crews had left behind in their kit and sending it home to their next of kin. On 8 June we were withdrawn to West Malling, and for 26 Squadron that was Dunkirk. It was later that summer that Lympne was bombed.

On 28 May 1940, security at Lympne was tested when an escaped PoW was reported as having been seen in Hythe. He was described as being 5 feet 8 inches tall, with close-cropped hair, very sunburnt, wearing a jacket and distinctive white plimsolls. The individual was later apprehended by police and returned to his PoW camp. During a reconnaissance flight the following day, Flt Lt Bryant and Plt Off. Stone flying Lysander P1689 of No. 26 Squadron were reported missing. In the morning, a telephone message was received from Stone to say they were both safe and at Camberley after being shot down off Dunkirk and that Bryant was wounded. May did not end well, as No. 16 Squadron lost Lysander P9127, shot down by 6./JG 27 over Dunkirk. Flt Lt G. R. Shipley was killed and Plt Off. C. J. F. Hare reported missing. This loss was followed by another, when Lysander L4793 was shot down by Maj. Freiherr von Berg of Stab III./JG 26 over the Channel near Dunkirk. The crew, Plt Off. G. M. V. Biden and Sgt A. Beard were reported missing.

At the beginning of June 1940, Sqn Ldr R. W. K. Stevens took over command of No. 26 Squadron from Sqn Ldr R. C. N. Perriers, who

The wreckage of Lysander L6863 which crashed on top of Fort Risban on 27 May 1940, P/O E. E. Howarth and LAC J. A. Bolton were killed.

remained as second-in-command. The same day, instructions were received from HQ No. 22 Group that the squadron would move to West Malling by 10 June. Operating from Lympne, Lysander N1253 returned damaged from operations over France, crashing at Hawkinge and killing Plt Off. J. C. Paterson and LAC A. Carter. Two hours later, at 8.40 am, Lysander L4761 was shot down by Lt von Moller of 1./JG 2 and crashed near Furnes, killing Plt Off. R. Wilson and LAC A. V. Fitzgerald. This was the pattern of events, with more air-raid warnings and a steady build-up of personnel arriving, until 15 June when Flt Lt T. Hogan arrived from RAF Lossiemouth and took command of Lympne, assisted by Plt Off. Rutherford-Jones.

A squadron of the French Air Force had arrived at Lympne at the end of May 1940. GC II/8 had been based at Deauville and their task was to fly escort to French aircraft operating in support of Allied troops at Dunkirk. It was rather an ignominious start to their short stay at an English airfield: one of their aircraft, a Bloch 152 piloted by S/Lt Delocque-Fourcault, was hit by gunfire by over-enthusiastic RAF pilots and returned to Lympne with damage to its port wing. On 9 June, another Bloch 152 of this unit, flown by Adjt Nicolle, was shot down by a Bf 109 and abandoned near Rouen. Nicolle baled out but was fired on by the German pilot Uffz. Heinbockel of 2./JG 21 and wounded in the head as he dangled from his parachute. The French pilot had been escorting a raid on Forges-les-Eaux by Chance Vought V-156Fs. The unit returned to France on 12 June.

During a routine tactical reconnaissance flight on 5 June, Lysander N1211 of No. 26 Squadron was shot down by Hptm. Muller of 4./JG 3 south-west of Abbeville and crashed at Ercourt. Both crew members, Plt Off. D. G. Fevez and Sgt R. D. K. Cochrane, were killed and the aircraft was a write-off.

On 9 June 1940, a care and maintenance party was formed at the airfield. This unit consisted of nine officers, 234 airmen, fourteen civilians and, in addition, four airmen essential to duties prior to arrival of personnel. The following day, Flt Lt T. P. Aldworth DSO, OBE arrived with 122 airmen from Morecambe. Being the only officer on the station, Aldworth assumed command until such time as an officer arrived on posting. Later that day an air-raid warning was given but nothing developed, more airmen arriving on posting.

H. V. Cossons, who was based at Lympne during 1940, recalls:

On the defence of airfields in the south-east of England during the Battle of Britain, for my battery, the 138th Light Army-Aircraft Battery, Royal Artillery, had a troop defending Lympne airfield during the Dunkirk evacuation. I well remember a squadron from the French air force operated from there at the time. They were equipped with Marcel Bloch fighters, armed with two 20 mm Hispano cannon mounted in the wings, and two machine guns in the body. They were led on patrol by a twin-engined Potez fighter with twin rudders, looking like a smaller and radial-engined version of the Messerschmitt 110. A huge Armstrong Whitworth Ensign airliner had crash-landed on the airfield and so had a Westland Lysander. In an adjacent field an Avro Anson was pitched up on its nose. I remember seeing Hawker Hector biplanes with Napier Dagger engines take off with supplies for the troops besieged in Calais. It may be news to some people that this is the last of a long line of Hawker biplanes that saw service in the Battle of Britain, or at least just before it. The 138th battery was divided into three troops and during the whole of the Battle of Britain one troop defended RAF Manston, another defended the radar compound between St Margaret's Bay and Dover, and the troop in which I served as a gunner defended Dover harbour itself. It seems incredible to realize that we never, to the best of my knowledge, had a man killed or a gun knocked out during the whole of that time. I don't think that there is another battery in the Royal Artillery which has helped to defend three such important objectives against such odds, without loss, at one and the same time.

On 25 June, the airfield was visited by Inspector General ACM Sir Edgar Ludlow-Newitt. However, it had been a frustrating month at Lympne, with many air-raid warnings but no action. It was not until 3 July that war came to Lympne, when during the afternoon some thirty bombs were dropped on the airfield by aircraft operating independently. Pilots were scrambled to intercept Dornier Do 17s and got into a fight with Bf 109s protecting them. There were no casualties, but one MT vehicle was hit and buildings were slightly damaged. Just after 2 p.m. on 11 July, as Spitfire Mk 1 P9398 approached the airfield, it was obvious that the pilot was struggling with his aircraft. However, Plt Off. D. G. Cobden, based with No. 74 Squadron at RAF Hornchurch, managed to crash-land it without sustaining any injury and P9398 was later repaired. Sadly, Cobden, a New Zealander, was shot down and killed on 11 August 1940 over the North Sea east of Harwich, flying Spitfire Mk 1 R6757. Following a 'circus operation' to France escorting a number of bombers, Sgt Lamberton of No. 72 Squadron, flying Spitfire W3171, also crash-landed at Lympne but was uninjured.

On a foggy and rainy day, 25 July, Flt Lt L. F. Henstock of No. 64 Squadron at Kenley force-landed at Lympne with a main supercharger bearing failure after combat over Folkestone. His Spitfire Mk 1, R6700 SH-K, was fitted with a new engine and returned to Kenley by Sgt J. W. C. Squire.

It was a sad day on 1 August for those stationed at Lympne when an airman on detachment to RAF Hawkinge was killed in a ground aircraft accident. The victim had most probably been sent there with a service flight. On 12 August, Bf 110s of *Erprobungsgruppe 210* attacked radar stations at Dover, Pevensey and Rye, and fifteen Do 17s of 1./KG 2 attacked Lympne. A total of 242 bombs were dropped. It was a surprise attack, coming in low over Romney Marsh before rising up over the escarpment to the airfield. Damage was caused to hangars, offices and the airfield, but repairs to the hangars were hindered by delayed-action bombs. One airman, LAC S. H. Bell, was killed, and two were seriously injured by a bomb which fell outside the airfield. The runway had also been hit and was unserviceable for forty-eight hours. The Luftwaffe was trying to knock out fighter bases and cause as much damage and loss of life as possible. Two Spitfires of No. 54 Squadron that force-landed had to swerve to avoid the craters left by the German raiders. Thankfully, both pilots were uninjured. Later that day, the station was again visited by Sir Edgar Ludlow-Newitt, who arrived by air and witnessed the aftermath of the earlier raid. Thirteen civilian aircraft that had been locked up in No. 2 hangar at the outbreak of war were totally destroyed. Perhaps they should have been moved or requisitioned!

The bombing at Lympne of 12-13 August was followed by a major attack on the 15th by fifty Ju 87B Stuka dive bombers of II./(St.)LG 1, escorted by Messerschmitt Bf 109s. Hangars were damaged and two wooden huts used as paint stores and an arms store were all burnt out, civilian firefighters being employed to put out the fires. All power and water services were cut. Worse still, there was a direct hit on the station's sick quarters, which had to be evacuated to empty houses near the airfield. The orderly room and the accounts section were also hit. Another bomb hit an air-raid shelter, seriously injuring five pilots, one of whom died from his injuries later that month. Consequently the airfield could only be used for emergencies until mid-September.

Sunday 18 August 1940 became known as the 'hardest day', because the RAF lost sixty-eight aircraft. The Luftwaffe lost sixty-nine. At 1.40 p.m. Flt Lt 'Squeak' Weaver shot down a Messerschmitt Bf 110C-4 of 3./ZG 26, which crashed in flames at Bonnington. When airmen arrived on the scene, they found in the burnt-out aircraft the remains of two German airmen, Obrfw. Willie Stange and Uffz. Hans Hesse, who were both reported at their base as missing in action. Their remains defied identification at the time and as a result they were both buried at St Stephen's Church, Lympne. On 22 August, Flt Lt Montgomery, the CO of RAF Lympne at the time, wrote to the Revd David Hall:

We have brought into Lympne aerodrome the bodies of two German airmen shot down last Sunday at Bonnington, about four miles west of here. Would you please be good enough to make arrangements for the burial of these men tomorrow, 23 August 1940.

It would appear from St Stephen's parish records that two unidentified German airmen were buried as requested. Two other unfortunate German aircrew were also shot down on the 18th and were recovered from the crash site at Rough Common, Harbledown. They were buried at Chartham private cemetery, but when the grave was exhumed in 1962 for transferring the remains to Cannock Chase, four bodies were found. So it would appear that they may all have been quietly buried together again by the Commonwealth War Graves Commission (CWGC) and that both Stange and Hesse were indeed buried at Cannock Chase in block nine, grave forty-six. The CWGC states that it 'cannot confirm or verify the names of the airmen in grave forty-six as they are classified as unknown'.

On 30 August at 3 pm, nine aircraft dropped 500 lb bombs, damaging the remaining hangar and killing six civilians during a direct hit on an air-raid shelter. There were no RAF casualties. The unfortunate civilians were buried at St Stephen's Church, Lympne. The Luftwaffe aircraft that carried out the latter raid had broken off from a large formation of bombers and

Soldiers inspect remains of Bf 110C-4 3/ZG 26, shot down on 18 August 1940 at Bonnington, in which both crew members died.

headed for Lympne to launch the attack. The surviving hangar, unscathed in previous attacks, was also in need of urgent repair.

RAF Lympne was informed of and dealt with many crashes in the area. One of these occurred on 1 September 1940, when Hurricane P2376 of No. 1 Squadron based at RAF Northolt, flown by Flt Sgt F. G. Berry DFM, was shot down at Brisley Farm, Ruckinge near Ashford. His body was brought to Lympne and later buried at Harrow New Cemetery, Middlesex.

At 3.32 p.m. the same day, following combat with a Do 17 that force-landed in the vicinity of Lydd, Plt Off. G. Allard of No. 85 Squadron broke away, noticing his oil pressure was low, and brought his Hurricane into Lympne as the engine died on him. As he was waiting for his aircraft's service to be completed by two airmen, the airfield was attacked by three Bf 110s that aimed two bombs at the Hurricane. One of the airmen, LAC S. Andrewartha, was killed and the other, AC1 C. T Thornton, was seriously wounded, some ten minutes after the all-clear had been given. The blast from the bombs also damaged Hurricane Mk 1 N2477, which was later repaired and returned to service. Allard was lucky to escape with his life – uninjured, he lived to fight another day.

Plt Off G. Allard, had contributed to the attack of Do 17Z of 9/KG76, which was on route to attack Gravesend, killing Gfr. Speiss, the remaining crew were taken POW

Sgt J. Metham of No. 253 Squadron flying Hurricane Mk 1 P2946 was shot down by Bf 109s over Thanet. He managed to bale out and landed uninjured. Only twenty minutes later, Plt Off. S. Skalski of No. 501 Squadron crashed at Horton Priory, Sellindge. His Hurricane Mk 1 V7230 was repairable but Skalski was injured.

Lympne received an unwelcome visit at 9.40 a.m. from German aircraft dropping thirty bombs on the site and leaving a few craters in the runway area, but these did not prevent emergency landings. This was fortunate for Flt Lt E. Graham of No. 72 Squadron, who crash-landed in Spitfire Mk 1 X4241 following combat. He was followed by Sgt H. C. Adams, who crashed unhurt on the airfield in Hurricane Mk 1 V7234 of No. 501 Squadron.

Uffz. von Stein force-landed his Bf 109E4 (1452) not far from Lympne Castle. He had been brought down during sustained combat with Flt Lt R. G. Reynolds of No. 43 Squadron and taken prisoner. On 1 September, Lympne was notified of a Bf 109E-4 of III./JG 43 that had crashed at Hurst Farm, Chilham. The pilot, Oblt Bauer, was killed and once again a party of airmen went to the scene to recover the body, which remained in the mortuary at RAF Lympne before being released for burial on the 3rd, later being moved to Cannock Chase. Sgt Jack Stokoe of No. 603 Squadron wrote in his combat report:

> At about 5.30 p.m. we were patrolling Manston at 12,000 feet when control informed us Canterbury was being dive bombed about five miles south of the town, when at about 3,000 feet a Bf 109, silver with black crosses, dived past my nose, flattened out about 50 feet up and headed south. I executed a steep turn, pushed in boost override, and sat on his tail. At about 50 yards, I gave one small burst with little effect, closed to 30 yards, and gave a longer burst. Black smoke poured from him as I overshot him. The aircraft crashed in a field, turned over two or three times and burst into flames in a clump of trees. Seventy bullets had been fired from each gun.

No. 74 Squadron were operating from Hawkinge on 2 September when their CO, Sqn Ldr Collins, was injured in his knee and hand during combat. Flt Lt Ted Graham took over command, only to be shot down himself in Spitfire Mk 1, crash-landing at Lympne. Graham was not injured, although his Spitfire was riddled with bullets. A few uneventful days followed, but on 6 September the airfield took charge of the body of Flt Sgt W. P. Cambridge of No. 253 Squadron, who was killed baling out of his stricken Hurricane Mk 1 P3032 that was shot down over the Kingsnorth area of Ashford.

Plt Off G. Allard, previously mentioned, made up for his disappointment the day before, attacked and brought down a Do 17Z of 9/KG76, which was on route to attack Gravesend. The damaged aircraft crash landed near a railway branch line, killing Gfr. Speiss, the remaining crew were taken POW.

Sgt G. W. Pearson of No. 501 Squadron in Hurricane P3516 was also shot down and killed near Ashford, his body being brought to Lympne for burial. Pearson had joined the squadron ten days earlier. He crashed at Cowsleas Farm, Hothfield, near Kempton Manor. Originally his headstone at St Peter's Church was simply marked 'unknown airman'. However, in 1982, his sister searched through official records and interviewed many people to in order to establish whether the grave was indeed that of her brother. After dealing with official obstacles she eventually identified his grave at St Peter's and a proper headstone has since been erected.

An invasion alert was received on 10 September 1940, which was to remain in force until further notice. On the 15th, Plt Off. A. Barton of No. 253 Squadron took part in a head-on attack on Do 215 bombers, during which his Hurricane Mk 1 V6698 was damaged by return fire, crash-landing at Lympne.

Having just been engaged in aerial combat with a Messerschmitt Bf 109, Plt Off. Albert E. van den Hove d'Ertsenryck's Hawker Hurricane Mk 1 P2760 exploded over East Stour Farm, Chilham, and he was killed, his aircraft coming down in the River Stour. His funeral, on 20 September at Lympne church, was attended by the Belgium air attaché accompanied by another Belgian officer. Sixty-eight years later, on 15 September 2008, Battle of Britain Day, the 'Spirit of Kent' Spitfire flew over the church, and members of the Hythe and Romney Marsh branch of the RAF Association, who held their annual ceremony in the churchyard at Lympne, unveiled a memorial plaque to commemorate Albert on the site of his original grave. In addition to former members of the RAF, people from the village of Lympne and elsewhere also attended the ceremony, as did pupils from Lympne School, one of whom read a moving poem, 'High Flight', by Plt Off. J. G. Magee of No. 412 (RCAF) Squadron. Albert, who was numbered amongst the twenty-eight Belgians killed during the Battle of Britain, is now at rest in his native Belgium, having been moved to the lawn of honour in the cemetery at Evere in Brussels. However, for many years to come he will be remembered by the people of Kent.

Damaged during combat with Bf 109s, Spitfire Mk 1 P9500 force-landed at Lympne on 20 September 1940. Its pilot, Plt Off. G. H. Bennions of No. 41 Squadron, was uninjured. The aircraft was later repaired and flew until March 1942, when it crashed killing its pilot. Plt Off G. Bennions again force-landed on the airfield later the same day in Spitfire Mk 1 X4101 following enemy action. He went to bed that night lucky but shaken. On 24 September, a German aircraft again dropped fifty bombs on Lympne, but there were no casualties recorded, the enemy continuing on its way in a south-easterly direction. Two days later, German aircraft approached from the south-east, having been turned away by gunfire from an anti-aircraft battery in the Folkestone area. They approached Lympne in a shallow dive, dropping twenty 500 lb bombs, including incendiaries that landed along the western side of the airfield. Several unoccupied shelters were demolished, including an army truck that caught fire. Four soldiers were injured but little other damage was caused and there were no other casualties.

Following the crash of Spitfire Mk 1 N3109 on 7 October 1940 at Hurst Farm, Godmersham Park, the body of Flt Lt H. K. F Matthews of No. 603 Squadron was conveyed to Lympne. He had been shot down by Bf 109s of II./JG 26. Another attack by a solo German bomber occurred two days later when two large shrapnel bombs and one oil canister were dropped on the north-east corner of the airfield but with no damage or casualties.

On 22 October, Sgt R. H. B. Fraser of No. 257 Squadron, North Weald, was shot down and killed, his Hurricane Mk 1 V6851 crashing at Shadoxhurst near Ashford. His body was brought to Lympne and dispatched to his next of kin on the 29th. Fraser is buried in his home city of Glasgow, at Craigton Cemetery. In 1973, Brenzett Aeronautical Museum recovered the remains of V6851, which are on display at Lashenden Air Warfare Muscum, and on 4 April 2013, a memorial was unveiled at Moat Farm, Shadoxhurst, in memory of Fraser. The owner of Moat Farm was the retiring High Sheriff of Kent, Michael Bax, who helped to organise the placing of the memorial and conducted the ceremony with ex-Battle of Britain pilot Bob Foster.

October came to an end it and it had been a wake-up call to the reality of war. The Battle of Britain had been a victory, but many pilots, airmen and civilians had been sacrificed. Several weeks later, Sgt Nilezwski had a narrow escape, on 8 December 1940, when he force-landed near Wye in Hurricane Mk 1 R4101, squadron code SD-P. He was uninjured and his aircraft, inspected by the engine officer from Lympne, was later taken to the De Havilland Aircraft Co. for repair. On 17 December, three crew members of Blenheim Mk 1 P6953 of No. 101 Squadron were killed when their aircraft crashed near Hastings. The bodies of Sgts W. Skipworth, W. E. Need and D. Stephenson were transported to Hawkinge. Later that day, Wellington Mk 1 T2461 of No. 99 Squadron crashed near Rye. Sgt Plt Miller and five crew members were uninjured and returned to their unit. A guard dispatched from Lympne was placed on this aircraft until the 24th of the month.

January 1941 was a particularly quiet month at Lympne, with the airfield non-operational for a few days as a result of snowfall. On the 10th of the month, Spitfire Mk 1 P7310 of No. 74 Squadron flown by Flt Lt Boulding force-landed at Lympne due to engine failure. Three days later, a work party of eight airmen arrived from the squadron, based at Biggin Hill, to repair Boulding's Spitfire at Lympne. Four days later, Spitfire Mk 1 P9516 of No. 222 Squadron, piloted by Sgt Plt Cockram, force-landed at New Romney due to fuel shortage, the pilot fortunately not sustaining any injury. The engineer officer and his team from Lympne were sent to inspect the aircraft, which returned to service.

On 9 February, AVM Trafford Leigh-Mallory, AOC 11 Group, arrived at Lympne and following inspections was able to talk to pilots and ground crew – a visit much appreciated by all concerned. Col. J. F. Turner, who had served with the Royal Engineers, had been brought out of retirement to take on the Air Ministry's decoy programme, a scheme in which dummy aircraft were located away from the main airfield to deceive the Luftwaffe into thinking they were satellite airfields, which, it was hoped, the enemy would attack rather than directing their full resources to the main airfield. These locations were known as K Sites, and the south-east area was K4. This project was one of many deceptions and on 13 February, accompanied by Wg Cdr Riley, Turner discussed the location of such a site at Lympne. They were joined the following day by Sqn Ldr Pritchard of Fighter Command, and Maj. Gen. Liardet, Inspector General of Airfield Defences. A location was agreed and thirteen airmen led by a sergeant arrived at Lympne on 20 February to erect dummy aircraft, which were simply bolted together in sections. The airmen, usually drawn from the RAF's less specialised trades, were required to move the aircraft around occasionally in order to suggest activity. Those used at Lympne would probably have represented Hurricanes or Defiant aircraft. Records suggest that the K site at Lympne remained until the end of May 1942.

It is also known that the future traffic manager of Skyways International in France served at Lympne in 1940 with the RAF, and recalled the decoy Hurricanes that were placed on the airfield, to deceive the Luftwaffe.

It would appear that Fifth Column agents were active, since whenever the wooden aircraft were pushed aside for the real aircraft to land, the airfield was subjected to attack. In fact the real aircraft were often pushed across the road into the woods around the grounds of Lympne Preparatory School. As with several airfields of the period, Lympne was mined for destruction should the country be invaded. Although recovered many years later, the mines would prove fatal, as will be revealed later in this book.

The Luftwaffe visited again on 26 February, three fighters and two bombers approaching the aerodrome flying in a north-eastern direction.

Some ten bombs were dropped indiscriminately over an area of 400 yards. There was no damage to the airstrip but some properties away from the airfield were damaged, although there were no causalities.

On the morning of 20 March 1941, Lympne was subjected to low-level dive attack from four Bf 109s flying south-west to north-east at about 950 feet, firing cannon and machine guns, dropping one bomb each. There were no casualties and no damage other than craters. Ground defences opened heavy fire but apparently with no results. At 10.27 a.m. the station was again attacked by low-level fire and bombs were dropped. Five Bf 109s, presumably the same formation, dropped about twenty bombs. All came within 200 feet of the ground and two at least came within six feet of the ground at one time. There were no casualties nor damage other than craters on the landing field. Ground defences again opened heavy fire, claiming a hit that was confirmed by the crew of another gun – the aircraft concerned was seen to be smoking very badly. Some bombs were released so low that they hardly penetrated the surface, running along the top of the ground.

Three days later, bombs fell from four Bf 109s coming from north-west to south-east, and diving to within 100 feet of the ground. Again, several bombs hit the ground horizontally, skidded along the surface and came to rest without exploding. Three huts were damaged and the petrol storehouse was half demolished. Some petrol was lost by leakage from several cans pierced by bullets but no fire was started. Two people were injured because unfortunately no warning had been received. Ground defences opened fire without hitting any of the raiders.

In the spring of 1941, a top secret plot was hatched that, if successful, would have changed the face of Europe. It was a plan to kidnap Adolf Hitler and fly him to Lympne aerodrome. Hitler was to be taken alive from the plane after a rapid descent over the Channel before being bundled into the back of a car and driven to London. Evidence of the plan can be found in official RAF documents kept at the National Archives in Kew.

The story began in the Bulgarian capital, Sofia, when a man named Kiroff walked into the British military attaché's office and claimed his brother-in-law, Hans Baur, Hitler's personal pilot, was planning to defect in Hitler's plane with the Führer on board and land at Lympne. The date set for their arrival, 25 March 1941, came and went. The aircraft never arrived, and Baur spent the rest of the war as Hitler's pilot. So was it really ever likely to happen? In fact, a few weeks later, Rudolf Hess did defect, landing in Scotland by parachute – a long way from Lympne and not quite the prize the RAF was hoping for.

RAF Lympne officially became the satellite airfield for RAF Hawkinge on 5 May 1941, on the same day as four Bf 109s returned to attack the airfield. Although no bombs were dropped, they managed to destroy Spitfire Mk 1 R7294, a presentation aircraft of No. 91 Squadron, christened 'Derrick'. Some personnel were slightly injured. At this time the squadron were tasked with protecting both RAF Hawkinge and Lympne. The following day, nine aircraft of No. 4 Squadron of JG 52 took off to attack Lympne. Led by Oblt Simschem, they carried out several attacks on parked aircraft. Gefr. Adolf Glunz flew Bf 109 F-2 over the airfield and shot down a Spitfire. It was his first victory. The attack did not last long, although two Spitfires on the ground were damaged by bombs and cannon fire. At 3.15 p.m. three Bf 109s attacked the airfield without dropping bombs. There were three casualties and a Bf 109 was reported to have been shot down in flames, falling into the sea.

At 9.24 p.m. on 11 May, twelve Bf 109s of 1./JG 51 dropped bombs and machine-gunned the airfield in a raid of no more than five minutes' duration. However, the day was not over yet, as during the early afternoon an Me 110 dashed across the airfield dropping two bombs, causing a few minor casualties and some slight damage. Anti-aircraft guns fired at enemy aircraft, causing some damage, and during a patrol Flt Lt Holland and Sgt McKay destroyed a Bf 109.

The Me 110s returned on 16 May to deliver four bombs. There were no casualties but one of the attackers was hit by anti-aircraft fire from Lympne. On 9 June, four Bf 109s strafed the airfield but no one was injured. Shortly after, a Handley Page Hector, G-AEGH, arrived from Rochester, piloted by Mr Simmons and accompanied by Wg Cdr Abraham and Mr Truebody. The following morning the aircraft returned to Shorts at Rochester.

On 9 July 1941, two Spitfire Mk IIAs of No. 92 Squadron – R7195, flown by Plt Off. P. L. I. Archer, and P8537, piloted by Plt Off. E. G. Brettell – crashed at Lympne. Archer was injured during a routine sweep. Brettell was one of the unfortunate pilots who, like Roger Bushell, was murdered following the mass escape from Stalag Luft III. On 23 July, Avro Avalon DG655, stationed at Lee-on-Solent with the FAA and flown by Lt Lewis, arrived with airframe fitters to repair Walrus W2794 of 1350 Flight.

On 11 September, six Spitfires of No. 72 Squadron had taken off from Gravesend to draw enemy fighters into combat, while escorting a small number of bombers. Returning from a rather uneventful trip, four landed at Detling and one at Biggin Hill, the only casualty being Sgt Lamberton who crash-landed at Lympne but was uninjured. Handley Page Hampden OL-C AE374, flown by Plt Off. Seward, having been damaged during operations, landed and overshot the airfield at 7 a.m. Following a call to RAF Scampton where the aircraft was based with No. 83 Squadron, Avro Anson N9909 of No. 106 Squadron, flown by Plt Off. Hartley, landed to ferry the crew back to base. Three days later, N9909, flown by Sgt Riley, arrived with a team of fitters to repair the damaged bomber. A replacement crew was ferried to Lympne in Hampden OL-H AE312, and on 12 October both Hampdens took off bound for Scampton.

Miles Magister P2501 of No. 73 Squadron was delivered to Lympne from Heston on 9 October, flown by Mr Simpson. Later that day, Puss Moth DC663, piloted by Mrs Forward, landed from Hatfield to collect Mrs Moore, an ATA (Air Transport Auxiliary) ferry pilot, returning to Hatfield airfield. Lysander V9483 landed from Hawkinge on 23 November, flown by Sgt Fletcher of No. 277 (ASR) Squadron with Plt Off. J. Spence, who was to be duty pilot. This is worth a mention as this particular aircraft later crashed in a forced landing at Foxholt in Kent, on 16 April 1941.

Squadrons often used Lympne for exercises not undertaken from their own airfield. On one such occasion, seven Lysanders of No. 16 Squadron detached from RAF Weston Zoyland arrived on 23 November with sixty-seven other ranks and five officers. Whilst at Lympne they flew air sea rescue flights before returning to their home base four days later.

CHAPTER 7

RAF support and defence units at Lympne, 1942-43; RAF squadrons using the airfield during the Dieppe raids; operations of squadrons based on the airfield; further attacks

At the beginning of 1942, No. 38 Works Flight arrived at Lympne to repair areas damaged by the recent attacks. 'A' Flight of No. 91 Squadron flew in from Hawkinge (Lympne being its satellite airfield) to take advantage of the facilities extended to them, operating between Hawkinge and Lympne until 23 November 1942, often due to extremely poor weather conditions when Hawkinge was affected by thick mist and fog. The move was not unpopular as officers were billeted at Port Lympne. Sadly, the squadron's stay at Lympne was overshadowed by the loss of two pilots. Flt Lt Gordon Dean and Flt Sgt Melville Eldrid were shot down and killed by Fw 190s of 6./JG 26 during a sortie over Dieppe. Both were reported missing, and they and their aircraft were never found. The following day, Plt Off. J. P. Lux was also killed by a pilot of 1./JG 26.

On 24 March 1942, RAF Lympne was visited by none other than Gen. Bernard Montgomery, in charge of South Eastern Command, to inspect the airfield and its defences and to meet RAF personnel. His visit may also have been in connection with Exercise Tiger – a combined forces operation involving 100,000 troops. Following on from the work that commenced in 1941, it was decided to improve and provide further dispersal and hardstanding areas at Lympne, a fighter pen and three Blister hangars, and work was begun to complete the extension of the airfield.

Miles Magister Mk 1 L5962, a communications aircraft used by No. 91 Squadron, crashed when coming in to land on 24 April 1942. This aircraft, often flown between Hawkinge and Lympne, was piloted on this occasion by Flt Sgt Young, who fortunately was not seriously injured. On 22 May, defences were strengthened when thirty-four men and other ranks led by an officer arrived from RAF North Weald. At the same time, C Troop 459

Battery RA arrived with one officer and seventeen men from RAF West Malling. With them came six Beaverettes – armoured vehicles used by the Army and RAF for Home Defence service and training. Later that month, defences were further stepped up when B Troop 175 Battery RA arrived with Bofors guns.

It was a sad day for No. 91 Squadron on 15 June 1942 when Plt Off. E. E. Sykes of the RCAF, flying Spitfire Vb AR370, went missing during a routine shipping reconnaissance off the coast of Dieppe. Neither he nor his aircraft was seen again, as was the case with so many pilots on patrols over the English Channel, although the air sea rescue crews recovered many downed airmen. By 30 June, Nos 72 and 133 Squadrons, both based at Biggin Hill, had been moved to Lympne, their mission to take part in fighter sweeps and coastal patrols and to cover the Canadian forces during the Dieppe landings. No. 133 Squadron was one of three that formed the American Eagle Squadron; however, the other two units, Nos 71 and 121 Squadrons, did not join them at Lympne.

Good news was received by No. 72 Squadron when Flt Lt Woods was awarded the DFC, and the same evening a celebration took place at the officers' mess. Cpl Jack Lancaster, a fitter with the squadron, was detailed to go ahead of the road convoy and call into a pub on the A20 to order up some beer for the weary airmen. Having been entrusted with £5, he duly placed the order, much to the delight and surprise of the landlord.

No.72 Squadron pilots were on readiness from dawn and two pilots on advance readiness sat in their aircraft ready for take-off. At the time, the squadron were still equipped with Spitfire Vb and Vcs, although these were later replaced by Spitfire Mk IVs. Twenty aircraft had been painted with white strips on the engine cowling and tailplane and were not to be flown near the English coast until their next sweep. This was ordered throughout Fighter Command and was intended to prevent the risk of friendly aircraft being shot down.

An incident which had serious consequences for the squadron's ground personnel occurred on the afternoon of 5 July. Plt Off. Daniel, piloting the unit's engineer officer, Plt Off. Tomlinson, to Biggin Hill, was caught in a sudden downdraught and crashed near Sevenoaks. His aircraft, Miles Magister T9765, was burnt out. Daniel escaped with slight burns and Tomlinson was badly shaken. The following day, six aircraft took off on convoy patrol but returned without incident or loss. On 7 July, six convoy patrols were flown by twelve aircraft and a replacement Magister was delivered to Lympne. At 6 p.m. the squadron were advised that they were to fly back to Biggin Hill the same night, which they did, accompanied by the ground crews and equipment. No. 72 Squadron returned to convoy patrols after what had been a very disappointing and unrewarding break at Lympne. On 30 July 1942, the RAF Regiment based at Lympne moved its headquarters to The Croft, a large house located at Stone Street, not far from the airfield. The following month, 2798 Squadron RAF Regiment arrived at Lympne from Debden, and 2744 Squadron RAF Regiment, who were already based at the airfield, were inspected by Brig. C. Britton.

Until 7 July, No. 133 Squadron had operated from Lympne, escorting Bostons to their target and seeing them home safely. On one occasion, they acted as cover for 'Hurribombers' of No. 234 Squadron. As it turned out, they were vectored to the wrong area and did not rendezvous with the squadron until they caught up with them on their flight home. No. 133 Squadron moved to Lympne from Gravesend on 31 July 1942, where they remained until 17 August, when, much to everyone's annoyance, they moved to Martlesham Heath on a gun-firing course, remaining there until the end of August, when they moved south to Biggin Hill, not returning to Lympne. However, preparations for Operation Jubilee began. The squadron were put on readiness, only to be informed that No. 65 Squadron were to take over their first patrol, but they were eventually scrambled. They took off for Dieppe, reaching 7,000 feet and managing to engage a formation of Fw 190s, destroying two. Another four patrols were flown on the same day, during which a Do 17 and a Fw 190 fell victim to the eager guns of the squadron. Despite worsening weather, all aircraft returned safely.

No. 401 (RCAF) Squadron had been posted to Lympne from Biggin Hill on 14 August and settled quickly into their new surroundings. Officers messed in Lympne Place, and were briefed to take part in the Dieppe raid and Ramrod operations. The following day, Green Section were scrambled at 9.10 a.m. to the Ashford area. On taking off, WO Flander hit a tree south of the airfield, damaging his starboard wing leading edge, cooling radiators, fairings and nose cowling, but despite this the pilot managed to land at Lympne shortly after the incident. On 17 August, Plt Offs Morrison and Murray were on patrol in the Canterbury area and reported a drifting barrage balloon at 16,000 feet. Morrison was instructed to shoot it down. Eager for action, he opened fire and watched as the balloon descended into the sea off Dover.

The same day, Spitfires of No. 401 Squadron joined Nos 411 and 64 Squadrons in support of 8th USAAF B-17s attacking marshalling yards in France. Flt Sgt W. E. Rowthorn's aircraft, Spitfire IX BR985, was attacked by fighters and received damage to his port aileron. Heading home to Lympne, he banked to port at 400 feet as he came into land but got into a spin, turning twice, and just managed to level off before hitting the ground. The port wing dug in and wreckage was scattered over a great distance. The aircraft had caught fire but Rowthorn was thrown clear, still in his seat, and was dragged away by a farmer and a constable who happened to be near the scene of the accident in a field adjoining the north side of the airfield. Although conscious, he had injuries to his forehead as well as multiple injuries to his legs, hands and face. Sadly, he died of his injuries in hospital on 20 August. Ironically, prior to the operation, Rowthorn had tossed a coin with Flt Sgt Rosser to decide who should fly on this mission. The winner kept the penny for luck, but his luck ran out. He was a popular pilot who had shown much determination. Plt Off. J. K. Ferguson was shot down on the same mission. At first it was thought that he had been taken prisoner, but he was in fact killed. Sqn Ldr K. L. B. Hodson, flying BS120, after combat with Fw 190s landed at Biggin Hill; Flt Lt N. H. Trask was shot down in Spitfire IX BR634 and taken prisoner.

Having flown operations from RAF Gravesend, Eastchurch, Martlesham Heath and Biggin Hill No. 401 (RCAF) Squadron moved to Lympne on 14 August, unaware that there was going to be a raid on Dieppe. Three days after their arrival, they escorted B-17s on a raid to Rouen, their first raid of the war. Don Morrison DFC, DFM was flying his usual Spitfire IX, YO-A BS119. During the operation one pilot was killed and another went missing.

Twelve aircraft of this first sortie landed at Lympne at 8.20 a.m. The same day, Blakeslee led No. 133 Squadron to fly top cover over Dieppe, during which seven pilots of the unit shared in damaging four Fw 190 fighters and three Do 217 bombers. One squadron's operations record book reads, 'A great ending to a good day's work. Subject to reassessment, the squadron score at the end of the day stood at six destroyed, two probables and eight damaged – for no loss.'

On 18 August, Flt Lt Blakeslee shot down a Fw 190 during a fighter sweep. During the late afternoon, No. 401 Squadron pilots were briefed by their CO, Sqn Ldr Keith Hodson, about the planned raid on Dieppe. Everyone was reminded that they were to support Canadian troops on the first large raid on occupied France. The following day, Canadian and British troops made their attack on the harbour town of Dieppe as part of Operation Jubilee. They were to be protected by a large array of RAF aircraft, the air operation being under the command of AVM Trafford Leigh-Mallory. In the gloom and cold of the early morning on the 19th, pilots and ground crew prepared for action. After breakfast, pilots walked over to the dispersal areas at Lympne. It was still dark, and there was a thick ground haze.

Twelve Spitfire IXs of No. 401 Squadron, operating from Lympne, led by their CO K. Hodson took off on 19 August at 01.25 a.m. to patrol the Dieppe area in support of the troops. Plt Off. Don Morrison, who destroyed several German aircraft to his credit, engaged a Fw 190 over

Dieppe, pieces of the stricken aircraft hitting Morrison's Spitfire. On fire, he baled out over the Channel and was picked up by the RAF air sea rescue launch HS177. The launch remained on patrol, assisting two other launches being attacked by Fw 190s. Noticing a semi-conscious seaman drifting away, Morrison dived into the sea, which was now covered in burning oil, and rescued the sailor. He later wrote a detailed account of the incident without mentioning his own courageous act.

Morrison remembers the day very well:

We woke up early on 19 August to the sound of bombs and gunfire from Dieppe, a short distance from Lympne across the Channel. We walked down to our dispersal and found to our disappointment that the B-17s were not scheduled to bomb Abbeville's airfield until 10.15 am. We were assigned to escort them along with 402 and 611 Squadrons. We were all flying Spitfire Mk IXs, the new, high-altitude aircraft with blowers that cut in automatically at 19,000 feet. They were also equipped with new belt-fed 20 mm cannons, a big improvement over the original 5 mm drum-fed cannons. We were keen to get airborne and naturally quite upset as we watched the other Spitfire squadrons flying over to and from Dieppe. We finally took off from Lympne at 9.35 a.m., climbing to 23,000 feet to rendezvous with B-17s over Beachy Head. We encountered heavy flak and turned back to the Channel; in the meantime we encountered German fighters dropping their bombs. We could see that no damaged had been done to runways but the airfield's buildings were damaged and the airfield put out of action.

We landed back at Lympne, having escorted the bombers safely home. After refuelling, we took off again for Dieppe. It wasn't long before we got into a fight with Fw 190s, after one was damaged by Flt Sgt Hodson in Spitfire BS172 and Flt Sgt Zip Zobell in BS120. They then headed back for Lympne. Crossing the Channel we saw Dornier bombers heading for Dieppe unescorted. Hodson attacked, damaging one. Zobell fired on another but was hit by return fire; slightly wounded, he managed to land at Lympne. I saw a lone Fw 190 and attacked. I scored hits and following the aircraft down, it suddenly exploded. I was caught in the explosion and realised I couldn't make it back to Lympne, so I baled out. As I left my Spitfire the parachute pack caught on the hood and I stopped suddenly, hanging from the cockpit looking down over the nose at the Channel, which was coming up to me quickly. I rolled over backwards and pulled the rip cord just in time, as I hit the sea. If this had happened over land I would have died. Two Spitfires circled over me but, low on fuel, headed back to Lympne. I was eventually picked up by an air-sea rescue launch; returning to port, I returned to Lympne the following day.

Morrison was again shot down and captured on 8 November. Injured, he was sent to Stalag Luft III, where he learnt he had been awarded the DFC.

Plt Off. Eric Doorly recalls his exploits on the first Dieppe mission during an encounter with Fw 190s heading for ships in Dieppe harbour:

> Suddenly I saw two more 190s to the left and slightly below me. I closed on them and fired one burst at long range. One aircraft jettisoned his bomb and headed inland, the other flying towards the shipping. I closed to within 300 or 400 yards, and gave him two more bursts. We both passed the entire convoy at 300 feet. The Fw 190 dropped its bomb, but I had no idea where it hit. I was still firing and observed strikes, the left wing broke off and he dived into the sea. I flew south, turning back over Dieppe, gaining altitude. I found three Ju 88s heading for the harbour, I fired at a deflection shot one more burst and I was out of ammunition; I headed back to Lympne.

Following Lympne's successful role in the Dieppe raids, the airfield was upgraded to enable prolonged operations by a squadron wing. Pierced steel planking (PSP) was laid on the northern side and at the south-eastern corner of the airfield. The work also included the construction of a much needed additional Blister hangar. On 20 August, both Nos 401 and 133 Squadrons were moved back to their home base at Biggin Hill and did not return to Lympne.

Wg Cdr Hughie Edwards VC, DFC, the CO of No. 105 Squadron, was returning from a sortie on 29 August 1942 in Mosquito Mk IV DK323, based at RAF Horsham St Faith, when twelve Fw 190s attacked some forty miles from inside enemy territory. The attack came head-on and it would appear that the German crew did not appreciate that they were attacking a Mosquito. They lost ground as they swept round for a stern attack and were unable to close. Over the Channel the port engine of the Mosquito had to be shut down due to a bullet through the coolant pipe. Edwards decided to land at Lympne, but the aircraft performed an unexpected belly landing. Both Edwards and his navigator, Plt Off. Thomas, were shaken but fortunately uninjured. Edwards had won the VC following a low-level attack at 50 feet on Bremen on 4 July 1941.

It was 1 October 1942, at RAF Drem, and No. 65 Squadron had just received orders that they were to move south and join 11 Group. Preparations were made and a train party left Drem that night bound for Lympne, arriving the next day. Eighteen Spitfire Vbs took off for Catterick to refuel before going on to Lympne, reaching the airfield in the afternoon. They were followed by two Handley Page Harrow aircraft, which provided transport for forty airmen. No. 65 Squadron became a temporary member of the Biggin Hill Wing. The following day, nine aircraft made sector reconnaissance. The period was one of suspense, as pilots were eagerly waiting for a briefing on an important operation. They were tasked to act as rear support for USAAF B-17 bombers heading for Lille in France. Twelve aircraft of the squadron, led by Cmdt R. Mouchotte DFC flying Spitfire Vb BL664, made ready with the other squadrons of 11 Group Biggin Hill, formating over Manston at 15,000 feet. During the mission, Flt Lt T. A. Burke in Spitfire Vb BM367 was hit by flak and returned to base, accompanied by Plt Off. A. Vale in Spitfire Vb AB259. Both landed safely at Lympne. The remainder of the flight returned without incident. On 10 October, the squadron were ordered back to Drem and left Lympne during the afternoon. It had been a brief stay in Kent.

Flt Sgt Cooper of No. 616 Squadron was shot down over St Omer, baling out close to the French coast. A Lysander of 'B' Flight 277 ASR Squadron at Hawkinge took off with an escort of four Spitfires of No. 91 Squadron operating from Lympne, and Cooper was soon located and retrieved from his dinghy. Also arriving in October was No. 347 Searchlight Battery, a much needed addition to the defence of Lympne. They were to be joined later by C and D Troops, 419 Battery LAA, who relieved 175 Battery also at Lympne for airfield defence. There was an unfortunate accident on 25 October, when personnel of 2744 RAF Regiment – ACs R. Hall and J. C. Bone – were injured by an exploding mortar bomb during range practice near RAF Hawkinge.

Although based at Hawkinge in October 1942, No. 91 Squadron used Lympne for operations, 'B' Flight moving to Lympne on 15 November. Eight days later, they were joined by 'A' Flight. Two of the squadron's pilots were posted missing on 6 December, following an encounter near Dieppe with Lt Kurt-Erich Wenzel and Uffz. Gerhard Vogt of 6./JG 26. Neither Flt Lt Dean nor Flt Sgt Eldrid was ever found. By incredible coincidence, Plt Off. J. P. Coudray, a Free French pilot, was also lost flying Spitfire Vb BL853 when he was shot down north-west of Calais by Fw. Franz Hiller of 1./JG 26.

Raiders returned to attack Lympne on 11 December 1942. The six Fw 190s could not have known, but their visit coincided with an inspection of Lympne by Sqn Ldr Gillingham of the Directorate of Air Force Welfare. There were no casualties, but several Spitfires were damaged at the dispersal point. A few days later, Maj. McClean of 125 LAA Regiment arrived to inspect gun sites, during which a Do 217 flew over the airfield but did not attack despite being fired at by anti-aircraft guns without any result. On the same day, a Spitfire Vb of No. 91 Squadron limped back to Lympne following combat with a Fw 190. The aircraft had been hit by 20 mm rounds, which had severely damaged the upper and the battery compartment door.

A 'blue on blue' incident occurred on the 18th when Sgt J. Chittick of No. 91 Squadron was flying a routine patrol with Sgt O'Shaughnessy and was attacked by Typhoons of No. 609 Squadron based at Manston. O'Shaughnessy managed to evade the attackers but Chittick was shot down and killed.

Operating from RAF Manston in 1942, No. 137 Squadron were equipped with twin-engine Westland Whirlwind Mk 1 fighters. On 22 December, Sgt T. Sutherland was flying on patrol over Abbeville. Having dropped four 250 lb bombs on a goods train and station, Sutherland was hit by heavy flak from each side of the station, receiving strikes on his starboard engine and the cowling on his port side. The engine seized up and caught fire as he approached the English coast, so he tried to land at Lympne but overshot and crashed. His aircraft, P6998, was a write-off, but he escaped uninjured.

Leonard Gilham spent thirty-six years of his working life as a train driver with the Southern Railway and in 1942 was operating engines out of the railway depot at Tonbridge. The Luftwaffe had embarked on hit-and-run raids across the Dover Strait and regularly sought out railway engines as their target. It was shortly before Christmas 1942, and the weather was dull and wet as Gilham eased the freight train out of Tonbridge – just another day's work, despite the war. The journey towards Hythe was uneventful, and on reaching Ashford he joined other trains waiting to take on coal and water. Suddenly he became aware of an aircraft coming out of low-lying cloud to the east. In an instant, the engine in front of his exploded, killing the driver, Sid Wiles, and the fireman, Harry Turner.

At the time, Gilham was unable to find out what happened to the lone aircraft that had made the attack, but nearly fifty-three years later a chance meeting answered the question he had often pondered. On leaving the Southern Railway, he joined the Distillers Co. in Tonbridge and was later transferred to Barry in South Wales. After retiring, he joined the Barry Men's Forum comprising like-minded men who enjoyed listening to guest speakers. He had often sat next to one particular member and they had exchanged views on many subjects but until that day had never talked about the war years, about which the guest speaker was recalling his experiences, telling his audience about an air raid he was caught in. On hearing this tale, Gilham nudged the person next to him, as he recalls:

'You know, I was involved in a similar raid at Ashford Goods Depot in Kent.' On hearing my comment, my friend turned to me with a look of utter amazement. 'You were in Ashford Goods Yard in December 1942? I asked, 'Do you know what happened to the aircraft that dropped the bomb?' He couldn't answer the question but suggested that the aircraft had returned to its base in France. My friend went on to say that he was serving with the South London Territorial Bofors gunners who opened fire on the aircraft, a Ju 88, at point-blank range, nine miles south of Ashford. According to him it was hit and went down in the sea off Hythe and that there were no survivors. The gunner, Tecwyn Cole Morgan, who was at the time with B Troop 425 LAA Battery, and the gun crew were located half a mile beyond the perimeter of Lympne airfield.

The gun was positioned on a gentle slope, and away to the left lay Ashford and to the right Hythe and the coast. Except during periods of maintenance, the gun was at readiness at an angle of 30 degrees and pointed in the direction of Folkestone which was the stand-by direction. The field telephone rang, and the order to take post was given. The crews' ranks swelled to a full complement and were at action stations within seconds. An enemy aircraft had crossed the coastline between Hythe and Dymchurch and was flying along the western side of Lympne airfield, heading for Ashford. Every few minutes, reports were coming in, updating the bomber's progress and confirming that the aircraft was indeed a Ju 88. Reaching the outskirts of Ashford, the intruder performed a series of zigzag manoeuvres, then went north of the town to the east and commenced a low-level bombing run to the Southern Railway Goods Yard, dropping a bomb on a freight train and then turned away down the Stour Valley, heading for the coast and home. The crew of the Bofors gun knew that action was imminent as the detachment commander caught a glimpse of the Ju 88 through his binoculars.

He yelled out, 'Target 10 o'clock, engage!' and the gun swung to the direction indicated, followed by the cry 'On target!' The DC bellowed, 'Fire!' The gun opened up and a white flash appeared in front of the aircraft's cockpit. They continued firing and pieces fell from the Ju 88. It started to wobble out of control, the starboard wing up-ended to allow the ventral gunner to strafe the Bofors gun position. An RAF officer making his way across the airfield flung himself to the ground and only just avoided injury or death. The Ju 88 was in trouble and was losing height and heading towards the Channel; the jubilant gun crew were told that it had crashed into the sea a few miles off Hythe. The following day, the owner of the airfield, a French lady who frequently visited the crew in her NAAFI van, handed out a double ration of chocolate! As a reprisal attack, within a fortnight, a lone Me 109 strafed the airfield, but the gun position had been resited overlooking Romney Marsh. However, they were able to fire a few parting shots as the fighter swiftly flew away.

Flt Lt Roger 'Sammy' Hall of No. 91 Squadron lost his closest friend on 29 December when Plt Off. I. W. 'Scottie' Downer, flying Spitfire Vb

Ground crew of 91 Squadron having a break from duties. The vehicle appears to be a mobile fuel bowser.

EN782, was bounced by two Bf 109s whilst on patrol in the Dungeness area and shot down off Beachy Head. Despite a search by 277 ASR Squadron at Hawkinge, both the pilot and his aircraft were lost. This loss was particularly hard to accept, as Downer had not long been married. In his book *Clouds of Fear* Hall recalls:

> The pilot I knew best, the one I liked the most and spent the best part of my time with, was Scottie. We often flew together on dawn and dusk patrols. I taught him to drive in my car; he was only twenty-two when he died.

It had been a difficult year for No. 91 Squadron, which was to move back to Hawkinge. At the time, Plt Off. Bob Spurdle, later Sqn Ldr Spurdle DFC, was in command of 'A' Flight and recalls the move to Lympne:

> My 'A' Flight was detached at Lympne aerodrome, a small satellite field just three miles from Hawkinge, our nominal base. It had been an aero-club before the war and to our huge glee we found that the underground fuel tanks had been locked and forgotten. We broke the locks, dipped the tanks and found them full of low-octane fuel, useless to our service aircraft but perfect for our vehicles. Being un-tinted it couldn't be detected by stains around our car's carburettors. The best-kept secret of the war, in my opinion, was the drawing off of this juice which, to my

certain knowledge, was still going on in April 1944. Aircraft fuel was tinted green to aid in the detection of misappropriated petrol. There was a continual struggle for petrol for our cars. Random checks were a serious hazard.

At Lympne, we were quartered in the great mansion of the late Sir Philip Sassoon, Under Secretary of State for Air. It was magnificent – a swimming pool, crushed brick tennis courts and even one extra special loo built like an armchair with a padded velvet seat. There were two old gardeners who pottered about trimming hedges and lawns. As our operational hours crept up and we slowly grew tired, our sense of propriety blurred and our excesses became bizarre. We drank far too much and any excuse for fun would start a party or madcap escapade. Heapo and I developed a dangerous sport. Donning our heavy sheep-wool goon-skins and steel hats, we'd position ourselves one at each end of a 50-yard lawn lined with high clipped hedges. As the sun set, tiny bats would flit along from one end to the other catching moths. We'd try to shoot them. It called for a lot of skill as they jinked about and at the flash of a gun you'd duck your head. Pellets would hiss past or ping off harmlessly. But you couldn't afford to blink in case you missed that red flash.

One of our most popular pilots was Sammy Hall, later to win the DFC and write a moving book, *Clouds of Fear*. He was a big chap and one hot day got well and truly plastered. He locked himself in an upstairs loo with a skeet gun and blasted a tray of drinks off the patio balustrade scaring a batman (who'd just put it down) and the rest of us almost rigid. Naked as Adam, Sammy climbed out the window and down the ivy, which tore off in a great dusty mess. We grabbed the giggling monster and tossed him in the pool to sober up. I encouraged a standing patrol of off-duty pilots to scour the fields and woods for game. We needed to augment our miserable meat rations with rabbits and hares, pheasants, quail, pigeons, and sometimes a duck, hen or goose got clobbered and local farmers got a trifle tetchy.

One night we took two of the cars out onto a gentle hillside overlooking Dymchurch. Using full headlights to chase rabbits, we were pretty merry when, pausing to drink up, we heard creaking of tank tracks. There were shouted orders and the sound of jeep engines. Taking fright, we zoomed back to Port Lympne and hopped into bed, boots and all! How were we to know a large rubber inflatable had been found on Dymchurch beach that morning and the wire defences cut?

For aerodrome defence, the RAF Regiment had some curious little Daimler armoured cars. They had dual controls so the vehicle could be driven from either end, forwards or backwards. On really pouring wet nights, when there was no chance of airborne enemy landings, the cars' crews were stood down. We found a way of jumping the ignition and used to take one pub crawling. We'd bait Army officers because as a breed, they were jealous of our war role and the fulsome newspaper coverage given to the aircrew. They called us Blue Orchids and we dubbed them Pongos. Apart from the rare commando raids and the thrashing our brown jobs were getting in the Middle East, they had nothing much to talk about – just years of hard training to look forward to. We gave them hell until, enraged, they'd fall on us and, outnumbered, we'd retreat to the car, pull down the hatches and roar away laughing our heads off. Just for fun, I insisted on forming a black section which threw the controllers into a tizz. Sections were usually red or blue etc.

As we were always putting up blacks [misdeeds], I thought it appropriate. It was a glorious spring and with the warmer weather, the garden of Kent came to life. I loved this part of England. We were very busy and between 5 April and 26 May, I flew seventy-four sorties, covering the whole gamut of our duties. On the last day we had a panic scramble to search for and find group captain Batchy Atcherley who'd got himself shot down into the Channel. Unkind rumour had it he'd gone up alone and by radio challenged a Jerry to combat and been obliged.

On 3 June our new VB Spits arrived – these had slightly heavier armour but this was not what we wanted. We wanted cameras. It was ridiculous to expect us to count and identify ships in heavily defended harbours at over 300 miles per hour. Sergeant Bill Sykes went missing on a recce to Dieppe. Damned shame – he was a very nice guy. Only bright thing about it was that I had his Ray Ban sun-glasses on approval and now inherited them. The Jerries were sending over lone weather recce fighters in increasing numbers and it became a mania to catch them. Heapo and I would scramble and be vectored around by GCI [Ground Controlled Interception]. We spent hours at it.

Sadly, 'A' Flight was recalled to Hawkinge and Port Lympne to a Yank squadron. With heavy hearts, we packed our gear and flew off and away from our lovely, idyllic, carefree home. We settled into Reindene mess. They sent us two Spitfire VIs. They had pressure cabins and could stagger around at over 42,000 feet. What earthly use were they to us? The hoods couldn't slide back but were clamped down over us on rubber seals. And again no cameras, so we didn't use them. Eventually they were replaced with standard Vs. At last – after nine scrambles hunting Hun recce machines, I got within 700 yards of one but it left me standing. Two more tries and no luck. The next time one found me, a Fw 190, the first I'd seen. In the ensuing dogfight a strange Spitfire horned in and jumped me and had a squirt which I answered, but missed. I really must go on a gunnery course!

'B Flight' No. 91 Squadron took off from Lympne back to Hawkinge on 11 January 1943, followed shortly after by 'A' Flight and 3028 Servicing Echelon.

It was common practice for personnel of RAF Regiments to be called out to attend crashed aircraft in the area, and on one such occasion airmen of 2823 AA Squadron RAF Regiment were called out to stand guard over Spitfire IX BS172 at Stone Green Farm. On 27 January, Flt Lt P. T. O'Leary of No. 403 (Wolf) RCAF Squadron based at RAF Kenley had been in combat over Dunkirk with Fw 190s of JG 26, the notorious and successful German fighter group, and had crashed at the farm. Sadly, the young Canadian pilot was killed.

On 9 March 1943, a Stirling Mk 1 bomber crashed into the sea a mile and a half east of Dungeness, returning from a raid on Nuremberg. The aircraft, BK610 of No. 7 Squadron based at RAF Oakington, had been hit by gunfire. The crew baled out over the Channel, but the mid upper gunner, Sgt D. R. Spanton, was lucky; having failed to hear the order given by Plt Off. L. L. V. Toupin (RCAF), he descended over land, being brought to Lympne with no serious injuries. The remainder of the crew – Sgts G. Bell, J. Goddard and H. Kilvington, Flt Sgt R. G. Thorne and WO2 Freeland (RCAF) – were all drowned.

Orders were given on 11 March that 2823 Squadron RAF Regiment HQ was to move from Lympne airfield to Barrington House on Aldington Road opposite The County Members public house. Two days later, Spitfire IX BR630, flown by Sgt G. T. Aitkin, crash-landed at New Romney ALG, Honeychild Manor, and a crash guard consisting of airmen of 2823 Squadron was placed on the aircraft. Aitkin's aircraft had run out of fuel following combat with Fw 190s of JG 26 and JG 27, but he was uninjured in the landing. The regiment had taken over anti-aircraft defence of Lympne from 4006 AA Flight, manning seven twin .303 Browning posts, one quadruple Browning Beaverette and four 20 mm Hispano cannon posts on 15 March, the guard returning from Honeychild Manor the following day.

On 15 March 1943, following only a seven-week stay at RAF Biggin Hill, No. 1 Squadron were moved again but given a choice – Lympne or Gravesend. This situation came about because Gp Capt. 'Sailor' Milan, the CO at Biggin Hill, did not want Typhoons on his station, and Sqn Ldr Wilkinson, the CO of No. 1 Squadron, did not hit it off with Milan. The choice of Lympne was made and the squadron had completed the move by the 15th. As it turned out, it was a popular move, because it was ideal for operations due to its proximity to the coast. Finding themselves accommodated in splendid old mansions overlooking the sea, and with the officers' mess being Port Lympne, it was no wonder everyone was happy. However, it was not long before it was felt that operations flown from Lympne would be difficult.

The Hawker Typhoon, although successful in its various roles, was not a forgiving aircraft to fly. Combine this with the fact that Lympne was not best suited for the heavy Typhoon to operate from, and it is not surprising that many incidents occurred on take-off and landing. On 18 March 1943, Flt Lt 'Zulu' Watson returned from an operation in Typhoon DN335 short on fuel and with no brakes. He overshot Lympne and dropped down onto a road, turning over in a field. He was rather surprised when a WAAF appeared on the scene and tried to stand on her head to check if he was all right as he hung upside down! On another occasion, when Zulu's undercarriage lights were not on, he was going around again and was unable to see the last Typhoon to have landed, which was taxiing up the middle of the airfield. In the ensuing collision, both pilots managed to remove each other's main-planes.

Returning from a routine patrol off Dungeness on 24 March, Flt Lt R. G. H. Dehaas, flying Spitfire Vb W3425, was attacked by Fw 190s of JG 26. The young Belgian pilot, on his first patrol with No. 91 Squadron, was killed. During the same combat, Flt Lt J. A. Anstey, flying Spitfire Vb BL410, was hit by gunfire. He nursed his aircraft, streaming glycol, back to

Officers and pilots of No.1 Squadron grouped in front of one of the unit's Hawker Typhoons. Seated centre is S/Ldr Tony Zweigbergk who took command of the squadron at Lympne from S/Ldr R. C. Wilkinson DFM and Bar.

Lympne and crashed short of the airfield. The Spitfire was a write-off but he survived with head injuries and bruising. Airmen from 2823 Squadron were sent to the scene to guard the aircraft. Next day, the unit were told that they would be taking on a main ground-to-air role, with ground-to-ground fighting as a secondary task, eventually manning eight 40 mm Bofors guns and four 20 mm Hispano cannons, and attending further Bofors training.

RAF Regiment units at Lympne were informed that a committee from RAF West Drayton would visit the station on 11 April to test eighty-one gunners affected by redundancy decisions. If they were found to be suitable material for re-registering, half of 2823 Squadron would be affected. In the event, only five airmen of the unit were selected. No. 2827 Squadron RAF Regiment had been formed at RAF Wittering, its main role being the defence of RAF airfields. On 15 April, the unit moved to Lympne, having also been based at Lasham, Hampshire. An inspection of the newly arrived regiment by Lt Col. Crabbe on 17 April was followed by a visit to Lympne and the RAF Regiment Camp by Col. Preston.

Also on 17 April, Flt Lt D. Haywood, then based at Hawkinge, crash-landed his Spitfire XII EN607 on New Romney Golf Course, no doubt upsetting the members, following a shipping recce. His Spitfire had been hit by anti-aircraft fire over Dieppe, but he had managed to bring it back over the Channel despite being in pain from an injured foot. A corporal and three airmen were dispatched to protect the aircraft. Eventually EN607 was repaired and was not struck off charge until the end of May 1946.

Nine Typhoon bombers of No. 181 Squadron and eight Typhoon fighters of No. 486 Squadron landed on the airfield on 19 April, before taking part in an operation. One returned to Lympne with engine trouble, and later, after completion of the operation, one fighter was forced to remain behind owing to a defective engine. The following day, a Lockheed Ventura, AE743 of No. 487 Squadron piloted by Sgt G. F. Whitwell, force-landed on the airfield with smoke pouring from the port engine. During a raid on Boulogne, an anti-aircraft shell had smashed into the cockpit. The fire service and an ambulance wasted no time in reaching the Ventura as it came to a standstill. The pilot, who was badly wounded in his left arm, had managed to drop his bombs in the sea before turning for home and was taken to the station's sick quarters. The Flying Control officer at the station commended the very fine effort put up by the pilot, who despite being wounded was able to land at a strange airfield of small size without causing damage to his aircraft.

Two Typhoons of No. 1 Squadron flown by Flt Lt H. T. 'Moose' Mossip and Sgt W. Ramsey were on a Rhubarb operation (a strafing mission by day or night) attacking a train near Armentières when they pulled out of a dive and Ramsey's aircraft was hit. His starboard wing was damaged and fuel was pouring from the tank. Resisting the temptation to bale out, he was determined to head for Lympne and was able to remove the cockpit doors, the roof panel releasing automatically. Ramsey managed to belly land in a field close to base, but overshot through a fence into a field planted with peas. When rescuers reached the scene, Ramsey was found beside his aircraft, R8752 JX-L, munching his way through some peas, unharmed, his aircraft a write-off.

During the period in the 1930s when the RAF shared the airfield with the Cinque Ports Flying Club, both Ann Davis and her husband Bill had looked after the RAF boys. Even when No. 1 Squadron arrived in 1943, Ann, despite her husband's tragic death, made it her job to look after the new influx of pilots and ground crew at Lympne, driving the NAAFI van around the airfield and aircraft dispersals. Even the drinks licence, which apparently had been overlooked by the authorities, provided the RAF with a supply of whisky from a small barrel. Ann became known to all at Lympne as Mrs Miniver or Mrs Mobile. On one occasion, her pet poodle gave birth to twelve puppies, one of which was christened by the

F/Sgt. W. H. Ramsey crashed in a field of peas, returning damaged to Lympne from an operation on 2 June 1943. His Typhoon R8752 JX-L flew again as did the pilot who was uninjured. Note the barbed wire to keep invaders out and perhaps protect the crop of peas.

squadron as The Honourable Sergeant Tiffy and can be seen in several of the squadron's photographs taken at Lympne.

The squadron continued with never-ending Channel patrols over the next three months, and was continually put on standby. At the time, several Typhoon bomber squadrons used Lympne as an advanced refuelling ground, much to the frustration of the patrol-weary pilots of No. 1 Squadron, who watched them leaving to take part in exciting missions over France. On occasion, escort missions for the 'Bombphoons' were flown by the squadron, giving the young pilots an opportunity to tackle enemy aircraft that might attack the bomb-laden Typhoon.

Sqn Ldr J. A. F MacLachlan DSO, DFC visited No. 1 Squadron, having been their CO prior to going to the USA on a lecture tour. Four days after his return to Lympne he was posted to the Air Fighting Development Unit (AFDU) where he flew the Mustang Mk 1. He was to introduce the use of Mustangs for long-range missions. Meanwhile, on 27 April, when returning from an operation, 'Moose' Mossip flying Typhoon R7865 on landing back at Lympne felt the aircraft bump and was astonished to see that the tail wheel had sheared off. The following day, Sgt Harry Bletcher also had a narrow escape when he crashed in Typhoon R8634 on Pevensey Marsh, writing off his aircraft.

With a view to the invasion of Europe, RAF Regiments undertook operational training to simulate taking over an enemy-occupied airfield. On 27 April, 2827 Squadron carried out an exercise at Kingsnorth, an ALG near Ashford, to simulate such an attack. Three airmen of the squadron used as decoys were captured; the remainder infiltrated successfully. Returning to Lympne the following day, having put on a convincing show, the squadron were ordered to move to Kingscliffe and later Boxgrove Common before returning to Lympne on 27 July. During August, the unit carried out Bren gun and rifle practice at Hythe Range. With Nos 2806 and 2742 Squadrons, they also instructed on the use of three mortars, two-pounder guns, signalling and section leader training. They were also trained in refuelling for operational use. This was essential work should they be called upon for other duties at Lympne. Gas exercises also took place, which meant that all airmen wore their gas masks with curtain helmets for half an hour following a gas warning, although, in the event, gas was not used against UK airfields.

There were changes coming for 2823 Squadron: on 10 May 1943, they were amalgamated with No. 4133 AA Flight. Of the sixty-one other ranks, half were drafted into No. 2 Bofors Flight for Bofors training and half went into Hispano Flight at Danehurst, taken over by the squadron for their accommodation, and seven twin Browning guns and four 20 mm Hispano cannons were brought on charge. The squadron strength increased to 231 airmen. A decision was made a few days later to move squadron HQ and the telephone exchange to cellars beneath Barrington House, the necessary work being done by squadron members. Besides being reasonably blast-proof, the combined exchange and control room in a centralised position helped make speedier transmission of air-raid warnings to gun sites possible when the squadron manned local Bofors guns.

A break from flying duties was offered to Flt Lt Wilkinson on 22 May, when he opened Wings Week, in which residents of Ham Street, a village not far from Lympne, were keen to participate. Lady Millais' Wings for Victory Week was a fundraising scheme to encourage civilians to save their money in government accounts, such as war bonds, savings bonds, defence bonds and savings certificates, cash being paid into post offices or banks. In much the same way as War Weapons Week, it coincided with a week of parades, exhibitions and other war paraphernalia. In 1943, it was decided that the national scheme would be themed around raising funds to purchase more bombers for the nation in order to take the fight to the enemy's homeland.

On 23 May, Sqn Ldr Wilkinson was posted to command the fighter wing at Gravesend and No. 1 Squadron waited in anticipation of the arrival of their new leader, Sqn Ldr Tony Zweigbergk. No stranger to the hazards of flying, Zweigbergk, a former pilot with Swissair, immediately fitted into life at Lympne as CO of No. 1 Squadron and was popular with ground crew and pilots alike. An entry for May 1943 in the squadron's operations record book reads:

> Squadron Leader A. Zweigbergk (the telephonists are going to enjoy themselves) came to take command of the squadron and everyone is pleased – as there were others in the running for the job. There was no flying for the squadron, owing to the bad visibility but although clearing later a scramble was ordered. Three sections took off by road – for the 1000 Hun Destroyed party at RAF Biggin Hill where a show was put on by Les Windmill Girls who were obviously under the impression that we were tired business men and how right they were! Or were they?

On 29 May, Flt Lt Julian, a member of the Aviation Candidates Selection Board, visited Lympne to eliminate all problems in connection with training and was offered facilities for interviewing volunteers for aircrew duties. A total of eighty-one airmen attended for this interview – a very gratifying response. Flt Lt O'Conner, command catering officer, visited the camp commandant in connection with the proposed erection of a ration store.

In certain areas of Romney Marsh, below Lympne airfield, minefields had been laid. It was the misfortune of a British soldier to have strayed into this area and it was not long before he was seriously injured in an explosion. Cpl Golding, a squadron medical orderly, on hearing of the incident jumped into a Jeep with two other men and set off to retrieve the injured soldier. Despite the obvious danger, the three men managed to navigate the minefield, bringing back the victim on a stretcher. Dr Golding, already the recipient of an MBE, was awarded the George Cross, along with his two assistants.

An amusing incident took place at Lympne as pilots watched a replacement Typhoon being flown into the airfield. To their astonishment, it did not appear to be piloted. Shortly after landing and taxiing close by, the cockpit was opened and out stepped a lady in ATA uniform. Being of short stature, she had blocks of wood strapped to her feet so she could reach the pedals. The pilot was none other than Diana Barnato, a well-known ATA pilot, who later wrote of her exploits.

On 4 June 1943, James MacLachlan returned again to Lympne flying his Mustang Mk 1 FD442, which he had fitted with four 20 mm Hispano cannons. MacLachan had lost an arm in combat but continued to operate long-range missions. It was said he was seeking revenge for the loss of his brother, Flt Lt Gordon MacLachlan of No. 616 Squadron. Recruiting the assistance of three of his former pilots and their Typhoons, they took off from Lympne on a long-range sortie, the idea being that the Typhoons would create a diversion, but the mission was unsuccessful and MacLachlan never fired his guns. This tenacious pilot was lost on an intruder mission over France on 29 June 1943. He was accompanied by Flt Lt Geoffrey Page (a famous Battle of Britain pilot). On the return flight his aircraft was thought to have been hit by ground fire or his engine caught fire. James MacLachlan was buried at Pont l'Évêque Cemetery in France.

Plt Off. J. M. Chalfour was on patrol with one other aircraft on 15 July 1943. Leading the section, he had taken off from Lympne at 9 p.m. The operation was uneventful but as they drew near to home the aircraft's tail section broke way and Typhoon EK228 dived from a height of 10,000 feet, crashing at Paddlesworth, near Hawkinge, killing its pilot. Structural failure of the tail had already claimed the lives of fourteen pilots, but this was the first occasion for No. 1 Squadron. Of the other pilots, only one had survived. By the end of 1942, modifications had been carried out, but this did not always cure the problem. However, following the addition of plates and internal stiffening, the accident rate dropped to 20 per cent. It was discovered that harmonic vibrations could cause structural failure of the elevator mass balance and flutter. It was not until the introduction of

The caption on the back of this photograph reads: '*Lads of Hut 46*', one of the many wooden huts used by the RAF. Ricky Flood's father with his chums at Lympne during the 1940s, by coincidence Ricky worked for Skyfotos at Lympne.

the Tempest with its much improved tail and fin design that the problem was cured. Chalfour, a charismatic pilot, was buried at Brookwood Cemetery in Surrey on 20 July, the service being attended by six officers from his squadron at Lympne.

Early on the morning of 22 August 1943, a convoy of various vehicles departed Martlesham Heath heading for Lympne. Orders had been received by phone that No. 3208 Servicing Commando were to move south. They arrived at the airfield at 4.30 p.m. and were informed that they were to be billeted under canvas. A suitable site had been selected and it was not long before tents had been erected. The following morning, in the absence of aircraft to be worked on, everyone was put on general airfield duties. West Malling, being the parent airfield to the unit, had a certain amount of equipment and stores that had to be collected, and the adjutant took this opportunity to make useful connections at RAF West Malling. As a result of his efforts, a sum of £10 was awarded to each airman towards comforts and entertainment. That evening the CO addressed the unit about their welfare. Next day, the CO left for RAF

Zeals, Wiltshire, to arrange for more equipment to be delivered to 3208 SC at Lympne. Shortly after, Spitfires of Nos 64 and 313 Squadrons landed for refuelling, and some airmen were later detailed to dig slit trenches for No. 609 Squadron. Work continued on servicing and repairing damaged aircraft as they returned to Lympne, the schedule being interrupted only by physical training and lectures. No. 3208 SC were to move to RAF Ford in Sussex on 4 October 1943. It had been a busy period for the unit, and valuable experience had been gained working on an operational base.

On 25 August, 2827 Squadron went to Lydd for training on manning the defence of an airfield, setting up HQ at Wheelsgate Farm. By 10 a.m. all vehicles and equipment were camouflaged and dispersed under trees and guns were position and manned, following which Sqn Ldr Preston inspected the regiment prior to the unit's return to Lympne. Exercises continued throughout August and September, including airfield defence operations at Lydd (Midley) ALG. They were again moved to Frimley for weapons training, returning to Lympne only to be informed that they were leaving for Popham on 8 October.

Flying a Ramrod mission to the St Pol area on 27 August, No. 41 Squadron, now based at Lympne, were attacked by Fw 190s of JG 26. During the dogfight, Flt Lt D. Haywood, who, as we have seen, had previously crashed on New Romney Golf Course, was again shot down – this time at sea. An ASR aircraft from Hawkinge sent to look for him found only a dinghy. There was no sign of his Spitfire XII, EN611, which most probably had already sunk. It was later revealed that he had baled out and been taken prisoner. Following his capture by the Germans, Haywood was sent to a PoW camp and issued with an identity card that although of little use within Stalag Luft III, did initiate the chain of events that would confirm he was safe to the British authorities and his family and bring Red Cross parcels to him.

Also posted to Lympne was No. 609 (West Riding) Squadron, having moved from Matlaske, Norfolk, on 18 August. The move included No. 3053 Servicing Echelon. Two Handley Page Harrows arrived at Lympne, followed by the squadron's road convoys. Some travelled to Kent by rail but were unimpressed when they realised that there was no stopping for tea. Fortunately, the squadron's Typhoon Mk IBs arrived with little problem. Dispersal consisted of an old farmhouse at the far side of the airfield and was approached by a road – not very impressive, as no electricity had been laid on and there were not even any tables. Although the NCOs and airmen were quite well billeted, they complained about the long walk. Officers had more pleasant surroundings at Port Lympne house. Most of the rooms were already occupied by No. 1 Squadron, and only two officers of the newly arrived squadron had been allocated rooms, the remainder being billeted in the servants' quarters, some in dormitories. Lympne, a satellite for Hawkinge, itself a satellite for Biggin Hill, was low on the supply list. It was felt by some that No. 1 Squadron were not that pleased to see them arrive, and there was some inter-squadron rivalry. Much to the amusement of the new boys, a one-time experimental Typhoon of No. 609 Squadron was found at Lympne that had been force-landed by Plt Off. Roberts during their stay at Duxford. Slowly the squadron were being re-equipped with new Typhoons fitted with long-range tanks. Flying consisted of formation gun and air firing practice, in an effort to bring the squadron up to readiness.

Everyone with No. 609 Squadron was wondering why they had been brought to Lympne. Rumours of an impending invasion were circulating, the squadron finally taking on operations on 28 August. On 4 September, Sgt Mike Bryan, returning from a routine patrol, overshot the runway and crashed, overturning his Typhoon and colliding with a hangar. Fortunately, neither he nor any ground crew were injured. On the 6th, No. 4659 Airfield Construction Flight arrived to lay Sommerfeld track for additional hardstandings, which were much needed at Lympne to solve the problem of dispersing the large Typhoons of both squadrons. The new hardstandings were completed by 14 September, and the following day was Battle of Britain Day. During the celebrations, Lympne was visited by the Commandant of the Belgian Air Force, Col. Wouvers OBE, MC who was entertained by No. 609 Squadron.

By this time, the airfield at Lympne was overcrowded. Despite this situation, Nos 41 and 91 Squadrons arrived with their Spitfires from Tangmere, tasked with protecting minesweepers in the English Channel. On 1 September, Spitfire FXII EN230 piloted by WO J. M. Bishop of No. 91 Squadron suffered engine failure and he was forced to ditch in the sea near Dover. In a desperate bid to escape the aircraft, Bishop managed to free himself at a depth of 30 feet. Fortunately, he was rescued by a vessel of the Royal Navy, but it was indeed a close call. The squadron's stay at Lympne ended on a high note when Sqn Ldr Kynaston, flying Spitfire MB803, was escorting Marauders to bomb St Pol and was attacked by Fw 190s but managed to destroy them from a range of 200 yards. Gray Stenborg, flying MB805, shot down another at 50 yards and damaged a second aircraft. Kynaston, who had been the squadron's CO since 19 August, was subsequently killed after being hit by flak and baling out off the French coast in Spitfire IX MK909 on 15 August 1944, flying from Deanland ALG in Sussex.

It may seem incredible, but at this time Lympne had a problem with rats, which seemed to have taken a fancy to both the WAAF and RAF regiment billets. The problem was finally resolved by Capt. G. W Knowles of the

Kent War Agricultural Committee, whose team quickly rid the buildings of the unwanted guests.

'Friendly fire' was sometimes a problem, and one such incident occurred on 29 September when Typhoons of No. 609 Squadron on a Ranger patrol to Juvincourt were engaged by British 20 mm anti-aircraft guns as they passed over the battery at Dungeness. Fortunately there were no losses. On a Ranger operation to Châteaudun by four aircraft of No. 609 Squadron, including Plt Off. Turek (from Poland), he was hit by flak and ditched. He managed to climb into his dinghy safely and was eventually picked up by a Walrus of 277 ASR Squadron which, unable to take off owing to high seas, was ineffectively shelled from the French coast, five miles distant. Fighter cover was provided by No. 609 Squadron, and eventually the Walrus took off and landed at Hawkinge.

The squadron had a busy day on 4 October when two aircraft in another Ranger patrol to the Châteaudun area damaged a staff car and shot up a gun post. Plt Off. Gueffen, a Belgian pilot, went missing; in fact, he had been hit by flak and managed to land his Typhoon, JP750, near Poix but was taken prisoner.

At Lympne, one popular pastime was picking mushrooms, which seemed to thrive at Lympne and proved very popular with Belgian pilots. One such, a pilot of No. 609 Squadron, was about to tuck into a meal of mushrooms in his room when he was summoned to answer a bogus phone call. On returning to his bedroom, he found that someone had already eaten them, so taking matters into his own hands, he rushed over to the anteroom where the suspected culprit was resting and slapped his face. At this, other Belgian pilots joined in. The next day the mushroom thief told the CO that he would forget the episode, but by then it had been reported and the offender was to be posted. However, the acting CO managed to get the posting cancelled. It was an amusing incident – and, yes, mushroom picking continued.

On 9 October 1943, prior to No. 486 (NZ) Squadron moving from North Weald to West Malling, Flt Sgt 'Mac' McCarthy overshot the runway at Lympne while landing in poor visibility. Along with other Typhoons of the squadron, they were on a raid to Metz. The CO had been flying from Tangmere to Manston to refuel prior to an operation protecting Mosquitos but decided to drop into Lympne to refuel because the weather was deteriorating fast. Unknown to the squadron, Lympne was an L-shaped airfield. Three pilots managed to put down, but Mac landed across the short runway and ran out of space, hitting the fence. Covered in blood from a head wound, although not serious, he was unable to take part in the operation. He took the train back to Tangmere, spinning a yarn to two soldiers about his experience, both of whom were alarmed by his appearance, as he was still wearing his bloodstained flying gear and goggles.

Flt Lt C. W. 'Chuck' Miller, a new Canadian pilot, arrived from No. 59 Operational Training Unit (OTU) at Milfield, who with Plt Off. A. S. Ross flew to Hawkinge in a Tiger Moth. Suddenly the Moth started to climb vertically, then stalled and dived inverted towards the ground. Hanging from his straps, Ross yelled at the new pilot, but as an operational pilot not wishing to show fear, he tried to remain calm while he watched the ground rise up. When it became clear that the pilot was bent on suicide, Ross could stand it no longer. Seizing the control column, he pulled the Moth out of the dive with a few feet to spare. The new pilot, of course, was under the impression that he was undergoing initiation to an operational squadron.

By 20 October 1943, No. 609 Squadron had good reason for a celebration – they had notched up their 200th kill. This honour fell to Plt Off. L. W. F. Stark when he destroyed a Ju 88 on patrol in the Châlons area. Many squadrons had pet mascots, and No. 609 had befriended a goat, affectionately named Wg Cdr Goat. A party was organised at the Majestic Hotel in Folkestone to celebrate the 200th kill, and during the celebrations Wg Cdr Goat was promoted to Acting Group Captain. No. 3053 Servicing Echelon had been asked to decorate the hall, which they did by surrounding the walls with two hundred swastikas, while above the dancers an enormous model of a Typhoon was hung. Bands from Lympne and Hawkinge took turns in friendly rivalry to keep the party rolling, while up on the balcony, on the way to the food, a series of photographs on the history of the squadron's progress was displayed. An enlarged photograph taken from Stark's gun camera showing the doomed Ju 88 with both engines on fire was an impressive site to behold. With over 600 people attending the celebration, it was a great success at a cost of £350, the directors of the hotel also contributing towards the cost.

At the beginning of November, the squadron had problems with their dispersal area at Lympne which became waterlogged. A request was made for an approach road to be laid, but nothing was done. Returning from operations on 2 November, WO Bovinton was told to land at Manston, but seeing a large bank of cloud and with evening falling, he decided to try for home. On making his approach at 150 mph in the middle of No. 1 Squadron's dispersal, he sheared off a wing, the tail and the cockpit of one of No. 1's Typhoons. Luckily he stopped at the end of the field after some unorthodox aerobatics, damaging his own aircraft, but was able to climb out uninjured. On 10 November, Army units arrived to take part in an exercise, upsetting No. 609 Squadron by taking over their cherished empty billets. They were soon moved on by irate members of the squadron. As if having to queue up with the Army for a morning shave was not enough, alarm bells rang when they lit a fire close to the fuel dump. An Armistice Day service was held at St Stephen's Church, Lympne, and the ground staff turned out in force for the parade. In the churchyard, wreaths were laid on the graves of airmen who had been killed in the present war, but the effect was rather spoilt by finding Army personnel occupying seats reserved for the RAF.

During the morning of 15 November, six Typhoons of No. 609 Squadron took off to search for some lost B-24 Liberators of the 93rd Bomb Group, based at Northrepps, that had got lost over the Channel. They managed to guide one into Lympne, but being a small airfield, the Liberator slid into a boundary hedge, stopping just clear of No. 4 Bofors post. For the following two days the airfield was unserviceable due to water-logging.

Morale was boosted on 20 November when Servicing Commando personnel arrived to build up the ranks of the resident servicing echelons, whose ranks had been depleted by postings. No. 3210 Servicing Commando arrived to carry out some repairs, although finding accommodation for them was a problem. With No. 609 Squadron's dispersal being knee-deep in mud and still no perimeter track or hard standings, aircraft had to be refuelled from tins, causing delays in getting the squadron's Typhoons airborne.

On 26 November 1943, Nos 1 and 609 Squadrons escorted Marauders on bombing raids. One of these aircraft, a B-26B, 41-31609 of the 553rd Bomber Squadron, 386th Bomb Group of the 9th USAAF based at Great Dunmow, Essex, was escorted back to Lympne by No. 609 Squadron. It crash-landed as No. 4 Bofors Post Pay Parade was taking place, coming to a halt close to the same spot where the Liberator had come to rest. The Marauder was not seriously damaged, and the crew were safe and made welcome before returning to their base. No. 609 Squadron's dispersal at Otterpool Farm having become impossible to use owing to mud, the CO and Intelligence Officer tramped about the site with the medical officer looking for a suitable alternative and decided the squadron would have to use the servicing echelon site as a dispersal area.

Tuesday 7 December 1943 was a bad day for the squadron. WO J. Fairbairn and Flt Sgt 'Spike' Watson were scrambled at 11.50 a.m. and vectored without success on to two German aircraft. By the time they were due to return, the weather had closed in at Lympne and they were instructed to land at Hawkinge. Watson made it, but Fairbairn, going round again, crashed into hills about three miles from Hawkinge and was killed instantly. His aircraft was completely destroyed, but the reason for the crash is not clear. The squadron lost not only a keen and capable pilot but a good friend. It was even more tragic, as his family and fiancée were living at Hawkinge, and Fairbairn had not long been engaged.

On 14 December, No. 137 Squadron were re-equipped with the Hurricane IV and moved from Manston to Lympne. The following day, they were operating Ramrod missions from their new base, supported by No. 609 Squadron. Armed with rocket projectiles (RP), they were formidable aircraft, diving on their target from 8,000 to 3,000 feet. The rockets packed a punch, with 60 lb high-explosive heads, and No. 137 Squadron were pleased with the excellent cover their new friends at Lympne gave them over the targets they selected.

Just before Christmas, No. 609 Squadron lost two pilots in a 'blue on blue' incident. They were escorting Marauders but only six Typhoons were available to look after them. Suddenly they were attacked by USAAF Thunderbolts, shooting down and killing Plt Off. 'Chuck' Miller and the CO, Sqn Ldr P. G. Thornton-Brown. A few days later he was posthumously awarded the DFC. Tragically his wife was due to join him the following day for Christmas. Returning from operations on 23 December, Plt Off. Albert L. J. M. Hue, better known as Pedro, was forced to land on Romney Marsh when he had problems switching over from left to right fuel tanks. He was uninjured, and eventually his Typhoon was recovered. Owing to poor weather conditions, several missions were abandoned and on Christmas Day they were ordered to stand down. There followed entertainment in the mess and by 2 p.m. they were enjoying a Christmas meal.

Hawker Typhoon Mk.1 serial EK176 squadron code JX-K of No.1 Squadron Lympne. On 16 August 1943 this aircraft crashed in forced landing south-east of Lydd, due to engine failure, killing its pilot Ft Lt L. J. Wood.

Additional airmen attached to a Works Flight were expected at Lympne on 27 December, and despite a shortage of equipment, some beds were to be delivered that day. When the lorry eventually arrived at the airfield, it made it to the airmen's huts but hit the anemometer (wind speed detector), running over one of its stays and toppling it to the ground. There were no casualties, but the driver was not very popular. The following day, the first new Typhoon 1B aircraft, with the new sliding hood, were delivered by ATA pilots to No. 137 Squadron and by the end of the month the squadron had flown their last operation in Hurricanes and were ordered to move to Colerne on 2 January 1944 to re-equip with the Typhoon Mk IIB.

On 30 December, returning from a raid on Ludwigshafen, B-17 Fortress 42-39867 crash-landed at Lympne. The aircraft had been severely damaged during the raid and although it had managed to reach the coast, four of the crew baled out too low and were killed. The pilot, 2nd Lt Frank Valesh of the 351st Bomber Squadron, 100th Bomb Group, based at Thorpe Abbotts in Norfolk, coaxed his aircraft into Lympne with both engines damaged and dead, managing to belly land the B-17. Although christened 'Hang the Expense II', apparently there had been no time to paint the name on the fuselage. The CO at Lympne was enraged because of the damage the sliding aircraft had done to the landing surface. However, the surviving crew were delighted with the RAF hospitality, the officers being quartered in the officers' mess at Lympne Place. They were even more pleased when they were offered a continuous supply of whisky. Valesh could not recall who paid for the drinks, but the crew were too pleased to be alive to care. The events surrounding the crash-landing at Lympne are described in detail by the aircraft's navigator Lt John R. 'Dick' Johnson in the 100th Bomb Group archive:

> Mission No. 11 started out bad and got worse. The date was 30 December 1943 and the target was Ludwigshafen. We were flying the Lockheed-built B-17G, 42-39867. The bomb load was 10 500 lb G.P. bombs. We were assigned the number two position, 2nd element, low squadron and the 100th was the low group in the wing. Not the best place to be when touring Germany! Take off was at 8.31 a.m. and at 9.42 a.m. our element leader aborted so we assumed the lead and an aircraft from the 95th B. G. joined our element. At 10.35 a.m. the lead PFF aircraft aborted. We were supposed to have fighter escort during the penetration with Spits at 1100, P-47s at 1128 and P-51s over the target at 12.30 p.m. None ever showed.
>
> Bombs were away at 1234 and the flak was big, black, heavy and accurate. No results were observed as we were over a 10/10 under-cast. En-route home, the P-47s did show up more or less as briefed and I'm

Seven B-17 Flying Fortresses named '*Hang The Expense*' were flown by 2nd Lt Frank Valesh of 100th Bomb Group 351st Bomber Squadron, he crashed each one. On 30 December 1943 he crash landed B-17 serial No. 42-39867 at Lympne following a raid on Germany. He is seen with his crew in front of '*Hang the Expense IV*' at Thorpe Abbots.

afraid we went to sleep as the Hun came out of the sun. I noted we were under constant fighter attack – Fw 190s and Bf 109s from 1.25 p.m. to 2 p.m. How accurate that log entry was I don't know, but it was the only log entry for the period. I recall one B-17 going down with flames streaming from the left liferaft storage area but other than that I was rather busy. I do recall the P-47s were still chasing their tails way above us. We had a large number of machine-gun bullet holes in the aircraft but the main damage was a large hole in the leading edge of the left horizontal stabilizer that was apparently caused by a 20 mm cannon shell. The stabilizer was flopping up and down, causing the aircraft to vibrate rather badly so as soon as we hit the enemy coast, we slowed to minimum air speed to ease the vibration. Even then it took the effort of both Valesh and Booth to hold the aircraft steady. I gave Frank a course for the closest point in England and all eyes were peeled for anything resembling an airfield. Someone spotted a field and we landed at 4 p.m. at Lympne.

It was a grass RAF fighter base and the CO later thanked us for landing on the edge of the field rather than the centre as the B-17 did dig some rather deep ruts in the soft turf. After ascertaining there were no wounded aboard, the next inquiry from the RAF was, 'Did you get the bloke what done it?' The gunners were taken to the sergeants' mess and the officers to the officers' mess where we were given a stiff drink of whisky and a call placed to the 100th. It was quite a place. The mess was some lord's home and the airfield his private golf course, all leased to the RAF for the duration. We were given a tour of the house which included the master suite complete with a 'secret' staircase leading to the outside in order that the lord's female guests could come and go without being seen by the servants. The master bath had a huge sunken, black marble tub and the commode had a wicker seat and arm rests.

The mess officer offered to loan us 5 pounds as he knew our intelligence types didn't let us carry money on operations. We gratefully accepted, figuring we would need it in the bar that evening. Then he decided we were not properly dressed for dinner so a hunt was made for suitable clothes. As the RAF could wear civvies off duty, I ended up with a brown tweed jacket and green Ascot tie to go with my O.D. shirt and trousers and G.I. brogues. I know we tied on one that evening but they refused to accept our money and the fiver was returned intact to the mess officer in the morning. Frank and John were assigned to one room for the night and Zet and I to the one next door. Just as he and I were getting into bed there was a knock on the door and a little WAAF popped in to inquire as to what hour we wished to be knocked up in the morning. We were a bit excited for a moment but quickly realized she meant awakened so we told her the same hour as the other Yanks. At the appointed hour she pops in and says, 'Good morning sirs, it's 6 a.m., here's your tray.' Then she grabs our shoes and takes off. We were finished with breakfast before she showed up with our shoes, apologizing for not having any brown boot polish but having done the best she could. Now mine were G.I. brogues that I used only for flying but she had them looking good.

After breakfast we went out to the aircraft to get our gear prior to returning to Thorpe Abbotts. For some reason I was late and when I got there, the rest of the crew was conducting a guided tour of the aircraft for any of the RAF personnel who were interested. They were going in the rear door and out the nose hatch and Zet was sitting in the nose handing our three or four linked .50 calibre cartridges to any who wanted them. I heard several of the RAF people refer to the 50s as bloody cannon. I was looking over the battle damage when I noticed a yellowish liquid dripping out of the machine-gun bullet holes in the belly area between the nose hatch and the flight deck. A couple of RAF airmen noticed it about the same time and remarked: 'They must have gotten a hydraulic line.' I knew there were no hydraulic lines in the area, nor had we had braking problems on landing, so I stuck my head in the nose hatch to check the source.

Apparently one of the tourists had accidentally knocked the flight deck pee can down to the catwalk and the now melted contents were running out. When I pulled my head out to explain, one of the two aircraftmen had just put his hand out to catch a few drops. He sniffed it, tasted it, and remarked, 'No. It's not hydraulic fluid.' I just walked away.

We had to take a train to Manston in order to catch the promised flight back to Thorpe Abbotts as Lympne was not suitable for large aircraft. How we paid the fare I do not know. There was no plane when we got to Manston and a call to Thorpe Abbotts revealed they had no intention of sending one. However, there was a B-17 from the 94th BG there, sent to pick up one of their crews who had crash-landed in the area. They gave us as ride to Bury St Edmunds. Upon arrival we again called Thorpe Abbotts and after a two-hour wait, they finally sent a truck for us.

30 December 1943 was a busy day for all at Lympne, with several crashed aircraft reported in the area some twenty miles away, all requiring guards. Lympne was becoming crowded, with the B-17 Fortress and two Thunderbolts still standing on the airfield, but 1944 was to prove even more hectic.

CHAPTER 8

Operations flown by Spitfire and Typhoon squadrons from Lympne; the V-1 campaign; losses and crash incidents; the Second World War ends; units still based at the airfield until closure

Towards the end of 1943, No.1 Squadron were to reach their potential when their Typhoons were fitted with racks that carried 500 lb bombs. Operations continued on 1 January 1944 when No. 1 Squadron, led by Tony Zweigbergk with Typhoons carrying two 500 lb bombs, attacked a target at Hesdin, at the same time supporting rocket-firing Hurricanes of No. 184 Squadron. All went well but on return to Lympne, Flt Lt Duncan McIntosh dropped the starboard wing of his Typhoon and decided to go round again. This time the wing dug into the ground, spinning the aircraft around, but McIntosh recovered the aircraft and landed with a bent-up wing tip and jammed aileron. Flt Lt Jimmy King was unaware that his RT was not working, so was amused when he saw ground crew running away as he came into land, not realising that a 500 lb bomb was still attached to his Typhoon. It finally dropped off as he came to a halt – but the bomb did not explode!

On 6 January 1944, being Twelfth Night, No. 1 Squadron adjourned to the Red Lion public house in Hythe. As celebrations got under way, someone decided to remove the decorations and put them in the fire. Not long after this, the door opened and the company were informed by a police constable that the pub's chimney was on fire and that the fire brigade was on its way. A hasty retreat was made back to the officers' mess at Lympne.

No. 1 Squadron embarked on many offensive operations over France on low-level Ramrod dive-bomb attacks. Following these attacks the aircraft would re-form at low level and fly hell for leather back across the Channel. Flt Sgt Harry Bletcher, one of the squadron's pilots, was a talented artist. As a result of outings to the Victoria Palace Theatre in London, 'Bletch',

The mural which Sgt Harry Bletcher so faithfully painted on the wall of No.1 Squadron's mess hut wall in 1943, surviving the war it was demolished in the 1970s, lost forever. Similar works of art have been preserved by museums located on disused American bases in East Anglia.

as he was known, decided to brighten up the squadron's dispersal hut. His efforts were aided by fellow members of the squadron who raised the funds to pay for the paint required. The result was an impressive mural depicting a scene at the Victoria Palace of scantily clad young ladies dancing on the stage, which was aptly named *No. 1 Squadron Follies 1943*. The painting survived the war years and was still visible in 1977, although a wall had been built 3 feet from the masterpiece, creating a corridor. On a visit in 1979 he was staggered to see his handiwork was still in existence. The dispersal hut had by this time been taken over by Skyfotos, which used the building for offices, which is most probably why the artwork survived. However, the hut later fell victim to developers and was destroyed to make way for an industrial estate that would eventually take over most of the airfield at Lympne.

Following a raid on Europe, a North American B-25C Mitchell bomber of No. 98 Squadron, FL674 based at RAF Dunsfold, crash-landed on the airfield on 21 January. Damaged by anti-aircraft fire, it limped back over the Channel looking for a place to set down. Fortunately for the crew, it found Lympne. Its USAAF identification was 42-72833, and like many US aircraft had been supplied to the RAF under the Lend-Lease programme.

On 26 January 1944, Bletcher was tasked with a reconnaissance flight to determine weather conditions over the Channel and French coast.

With limited space at Lympne in 1944 large bombers such as this B-17 of the 379th Bomb Group which landed at in February, were not always welcome. With one of its engines missing and low on fuel, it is a miracle how some of these bombers returned home a tribute to the pilots and their crews.

As he taxied out in Typhoon Mk I EK139, he was totally unaware that clamps that secured the aircraft's flaps at night had been removed and thrown into the cockpit. The control column jammed as the Typhoon picked up speed, and with Bletcher unable to control the aircraft, it hurtled towards the perimeter. With a resounding crash it collided with a pill box, removing its top, and severely damaging the Typhoon, which was a write-off. Fortunately, its pilot was not injured and was able to climb out of the wreck, the only damage being torn trousers and shock. Zweigbergk, in collaboration with the engineering officer 'Chunky' Brown, saved the airman responsible from a court martial and entered a report in the squadron's operations record book to the effect that the Typhoon's engine had failed. As we have seen, the fortunate pilot had also survived a similar incident when he crash-landed in Typhoon R8634 on Pevensey Marsh on 28 April 1943, the aircraft being a write-off or 'Cat. E'.

Later that day, Lympne played host to a unit of the 141st Regiment, Royal Armoured Corps, based at Ashford, who arrived with a Churchill tank and a Bren gun carrier. Having given the Army boys a tour of the airfield, they pilots were offered a turn in the Army vehicles. Bletcher wasted no time in having a spin in the Bren gun carrier, but soon realised it was not like driving a car, colliding with one of the pillars supporting the entrance gate to Lympne Place. Following the war, Bletcher became an art teacher.

On 15 February 1944, No. 1 Squadron received orders that they were to move to Martlesham Heath. Despite their sad losses during their time at Lympne, the squadron were loath to leave the airfield, and to show their appreciation of the efforts made on their behalf by Ann Davis, she was presented with an engraved cigarette case.

Consolidated B-24 Liberator 41-29231 'Impatient Virgin' of 67th Bomber Squadron, 44th Bomb Group, crash-landed at Lympne on 24 February, being low on fuel following battle damage sustained in a raid on Fürth. The aircraft was forced to crash-land at 4.30 p.m. after eight of the crew had baled out, one sustaining injuries. The pilot and co-pilot then landed with considerable damage to the aircraft. But for one crew member, Lt Hill, and most of his crew this was mission number twenty-five – their combat tour was over! Prior to landing, Hill buzzed the airfield with full power and at an altitude too low to estimate. He then climbed at a steep angle, rocked the wings and landed the Liberator safely.

At the beginning of January 1944, No. 186 Squadron were equipped with Typhoon Mk IBs and were based at Tain. However, in February they were re-equipped with the Spitfire Vb, and moved to Lympne on 1 March. For several days the squadron carried out formation flying and shipping reconnaissance and escorted Marauders on a mission to bomb Coxyde airfield in Belgium. Then, on 5 April, the squadron was renamed No. 130 Squadron at Lympne and started operations the same day.

A total of sixteen sorties were flown that day on air sea rescue patrols in an attempt to find a dinghy believed to be eighty miles off Deal. At 2.45 p.m. Flt Sgts Hirock and Clay made contact, but a later search by the squadron could not relocate the dinghy. Several patrols were flown over the next few days, but the weather was very poor with visibility being down to two miles on occasions, and some operations were flown from Tangmere. On 7 April, thirteen Spitfires and a Tiger Moth of No. 130 Squadron returned to Lympne from Tangmere and were immediately placed on readiness. Night flying operations took place that month, with aircraft of No. 130 Squadron flying to Ford, but the weather caused havoc and there was no contact with the enemy. However, several aircrew were located in the sea and successfully rescued by ASR Walrus aircraft.

On 28 April 1944, Flt Sgt Spurdle led four aircraft on patrol, with nothing to report, but Plt Off. G. Jones sustained slight injuries when his Spitfire VC AD348 overshot and crashed on landing when returning to Lympne. His aircraft was a write-off. By noon the following day, No 130 Squadron were on the move again, this time to the ALG at Horne in Surrey. A party consisting of one officer and twenty airmen of No. 74 Squadron

A Spitfire IX of 403 (Wolf) Squadron RCAF flown by Ft Lt L. P. Boucher at Lympne, winter 1944. The squadron was also based at Lashenden and Headcorn (Egerton) Advanced Landing Grounds, Kent in 1943.

Pilots of No.165 Squadron on a muddy day during a pause between operations at Lympne in 1944. To the far left looking at the camera is F/Officer S. R. Chambers who shot down a V1 and claimed a share in two others destroyed by the squadron during the V1 Campaign.

A fascinating aerial view of Lympne, the bomb craters bear witness to the damage caused by German bombing during the early years of the Second World War.

left North Weald at 6.60 a.m. on 13 May and headed for Lympne by train, arriving at Westenhanger later that day. They joined Nos 33 and 127 Squadrons already based at the airfield. The general opinion of their new surroundings was favourable. As well as being billeted in huts near the dispersal area, an empty house was also made available. By 19 May, the squadron were on dawn readiness, commencing operations against 'No Ball' (V-weapon) targets.

Later that month, returning from an operational flight, Flt Sgt Bletcher of No. 1 Squadron was struggling with his damaged Typhoon Ib JP841. Despite his best efforts, he overshot the runway and crashed into trees in Tory Wood. The aircraft was badly damaged but fortunately the pilot survived without serious injury. Two days later, Flt Sgt L. E. Watson in Typhoon Ib JP498 went missing on operations and was killed. He was buried in St Pierre Cemetery at Amiens. WO J. W. Mackenzie had a narrow escape when coming into land. The engine of his Typhoon Ib JP841 failed and he landed short of the runway, dislodging the aircraft's undercarriage. Although the Typhoon caught fire, Mackenzie was uninjured.

It was a relatively quiet day at Lympne on 28 May, until a Spitfire returning from patrol crashed into a hut containing the station's ammunition. That day, four aircraft of No. 130 Squadron carried out

Plt Off. Gates of 137 Squadron during a pause in operations. In the background are Hawker Typhoons of the same squadron, being serviced by ground crew. A Blister hangar is just visible to the left.

a defensive patrol off the Thames Estuary but had nothing to report. A further four of the squadron's aircraft carried out a similar patrol, and a third patrol was also carried out, two aircraft being diverted to Manston.

Plt Off. Jones, flying Spitfire AB794, on his return to Lympne hit the hut and his aircraft caught fire. Without thought for his own safety, Sgt Cockburn of 2823 Squadron RAF Regiment ran over from No. 4 Bofors site, pulled the unconscious pilot out of the wreckage and carried him to safety, undoubtedly saving his life. The aircraft was a write-off. Jones, who was taken to hospital with abrasions on the face, was extremely grateful to Cockburn, but there does not appear to be any evidence that the sergeant was given any award for his actions, other than perhaps a few drinks with his chums.

After returning from the Mediterranean, No. 127 Squadron enjoyed a short stay at North Weald, but this ended on 16 May 1944 when, with new Spitfire IXs, they moved to Lympne. Tasked with flying invasion sweeps and bomber escorts, each aircraft carried bombs to attack marshalling yards at Douai. Everyone was looking forward to being involved in operations from Lympne, and it was not long before the squadron settled into their new surroundings. They joined a wing led by Wg Cdr Harris DSO, DFC, consisting of Nos 33 and 74 Squadrons operating from Lympne. Harris led the squadrons on their first fighter sweep on 20 May over the Cayeux area.

Two days later, the squadron were scrambled to attack targets in the Creil area, the main target being the marshalling yards. The squadron suffered their first loss when Flt Lt N. O. Thomas, flying Spitfire IX ML172, was hit by flak and crashed near Compiègne. When Spitfire IX ML187, piloted by Fg Off. A. R. Moulden (RCAF), was hit by flak and a shell exploded just behind his seat, a large hole was blown in the fuselage. The long-range 45-gallon tank was blown off and the wings were peppered with holes, but Moulden was lucky and survived to tell the story.

On 27 May, when No. 127 Squadron took off to attack a 'No Ball' target in France, Sgt Macey dropped his bomb en route and had to return to Lympne with engine trouble. The remaining flight following a successful attack headed for home, but Flt Sgt A. C. H. White's Spitfire IX MK696 was hit by flak over Le Tréport V-1 site and headed for the coast. However, he was too low and ditched in the sea, eventually being rescued by an ASR Walrus. On a similar mission, to Vacqueriette, Pas-de-Calais, on the 30th, Plt Off. Lloyd hit another aircraft on take-off and had to jettison his bomb. Unable to lower the undercarriage, he was told to crash-land at Manston, which he did successfully. Later that day Plt Off. Campbell and WO J. V. Pearson took off on a shipping reconnaissance flight. Flying at low level in poor visibility, Campbell called up his No. 2 on the RT but there was no reply – Pearson had been hit by flak near Dunkirk and had dived into the sea, unable to escape from his stricken Spitfire, ML234.

On 6 June 1944, D-Day, the tension at Lympne was terrific and squadrons based there were in the thick of it. Twelve aircraft of No. 74 Squadron carried out a convoy patrol from Dover to the Isle of Wight, while six aircraft of No. 127 Squadron and sixteen others from No. 74 Squadron carried out further patrols over 'Cannymead' (codename for the convoy) off Dungeness. Four aircraft of No. 127 Squadron were scrambled over a convoy just north of Dover, and eighteen other aircraft from the squadron patrolled continuously over 'Shark', which was also escorted by eight aircraft of No. 33 Squadron. Eleven other aircraft from No. 33 Squadron were sent to cover glider formations to the eastern beach area. Two Marauders crashed, the first one burning out, killing five crew members and slightly injuring one. The second blew up completely.

On 13 June 1944, the V-1 offensive began and some squadrons were detached to Lympne to join in the battle against the formidable *Vergeltungswaffe* (revenge weapon). It was an indiscriminate flying bomb, known also as the doodlebug, diver or buzz bomb, unleashed on the British public in order to kill and maim, destroy houses and factories, and attempt to break the morale of civilians. Having located many of the permanent launching sites and factories in France, the Allies launched 'No Ball' bombing operations against them. Many of these were attacked successfully by aircraft of the RAF and its allies, despite the V-1s often being launched from concealed ramps that were easily assembled, thus enabling them to be moved to other locations. Some 6,725 were known to have reached the English coast, but many RAF and USAAF fighter units destroyed them in flight, disaster often being averted by them being brought down by gunfire or in some cases 'tipped over' with the fighter's wing tip. Many were also destroyed by Ack-Ack units based strategically around London and along the coast.

Air Ministry wireless operators were also based at Lympne in the summer of 1944, located in the DF (Direction Finding) station on the airfield. J. V. Reilly looks back on those days:

I vividly remember the summer of 1944, and the first night the V-1 came over. I was on duty at our Adcock DF station at Court-at-Street and we were somewhat mystified by the strange aircraft engine noises that we could hear in the distance. By the time that it was daylight we still had not received the usual all clear message, but shortly after taking down our blackout shutters we saw our first doodlebug – a black evil-looking object, making an incredible racket from its flame-belching, rear mounted, engine. We were to become very familiar with this rather scary sound in the ensuing months, and I counted as many as fourteen one evening from a viewpoint on The Roughs overlooking the Romney Marsh.

One other hair-raising incident happened to one colleague of mine when on his way to post a letter in a pillar box near to his home in Berwick Lane, Lympne. He heard a loud swishing noise and, on looking up, he saw this large black object no more than 20 feet above his head. He told me that he could actually see the welding on its bodywork, but had no time to do anything but throw himself in the ditch. It came down only about 400 yards from where he lay, near an RAF Regiment Ack-Ack gun site, killing two airmen. Incidentally, the blast from this particular explosion blew everything off our dining room table (we had been advised at this time to leave our windows open), where my wife and I were sitting having breakfast. I have a distinct recollection of spilt milk and puffed wheat all over the floor!

On 18 June 1944, aircraft of Nos 33, 74 and 127 Squadrons carried out a fighter sweeps, the Wing having to fly above cloud. Twelve aircraft of No. 74 Squadron carried out convoy patrols in the Dover and Hastings area, and twenty-four aircraft of Nos 74 and 127 Squadrons swept Evreux and Caen, but the patrol was uneventful. Two aircraft of No. 33 Squadron escorted a convoy off Herne Bay, while twelve other aircraft from the squadron swept Evreux and the beach area in 10/10 cloud.

Capt. Coe USAAF (Med) ceased attachment and Capt. Granger USAAF (Med) came to take over. A Marauder crashed on Romney Marsh and Newchurch ALG dealt with this. The month of June continued with all squadrons engaged on escort, bombing and reconnaissance operations as well as beachhead patrols over D-Day landings. ACM Sir Roderic Hill visited the station with Wg Cdr Dow and Sqn Ldr Shields, from HQ Air Defence of Great Britain (ADGB).

On 28 June, everyone was amazed when a Tempest appeared over the airfield firing at a V-1, which suddenly blew up. The explosion took place 400 yards east of No. 127 Squadron's dispersal. Three Nissen huts were demolished and two damaged. During the afternoon of the 29th, Flt Lt D. E. Llewellyn and Sgt J. Dalzell, both of No. 74 Squadron, were airborne and on V-1 patrol in the Lympne area. Later recording the event, Llewellyn stated:

I was, as 'B' Flight commander, designated to lead the squadron that day. We were suddenly told we could send up an anti-diver patrol of two aircraft for the last hour of the daylight readiness. I took Sgt [Paddy] Dalzell as my partner. I had a nasty suspicion that the controllers might favour the more regular patrols, so we ignored their instructions, until

they put us on to one which was directed (as we expected) over Lympne.
As we approached from the west it was crossing from right to left at our
height, just below the cloud level (about 4,000 feet, I think). Because they
were supposed to be fast, I pulled up into the cloud, did a 90 degree turn
and came down directly behind it with speed, lined it up and fired. At that
moment one of those damned freelance Tempests came up from below,
right in front of me, and I hit him in both wings, directly above Lympne –
pieces of aircraft fell on the field and were shown to me afterwards. Since
I could do nothing about the Tempest, I went on and shot down the
Doodlebug. It turned over to the left and went into a field somewhere to
the north of Lympne. When I later phoned to say I had accidentally shot
down a Tempest, a bored WAAF said, 'Oh, what, another one?' and rang
off. It did not matter anyway. The Tempest was flown by the Newchurch
Wing, Wg Cdr R. F. Aitken OC 150 Wing, and there were far too many
Tempests (and wing commanders) floating around in everybody's way, in
June 1944!

It was soon evident that the flight path of the Doodlebugs from one
particular launch pad passed directly overhead, but we were incensed that
we were not allowed to go up after them. The Spitfire IX was considered
too slow and the Tempest and the Spitfire XIV squadrons were the ones
used to combat the V-1, although a number of wing commanders and
squadron leaders ignored these rules, and went up freelance. Naturally,
we and the other squadrons on the Wing complained.

Paddy Dalzell remembered the same incident:

I landed at Lympne and a couple of cars met me on the airfield and
enquired if I was all right. It turned out that Llew had been firing at a
V-1 and a Tempest appeared between him and the V-1 into the line of
fire, hitting and knocking off his wing tip. They thought it was me. I
had changed frequency to one used by the Ack-Ack to hear of any V-1s
approaching Kent and therefore did not receive any calls from Llew or
base.

One aircraft of No. 74 Squadron, Spitfire NH181, crashed on take-off on
30 June when a tyre burst, swinging round and hitting an air-raid shelter.
The aircraft was a write-off. Plt Off. D. N. Maxwell was injured and
admitted to Willesborough Hospital, Ashford.

At the beginning of July 1944, information was received from HQ
ADGB that Nos 33, 74 and 127 Squadrons, along with their servicing
echelons, were to be transferred to 84 Group, 2nd Tactical Air Force
(TAF). They were being replaced by 134 (Czech) Wing, comprising

Nos 310, 312 and 313 Squadrons, and exchanging their aircraft with the departing squadrons. A special train arranged for all other personnel departed from Westenhanger at midday. Servicing echelons arrived to join their squadrons, by which time the Czech Wing was already engaged on escort and convoy patrols.

On 4 July, No. 127 Squadron were transferred to Tangmere, with some of the pilots and other ranks being flown from Lympne in a DC-3, while others went by rail. Eleven pilots eventually flew their Spitfires to Tangmere, arriving late the in the evening.

It was not long before the newly arrived Czech squadrons were involved on anti-V-1 patrols. In fact, Flt Lt O. Smik of No. 310 Squadron, flying Spitfire IX EN527, destroyed three. His combat report for 7/8 July 1944 states:

I was airborne from base at 9.25 p.m. I reached a height of 5,000 feet, speed 300 mph. I dived and attacked it from port quarter and below, using cannon only and giving two-second bursts. I saw red flashes on its fuselage and it crashed near Ashford. I resumed patrol and at 9.45 p.m. again at 5,000 feet, saw a diver at 2,000 feet, speed 280 mph. I dived and made stern attack with machine guns only, giving finishing burst with cannon. Scored hits on the fuselage, and both wings flew off. Diver crashed north-east of battle. At 10 p.m. I was over the Channel at 4,000 feet. Saw no strikes owing to heavy rain but the diver exploded and fell near Tenterden. I landed back at Lympne airfield at 11.35 p.m.

Sqn Ldr M. A. Liskutin remembers an incident on 8 July, shortly after getting airborne from Lympne on an air test:

I saw, by chance, a flying bomb crossing over Dover on its way towards London. My new Spitfire IXA, MK670 DU-V, accelerated easily to about 300 knots, and the interception occurred above the main road between Ashford and Maidstone. It was quickly getting dark and becoming difficult to judge the distance behind this glowing jet-pipe. My height over the high ground of the Quarry Hills was under 500 feet. When I thought I was about 250 yards behind the infernal machine, I took careful aim and fired a one-second burst from my cannons. It happened, literally, in a flash. I did not even see the strikes before flying right into the fireball and out the other side. Fifteen minutes later I landed back at Lympne. My aircraft wasn't seriously damaged, but something had happened to my self-assurance. Between pressing the firing button and entering the fireball … I had a momentary sensation that I was looking at the V-1, and my Spitfire, from some 500 yards away to the left. It was quite clear, despite the darkness, and I must have been a good deal closer than 250 yards from my target.

The incident does not make any sense. It had occurred very briefly, probably in less than a second. But why was the vision so vivid, and why do I keep remembering it still? People claim to have seen flying saucers. Was it something like that? Or was it just a quirk of my imagination? Obviously, I shall never know the answer. Despite this the aircraft was not badly damaged and returned to Lympne, successfully landing without further incident.

Sgt J. Pipa of No. 310 Squadron succeeded in destroying two more V-1s over Folkestone. This he did after returning to Lympne from a particularly hectic escort mission, but his hatred for this new weapon did not prevent him from refuelling his Spitfire and taking off again:

> My feeling was one of gleeful satisfaction as I reported my success to Flying Control. The ever gentle voice of a WAAF guided me through the darkness to a safe landing and a night of dreams about the body and soul that was attached to an angelic voice – I slept well.

After only a brief stay at Lympne, 134 (Czech) Wing moved to RAF Digby on 11 July.

The following day, No. 165 Squadron was moved to Lympne from Detling, not far from Maidstone, the squadron flying eighteen non-operational patrols. The same evening, six anti-diver patrols were flown without any notable event occurring. The following morning, twenty-four aircraft were involved on anti-diver patrols and Flt Sgt A. F. A. McIntosh destroyed a V-1, which blew up over the Ashford area at 4.25 p.m. At 3.10 p.m. on 14 July, another was shot down by Flt Sgt O. Bundara and blew up over Elham.

Serving with No. 165 Squadron at the time of their move to RAF Lympne was P. R. Murdoch, who had joined the RAF and become an airframe fitter. He recalls:

> I was a fitter in the servicing echelon of 165 Squadron. The unit was stationed at RAF Detling as 2nd Line Defence against the flying bombs, flying the Spitfire Mk IVe with modified engines to take 150 grade fuel to combat the V-1s. [This fuel caused painfully sore hands when it came in contact with the skin.] Here we watched a Spitfire land, which was entirely black, thinking it to be some kind of night fighter. It turned out to be a Squadron Spitfire having hit a Doodlebug which exploded in front of it and completely blackened the aircraft. Trenches were

A pilot of 137 Squadron pointing out damage to the leading edge of his Hawker Typhoon, following his safe return to Lympne during the winter of 1944.

provided between the huts for shelter but after spending a few lights in the trenches we all returned to sleeping in the huts when we moved to Lympne. Here it was said was one of the biggest ever concentration of guns ever assembled on the Romney Marshes. Five lanes of Doodlebugs crossed at RAF Lympne. The squadron operated 1st Line Defence along with another squadron of Spitfire IVs. All maintenance of aircraft was carried out in the open (no hangars). During the period I was there, we worked until dark every night and I was never off camp. I recall only one flying bomb landing on the edge of camp, a direct hit on a gun emplacement killing all the gunners. The blast blew a Spitfire over. All the time we were at Lympne our aircraft patrolled the sky from dawn until dusk.

For the squadrons involved in ant-diver patrols, 15 July was a busy day. Flt Sgt Vassie of No. 1 Squadron opened the score, destroying a diver five miles east-north-east of Detling. Sixteen of his squadron's aircraft, together with sixteen of No. 165 and eighteen of No. 41 Squadron carried out anti-diver patrols. Flt Lt Porteous of No. 165 Squadron destroyed a diver north-west of Folkestone, while his colleague Plt Off. Scott destroyed a diver ten miles south-east of Dungeness. Flt Lt Williams of No. 1 Squadron destroyed a diver two miles south of Maidstone, and Fg

Off. Fisher of No. 41 Squadron carried out anti-diver patrols. During the day the station was visited by Capt. Harold Balfour, Parliamentary Under Secretary of State for Air, flying a Miles M.28 Mercury, an aircraft used for communication flights, who succeeded in frightening several pilots with his very low approach before landing safely, much to the relief of everyone watching.

A fire broke out at 3.05 p.m. in the Duty 'E' and Crew 'E' sleeping quarters but was hastily extinguished, although damage was caused to barrack equipment in the Air Ministry building and several naval issue kits were destroyed. There was one casualty, aircraft fitter V. Graham, a naval rating, who received burns and became seriously ill. The cause of the fire was not known and a formal investigation was ordered by the station commander.

The following day, twenty-one anti-diver patrols were flown, but the weather was very misty later in the morning. The CO took the opportunity to call a meeting regarding V-1 operations during which pilots were able to view film footage taken by their aircraft's gun cameras. In the afternoon, 'B' Flight of No. 2714 Squadron RAF Regiment arrived to add to the airfield's defences and carry out additional duties.

An accident occurred on 17 July, when a Spitfire of No. 41 Squadron collided with the squadron's Tiger Moth, DE575, killing both pilots who were twenty-one years old. The collision took place about one mile north of the airfield at a height of 200 feet. Flt Sgt C. Oddy, flying Spitfire XII MB877, was buried at Armley Cemetery, Leeds, and Flt Sgt R. L Short at Hawkinge RAF Cemetery. The subsequent inquiry concluded that Short had carried out unauthorised low flying and in doing so had crossed the path of the Spitfire during a formation take-off. The same day, two crew baled out of Halifax MZ313 of No. 466 Squadron over the airfield, the aircraft then blowing up and disintegrating, scattering pieces over a wide area. The two escaped certain death and were uninjured, the remainder of the crew having already baled out over the Channel. The Halifax was based at Driffield, Yorkshire, and was returning from a raid on Vaires-sur-Marne. The following day, thirty-six Typhoons of No. 1 Squadron, thirty-three Spitfires of No. 165 Squadron and eight of No. 41 Squadron carried out anti-diver patrols, during which four V-1s were destroyed. On 19 July, the crew of a B-24 of 34 Bomb Group 8 USAAF had to abandon their aircraft just before it was seen to crash into the sea.

At 2.32 p.m. on 23 July, a V-1 was shot down by anti-aircraft fire and made a direct hit on one Nissen hut, the centre one of three housing RAF Regiment personnel on the eastern boundary of the airfield. All three huts were completely destroyed. The main SAA store was damaged by the blast, the roof being lifted from the pillars and various beams fractured.

LAC R. H. Pritchard, a gunner, was killed and another gunner, LAC C. E. Moore, died of his injuries in Willesborough Hospital, Plt Off. R. K. Crowther sustaining serious injuries. Other gunners injured were LACs N. Wooton, A. E. Trevillion, H. G. Allen and G. A. Gee, and Flt Sgt T. K. Winnis. Despite the loss of personnel, the operational capacity of Lympne was not affected, but requisitioned houses located along Stone Street used as hostels and quarters for RAF and WAAF personnel were damaged in the explosion. These included Falujah bungalow, Channel View House, No. 4 Council Cottage, Bengor bungalow, Studfall House, Cranchester House and Wessex House. The section officer visited Lympne immediately and Works Flights and Air Ministry Works Department personnel began repair work on the damaged quarters immediately.

On 27 July 1944, Flt Sgt Cameron of No. 165 Squadron destroyed a diver a mile north of Marden. Anti-diver patrols were carried out by twenty aircraft of No 1 Squadron, eighteen aircraft of No. 41 Squadron and fifty six of No. 165 Squadron. A diver struck over the coast by anti-aircraft fire lost height and crashed 300 yards due south of No. 7 (Baker) Site at 1.06 a.m., three Nissen huts housing RAF Regiment personnel receiving superficial damage. At 12.10 p.m. the ceiling plaster at the RAF officers' (ante-room) mess at Port Lympne fell down in one large piece due to blast from the crash. Later that day another diver was also shot down by anti-aircraft fire over the coast, lost height and crashed 200 yards due south of Aldergate, a requisitioned house used as a WAAF hostel, and a third diver was shot down by Bofors guns No. 8 Site, 2823 Squadron RAF Regiment, and crashed 600 yards due south of the RAF officers' mess, causing superficial blast damage to the building as well as to French House, the sergeants' mess. Fortunately, none of these incidents caused any casualties to personnel.

The following day, Plt Off. F. Town of No. 1 Squadron destroyed a diver two miles west of Staplehurst and another near Lenham. His colleague, Fg Off. J. O. Dalley, destroyed another mid-Channel, and Plt Off. S. R Chambers of No. 165 Squadron destroyed a diver ten miles north-west of Ashford. Anti-diver patrols were carried out by forty-nine aircraft of No. 1 Squadron, fifty-two of No. 165 Squadron and forty-four of No. 41 Squadron. That evening, a diver was shot down by anti-aircraft fire over the coast and crashed at 10.30 p.m. in a field one mile due south of French House off the airfield, causing blast damage to Cranchester House in Stone Street, an airmen's billet, Port Lympne and a cottage used by WAAF officers as sleeping quarters. Another diver was shot down in the same manner at 10.30 p.m. and crashed in the area of Folks Wood, some 800 yards north of Berwick Cottage, Stone Street, a requisitioned property used as sick quarters for RAF Lympne away from the airfield. At

10.35 p.m. a diver landed in the vicinity of the airfield, cutting off mains electricity in the area. In Flying Control the lighting and RT failed while aircraft were stacked up in the circuit, awaiting their turn to land. The aircraft whose patrol did not allow for diversion landed on the standby battery RT and the remainder were diverted to Manston.

Flt Sgt Godfrey Tate of No. 1 Squadron failed to return from an anti-diver patrol over the Channel on 30 July, following engine trouble while flying Spitfire LFIXb MJ422. He baled out and landed in the sea but apparently drowned. Fg Off. Dennis Davy, who was leading Yellow Section, remembers what happened:

> While on patrol, Yellow 2 [Flt Sgt Tate] called up saying his engine was running rough. Control instructed section to return to base. Yellow 2 led me almost a mile and owing to haze was not visible. Shortly after, Yellow 2 called up saying engine was cutting and he was losing height, finally saying he was baling out. Visibility at the time was varying between 500 and 1,000 yards and I was still unable to see him. So I came down until I could see the water and was just in time to see a large splash created by an aircraft entering the water. I orbited the spot, searching for the pilot, but there was no sign, only a small oil patch. Another section and a Walrus was on its way out, but owing to fuel shortage I left the scene of the crash before they arrived, some 15 miles south-east of Dungeness.

The subsequent search found nothing. His body was later washed up on the Belgian coast and buried in Leopoldsburg War Cemetery.

By 31 July, pilots and ground crew were exhausted but were coping well, not only with the additional flying and aircraft maintenance but also the constant danger of V-1s exploding and crashing in the area, let alone the damage caused to buildings.

Throughout August 1944, the squadrons based at Lympne were on constant anti-diver patrols, but credit must also be given to the RAF Regiments defending the airfield. On 11 August, Gp Capt. Colin Gray DSO, DFC, Wing Commander Flying at Detling, was posted to Lympne in the same role. The three squadrons under his command at Detling – Nos 118, 124 and 504 – had been moved to Europe to join the 2nd TAF. At Lympne he commanded Nos 41, 130, 350 and 610 Squadrons. Gray was not pleased with the move to Lympne as the wing under his command was involved in shooting down V-1s, and although they had the new Spitfire XIVs, he felt that the squadrons would be doing the job for much longer. The Mk XIV was fitted with the Griffon 65 engine of 2,050 hp and had a top speed of 448 mph at 26,000 feet. Designed as a high-altitude fighter, it was slow at low level – too slow for the V-1, which moved at 350-400 mph. Over the following two weeks, Gray spent many hours on V-1 intercepts and recalls the campaign in his book *Spitfire Patrol*:

> Because the bombs were coming over at very low level, we did not get enough radar warning to patrol successfully in the outer zone and were mostly allocated to the inner zone. By the time we arrived on the scene the guns were getting pretty accurate and they almost invariably shot down the slower bombs. We had had to patrol very fast, about 350 knots, which cut down our endurance, and some 3,000 to 4,000 feet above the flight path of the bombs to give us some extra dive speed. There was precious little time to get in a firing pass before the balloon barrage appeared – less than five minutes at the speed we were going. Also firing times were quite unpredictable, so as always one had to be in the right place at the right time.
>
> On one occasion I thought I had it made, but was cut out by a Tempest and a Meteor – both of which were faster at low level than I was, so I left them to it. Another time, I was on patrol near Lympne and was again about to open fire when I was thwarted by our local air defence Bofors guns and had to break away. By the end of August 1944 it became evident that the flying bomb campaign was petering out, and I was not surprised to be told that we were stopping our anti-diver patrols and reverting to our proper role as air superiority fighters. I had a narrow squeak on one occasion when I decided to lead 41 Squadron on a sweep over the Continent in one of their old Spit XIs. The engine of this machine was very hot, as it had just come down and been refuelled after chasing buzz bombs, and I found it a bit difficult to start. When it finally did get going it kept cutting on take-off and was so bad that I finally decided to give up. I pulled up a few yards from the far hedge, missing some workmen and a tractor by inches. I thought the trouble was probably due to petrol vaporisation caused by the hot engine. When the machine was inspected, one of 41's pilots then took it up on air test. Not surprisingly perhaps, exactly the same thing happened again, but the pilot was not quite quick enough and finished up upside-down in a neighbouring maintenance unit, writing the aircraft off, but fortunately not injuring himself.

Returning to Lympne for a second stay, No. 130 Squadron were delayed by poor weather and did not arrive until the afternoon. They immediately started to organise patrols for the following day against the V-1. It was Flt Lt G. Jones, flying Spitfire XIV RM750, who successfully destroyed the squadron's first V-1 over Rochester.

Early in the morning of the 16th, four sections of No. 1 Squadron's Typhoons were scrambled to carry out air sea rescue operations, during which Ft Lt L. J. Wood developed engine problems and crash-landed on the beach two and a half miles south-east of Lydd. His Typhoon, EK176, touched down on rough ground and in the ensuing crash Wood received serious head injuries, dying the following morning. A popular pilot, he was sorely missed by all who knew him. On the same day, the squadron escorted Bostons of No. 88 Squadron on a raid on steelworks at Denain, during which four Bostons were shot down. Added to the loss of Flt Lt Wood, it had been a terrible day for the squadron.

Later that day Sgt P. E. H. Standish in Spitfire RM744 and Plt Off W. W. Brown destroyed two more over the Tonbridge and Rochester areas. During the attack by Standish, three Tempests and a Mustang joined the party, and he claimed that he received fire from all these intruders. Engine failure caused Plt Off. E. C. Matthew to crash-land at High Halden ALG. He was slightly injured but his Spitfire XIV was badly damaged. During an operation over the Amiens area, Flt Lt T. A. H. Slack of No. 41 Squadron had problems with his aircraft's fuel cock and was unable to switch to his main fuel tank. He was last seen at a height of 200 feet, heading for open fields near Hesdin where he crashed Spitfire XII EN226. Slack managed to get out of the aircraft but was caught and later taken prisoner.

At the height of the V-1 campaign, one of the constant fears was that of mid-air collision. One such accident happened on 18 August after Fg Off. R. Keating had taken off from Lympne on evening patrol. Flying over Romney Marsh at the same time was a Mustang Mk III, FB206, one of several climbing away from the ALG at Brenzett. Unbeknown to Keating, the Mustang was underneath his Spitfire, and before he could take evasive action both aircraft collided. Keating managed to pilot Spitfire XIV NH713 to a controlled crash-land near Woodchurch and survived, but the Mustang pilot, from Poland, Plt Off. Feliks Migos of No. 306 (Torunski) Squadron, was killed, his aircraft losing a wing in the collision and crashing near Ham Street. No. 306 Squadron formed part of 133 Wing with Nos 315 (Deblinski) and 129 (Mysore) Squadrons. The Wing was part of ADGB and was held back from Europe for the V-1 campaign.

The following morning, Plt Off. R. J Martin and Flt Lt K. J Matheson, 130 Squadron destroyed a V-1 before breakfast! On 25 August, WO B. Weeds piloting Spitfire XII MB875 experienced engine trouble as he was about to take off from Lympne. He switched off the engine and braked hard but hit a bank on the boundary of the airfield.

Despite the increased operations against the V-1, life continued relatively normally – there was even time for lectures. W. H. Goodchild of the India Office visited No. 130 Squadron to give a lecture about India, as the squadron were named after the Punjab. Later that evening a dance was held at which the visitor was a welcome guest. It was a good end to August for the squadron. Despite poor weather conditions, they had many V-1s to their credit.

An unusual event occurred on 1 September 1944 when fire and crash tenders were sent to a crash reported on the outskirts of Ashford. On arrival at the scene there was no sign of any crew or pilot, but closer inspection revealed that the crashed aircraft turned out to be an unmanned Mistel, a modified Junkers Ju 88 A-4 fitted with an explosive warhead. Mounted on top of the drone was a Bf 109 F-4 (later types used a Fw 190 F-8). This, piloted, aircraft guided the combo towards its target, the pilot in the fighter releasing the bomber. These composite aircraft were also used against shipping. Later in the war one was captured and the fighter used, a Fw 190, and is on display at the Imperial War Museum in London. This particular Mistel was one of two dispatched across the English Channel by II./KG 10. One crashed at Warsop; the other went in the opposite direction and crashed at Hothfield, the explosion creating a crater 12 feet deep and 40 feet wide.

By this time, No. 127 Squadron, which had flown from Lympne in July 1944, was based at B16 airfield at Villons-les-Buissons in France. Operating in the Lille area, Flt Lt D. J. McNally, flying Spitfire IX NH596, and Flt Sgt R. M. Housden, flying Spitfire IX NH543, were diverted to Lympne short of fuel. Both collided on landing and Housden died, McNally being badly burnt in the ensuing explosion. Sqn Ldr Bradley reported:

Last night, we had an unnecessary crash at Lympne. Typically it was not caused by enemy action. It was caused by pilot error. We were diverted to Lympne, because one pilot failed to obey the rule to continue taxiing down to the end of the runway. He attempted to turn off at the first intersection and was rammed by the following aircraft. Sergeant Housden is dead and Flt Lt McNally is in hospital with burns. In future, remember the unbreakable rule. Never turn off the runway until you have to – at the end. That is all.

McNally should have been commended for his bravery; he ripped off his harness and oxygen mask and ran over to Housden's Spitfire, leaping onto the port wing. There was a flash of fire as he grabbed his friend's head and shouted, 'Out! Out! Get Out!' He then saw that Housden was dead from a broken neck. At that moment the Spitfire's fuel exploded and McNally was blown back about 15 feet. Ammunition started to explode, cannon shells and machine-gun bullets flying everywhere. McNally was protected somewhat by his helmet and gloves, but with his goggles up and oxygen mask removed he was still caught in the blast. The injured pilot spent some time in Archibald McIndoe's care at the famous burns clinic at East Grinstead. Much to everyone's surprise, McNally visited his chums but was posted to the UK, tour-expired.

Plt Off. P. B. Graham, flying Spitfire XII MB831 of No. 41 Squadron, went missing on the same day. He was shot down while attacking a train near Ghent. On a Rhubarb mission near St Omer, he came across a train carrying the dreaded new weapon, the V-2 rocket, a priority for both pilots flying that day. As they came into attack, the flak wagons guarding the deadly cargo opened up. In his book *Skypilot,* Peter Graham recalls the events of 1 September 1944:

I decided to come in at tree top height from the flank and aim for the driver's cab initially and spraying the engine forward from there. As I passed over the engine there was an explosion. However, it was quite impossible to say what hit my Spit, because all the guns on the train were blazing away at me. Everything seemed OK but as I pulled away my engine temperature began to soar. I was losing glycol fast.

My number two stayed with me as I climbed steeply and headed north-west for the coast, thinking that there would be naval ships in the Channel; one would pick me up. The engine seized and I pulled back the canopy. I rolled the Spitfire over and fell out. As I came down my chute caught on a branch of a tree and I was swung violently upwards. I fell to ground on my back. I disengaged myself from the parachute, and dived through a hedge, where I was confronted by a German motorcycle combination. The driver pointed his rifle at me, his companion his machine gun, I was told to 'alt'. I 'alted. I was marched into Esquelbecq.

Graham spent the rest of the war as a PoW. On his return to England he later married and following an earlier calling he was ordained into the Church in 1952.

By the beginning of September, Lympne Wing was involved in armed reconnaissance and bomber escorts. As a result, targets were becoming out of range for units operating from bases at home. Later in the month, squadrons at Lympne were escorting DC-3s and Stirling towing gliders to Arnhem and were tasked with silencing any flak en route, being airborne for two and a half hours before heading home to Lympne. On the 18th, a large airborne force consisting of aircraft towing gliders and carrying paratroopers was being escorted to the Netherlands to take part in the battle for Arnhem, No. 610 Squadron forming part of the fighter escort across the North Sea. During the flight they attacked a flak barge, which caught fire. Unfortunately, Spitfire XII NH709 was hit by return fire from the barge. Flt Sgt Shaw headed for Lympne, but the aircraft speed dropped as he was landing and he crashed. He had a lucky escape, as the Spitfire was written off, both wings having been torn off and the spinner pounded nearly flat. Bystanders reported that the aircraft did three somersaults. One side of the Perspex cockpit cover was broken open and Shaw climbed out of the hole without a scratch.

At the end of September 1944, No. 130 Squadron were to join the 2nd TAF in Europe, but first they had to move to Hawkinge to take over the XIVs of No. 350 (Belgian) Squadron. However, one aircraft, Spitfire XIV RM761, hit a ridge on take-off and its starboard wheel was torn off, the undercarriage leg being forced into the ground. The remainder of the Spitfires arrived at Hawkinge without further mishap. From there they moved with No. 402 Squadron to airfield B70, a 2nd TAF ALG at Deurne in Belgium. On 29 September, Lympne played host to twelve aircraft of No. 350 (Belgian) Squadron, including nine Dakotas with glider pilots and soldiers from Arnhem, who landed due to poor weather and stayed for three hours. Approximately 180 Arnhem men landed and, needless to say, the bar and cigarette stocks were soon depleted, much to the annoyance of everyone at Lympne.

By 1 October 1944, the move to Lympne by No. 350 Squadron had been completed when No. 6350 Servicing Echelon moved to the airfield

Squadron Leader R. A. Newbury DFC and Bar, CO of No. 610 Squadron Royal Auxiliary Air Force (RAuxAF), seated front row with the unit's dog.

from Hawkinge by road. Having just arrived, a warning was issued to the effect that Nos 41, 350 and 610 Squadrons and their servicing echelons would be required to move to the Continent as soon as possible, to be transferred from ADGB to the newly formed 2nd TAF. However, orders were received the following day to the effect that the squadrons would stay at Lympne until further notification was received. Another accident occurred, involving Spitfire XV RM793 flown by Plt Off. Gibbs. As he was taking off from Lympne, the propeller hit the ground; the pilot selected 'wheels up' and the drop tank caught fire. Fortunately, Gibbs was uninjured.

Sqn Ldr Michael Donnet DFC, the CO of No. 350 Squadron, was not pleased with their move to Lympne:

> To add insult to injury, 83 Group 2 TAF took our Spitfire XIVs and left us with 130 Squadron's worn out machines. I made the phone wires hot with complaints to the Belgian Authorities and eventually wrung from them a promise of a certain move to Belgium before long and that something would be done about our Spitfires. Then they got their own back on me by telling me that although the squadron might go, I wouldn't! Instead I was posted to Hawkinge as wing commander flying for the RAF Wing there.

Returning to Lympne from an operation escorting 120 Halifaxes on 6 October 1944, Flt Lt Hoormarkt reported he had engine trouble. Making a low approach to land, Spitfire MN-F of No. 350 Squadron hit a fence north-west of the airfield and crash-landed. The pilot was uninjured. The following day, the rear party of 2847 AA Squadron RAF Regiment moved from Hawkinge to Lympne, quickly settling in, and by 11 October were fully operational.

No. 350 Squadron had a bad day on 25 October, when five of the Spitfire XIVs had to make force-landings. One of these, RM615, made a heavy landing at Lympne, in doing so tipping onto its nose, but Plt Off. L. Lambrechts climbed out uninjured. All of these aircraft were later repaired and returned to service. At the end of October, during an operation involving Nos 41, 350 and 610 Squadrons, three vertical trails seen twenty to thirty miles east of Rotterdam indicated that V-2 rockets were being launched from this area. The target was London. Unlike the V-1, the V-2 was unstoppable and it was not long before Londoners were subjected to horrific casualties. It would be fighter squadrons of the RAF that would mount attacks on V-2 sites in Europe during 1944 and 1945. Codenamed 'Operation Big Ben', they proved successful but many pilots were killed.

Plt Off. J. J. F. 'Johnny' Morel Mathieu had been posted to No. 350 Squadron as a flight sergeant in January 1944, becoming a commissioned pilot officer on 30 July. Like many Belgians who wanted to join the RAF, he had evaded capture in Belgium in 1941, but on reaching Spain was imprisoned at Miranda before eventually escaping to Britain in September 1941. He was assigned to Belgian forces on 20 October 1941 and later enlisted into the Belgian Section of the RAF on 12 February 1942. Sadly, Morel Mathieu crash-landed Spitfire XIV NH716 MN-X on his return to Lympne from high-altitude formation flying practice on 11 November 1944 and was killed.

On 22 November, two Dakota ambulances from Liège landed at Lympne. On board were twenty-three wounded soldiers who stayed overnight. The same day, another Dakota ambulance crossed the English coast. With low cloud everywhere and having no idea of his position, the pilot flew up and down the coast for half an hour, seeing only glimpses of sea and ploughed fields. Hearing the sound of distant engines, Lympne fired pyrotechnics and called on 'Darky' (British backup homing system) continuously. The pilot of the Dakota saw the mortar flares from seven miles away and made for airfield, circling in cloud at 100 feet. With radio transmission intermittent, the aircraft made its first approach blind and touched down travelling straight towards buildings, but was sent round again by RT, clearing the roofs by just 15 feet. The pilot was then instructed to land over flares and landed without further incident. When questioned, he stated that his instruments were u/s and that he had been contemplating landing in open country. The injured soldiers and the three Dakotas' crews were billeted overnight and the following day, despite the waterlogged airfield, one took off for Ramsbury.

During the month of November the WAAF strength decreased when the RAF station at Hythe closed and Cranchester, Studfall and Aldergate WAAF hostels were disposed of. By the end of the month, only four hostels were occupied by the WAAF and in three of them there was sufficient space for a rest room, which was much appreciated by the young girls serving at Lympne airfield. The period from November through to Christmas 1944 proved to be a trying time as the airfield was unserviceable on several occasions. Despite this, Lympne played host to many visitors.

In December 1944, Fg Off. A. J. H Wilson was put in charge of a detachment of thirteen airmen of 2707 AA RAF Regiment at RAF Hunmanby Moor, where they were on an advanced Bofors gun refresher course with No. 3 Anti-Aircraft Wing, and instructed to move to RAF Gravesend. Sqn Ldr E. L. Eldridge proceeded to Lympne to make a reconnaissance prior to the final move, and a detachment of men had already arrived at Gravesend with small arms and other equipment on

29 December. The following day, 'A' and HQ Flights reported to RAF Lympne and were joined the next day by 'B' and 'C' Flights. Within a day, 'A' Flight's guns were deployed and fully operational. A message was sent to HQ 11 Group and the local defence adviser at RAF Hawkinge, advising that 2707 AA Regiment were ready for action. Flights 'B' and 'C' began Bofors training and site construction, fulfilling the commitment of No. 1334 Wing RAF Regiment, of which the squadron were now a unit at RAF Lympne. As it turned out, 2707 Squadron were sent on another refresher course and operations were taken over by 2823 Squadron RAF Regiment.

With attacks by enemy aircraft unlikely at this late stage of the war, route marches and rifle practices were organised for the RAF Regiment and shooting competitions held. On 29 March 1945, the squadron were informed that ninety-nine other ranks would be discharged from the RAF and enlisted in the Army, and that as many guns as could be operationally manned might have to be moved at twelve hours' notice to carry out an operational task. By the beginning of April, the squadron were moved to RAF Swingate, but for administration reasons they would be officially based at RAF Hawkinge, the move to Swingate being effected for accommodation and rations only. By the end of April the squadron had moved back to Hunmanby Moor and did not return to Kent.

Since 14 November 1944, No. 567 Squadron 70 Group had operated between Hornchurch, Hawkinge, Lympne and Eastchurch. Their job was anti-aircraft co-operation and duties included target-towing with Miles Martinets, gun-laying and searchlight practice with Airspeed Oxfords, and simulated attacks on exercising troops with Hawker Hurricanes. The CO decided to merge both 'C' and 'D' Flights of the squadron and make local arrangements with RAF regiments based at Lympne.

As with all units at the airfield, flying suffered due to the poor weather and on 2 February 1945 no flying took place. On the 10th, WO Robinson had a taxiing accident, but although his aircraft was damaged, he escaped serious injury. At the beginning of March, three Miles Martinets arrived from No. 598 Squadron on attachment; these were needed to meet a new commitment with Newhaven Gunnery School in No. 1 AA Group. However, they remained grounded until the arrival of their fitters and ground crew picked for the job, but were soon joined by four Hurricanes and seven airmen from No. 289 Squadron. On 12 March, they were also joined by a detachment of five airmen and four ground crew of No. 598 Squadron from Peterhead, with WO Steele flying WO MacDonald in to join them.

On 3 April 1945, a signal was received from Fighter Command instructing the detachment to be reduced from twelve aircraft to six and stating that the order had to be complied with the same day. Later that day, six aircraft co-operated with RAF regiments based at Bell Farm and Bartons Point, returning by 7.45 p.m. During April, the unit was converting to a new aircraft, the Vultee Vengeance. Then, on 22 May 1945, 'D' Flight of No. 567 Squadron was ordered to move to RAF Hawkinge pending the closure of Lympne. No. 598 Squadron were disbanded on 30 April 1945, and No. 567 Squadron on 15 June 1946, after having moved to Manston, Eastchurch and West Malling. The last unit to be based at RAF Lympne was No. 659 Air Observation Post (Air OP) when they visited Lympne on 4 July 1945, having returning from their base at Nijmegen. Later they were sent on leave, apart from the duty officer, for an unspecified period. On 7 July, No. 659 Air OP re-formed at RAF Hornchurch and were immediately sent on leave again, for a further forty-eight hours, returning on the evening of the 9th in preparation for travelling to RAF Matlaske next day.

It is worth closing this chapter by stating that, during 1940–41 Westenhanger was used as a decoy airfield probably for Lympne and in April 1944 was used by Auster AOP aircraft of No. 660 Squadron, No. 84 Group, 2nd Tactical Air Force from East Grinstead for exercise with the Army for the invasion that year. They moved to Weston Zoyland in May 1944, returned to Westenhanger and finally moved into Europe in July 1944.   Following six years of RAF occupation the airfield at Lympne returned to a peaceful existence, Lympne Flying Control ceasing to function on 22 May 1945. Lympne had proved to be an important airfield for the RAF, but its future now hung in the balance.

CHAPTER 9

Civil flying returns; air races during the late 1940s; the Stowting air crash

Air racing returned to Lympne in 1946, when the Folkestone Aero Trophy was again competed for that year, and it seems appropriate at this point to look back at the pre-war Folkestone Aero Trophy, the first race being held in 1932. The major air racing event of pre-war years had been the King's Cup, presented each year for a flight round Britain. Several lesser events took place annually and were handicap races, the chief ones being from Heston to Cardiff, Heston to Newcastle, and Heston to the Isle of Man. In addition, there was the Devon Trophy Race at Exeter and the Folkestone Trophy Race at Lympne. This last-named event, organised by the Cinque Ports Flying Club, differed from the others in that it attracted foreign entrants and was flown over a closed circuit.

The Gipsy Moth was in its heyday, while the more competitive owners flew the Comper Swift. It was in one of these that A. J. 'Bill' Styran won the first race, reaching a top speed of 141 mph. The course was three laps, a total of fifty-eight miles, and observers were stationed at each turning point. Initially, the finish was over Folkestone Pier, but later it was a line across the airfield at Lympne.

With memories of the halcyon days at Lympne during the 1930s still vivid in people's minds, and blitzed hangars bearing testimony to the war years, Lympne staged the return of the Folkestone Aero Trophy on 31 August and 1 September 1946. On the first day there were to be three heats, flown over three laps of the pre-war course. The competitors would have to take off to the south-west in strong winds, necessitating a sharp turn on the first leg towards Capel airship shed near Folkestone. A 300-degree turn to starboard would take them to the Folkestone harbour light. This would be followed by eight miles of surf hopping along the coast to the Hythe gasometer followed by a short climb up to the fourth turning point in the centre of the airfield.

The two handicappers, Messrs Rowarth and Dancy (who had handicapped all the chief pre-war races), based their calculations on the known performance of the aircraft type in question. They also made a thorough check on each of the machines, because competitors often fitted smaller wheels or raised the engine compression, hoping that the handicappers would not appreciate the advantage of such modifications. Amongst the judges was AVM J. N. Boothman, CB, DFC, AFC, outright winner of the Schneider Trophy in 1931. One of the stewards was Sir Frank McLean, who had played a prominent part in British aviation during the 1920s. His Sopwith Gnu, G-EAGP, had been the winner of the Grosvenor Cup Race at Lympne back in 1923. Other stewards were H. Duncan Davies, who managed the Brooklands Flying Club before the Second World War; Whitney Straight, known for his provincial airports; and C. D. Hunting, who at that time controlled the Cinque Ports Flying Club.

The winner of the trophy also received £100 donated by the people of Folkestone. Second prize was a silver cup presented by Hunting Flying Clubs Ltd and £50 donated by the people of Folkestone, the third prize being a medal and £25. A speed trophy and £10 was given by the Cinque Ports Flying Club for the fastest time. The entries fell into three categories: (a) private owners; (b) aircraft entered by manufacturers or operating companies flown by company pilots; (c) aircraft entered by the clubs and flown by members or instructors. Of the original twenty-two entries, two did not materialise. These were No. 5, Percival Q.6 G-AFIX, piloted by Flt Lt Ian McLaren, and No. 22, Auster G-AHAX, flown by G. W. Derbyshire.

During the afternoon of the first day, Saturday 31 August 1946, in rain and strong winds, all entries were picketed. At 3 p.m. the seven competitors for the first heat assembled on the starting line at the north side of the airfield. Taking off past the enclosure, they carried out a sharp run round a haystack on the west side and so on to the course. The flag was raised, throttles opened. When the flag fell, tails were up before the wheels began rolling. Piloted by P. Landaur, the Piper Cub had rather a long start, arriving back bucketing and pitching as it hit the rising air currents over the southern boundary before some of the faster competitors had started. Even before the start of the heat the yellow Walrus, G-AHFN, flown by J. Grierson, was the favourite to win. The Supermarine Walrus, an amphibious single-engine biplane, had a manually operated undercarriage and the co-pilot could be seen frantically working to retract the gear as the aircraft was brought round the haystack in a near-vertical bank, close on the tail of the Taylorcraft Plus. Passing one of the three aircraft on each

Supermarine Walrus G-AHFN flown by J. Grierson during the first Folkestone Aero Trophy at Lympne to be held since the War on 31 August and 1 September 1946.

lap, he roared over the finish. A speed of 114.5 mph was recorded.

Handicapped out of the race, Tom Rose in his Miles M.28 could not catch up with the Proctor 1 aircraft flown by the Luton Club's chief instructor, which came second. Heat two was not so exciting. The scratch man, L. T. Carruthers, flying Jean Batten's Percival Gull Six, passed all the others easily to finish first at 144.5 mph, with the Proctors in pursuit. The Czech Sokol monoplane took part in the third heat, the only foreign competitor, owned and flown by K. R. Drbohlav. The limit man (D. R. Robertson, the first to take off) maintained his lead in Tipsy B G-AFJT. Close behind him came Wg Cdr H. C. Kennard flying the Messenger. Catching up with the Czech, he was himself pipped at the post by D. M. Bay in the Field Proctor 1, who finished first.

On Sunday, the weather changed and the event was bathed in sunshine. First on the agenda was the Siddeley Trophy, a two-lap course, organised as an inter-flying club event, the member gaining the highest placing in the Folkestone Aero Trophy representing his club. There were only two contestants: R. Pomfret in Tiger Moth G-AHNX of the Cinque Ports Flying Club, and R. Paine in Hawk Major G-ADCV of the Wolverhampton Flying Club. It resulted in a victory for the local club. Despite the Hawk Major flying a perfect circuit, it finished twenty-two seconds behind Pomfret, who was presented with a trophy and £10 from Lord Kenilworth.

Entries for the final of the Folkestone Aero Trophy comprised the first three aircraft in each heat. The Walrus took the lead, passing the Messenger on lap one, reappearing over the trees 'simply quivering with endeavour', as the commentator remarked. Bunched together, the four Proctors with the Sokol swung into the haystack turn. For a brief moment a collision seemed inevitable but, with sighs of relief, all watched as the group of aircraft disappeared in the direction of Capel pursued by Carruthers in his Gull Six, G-ADPR, Drbohlav in the Sokol, and Bay in his Proctor 1, G-AHMV. However, none could catch the Walrus, which had gained another 7 mph since the heats. Grierson sped over the airfield, parting the grass with the aircraft's keel and finishing with a speed of 121 mph. When interviewed, he remarked that it took the strength of both himself and the co-pilot to haul the Walrus around the turning points. Checking the oil pressure and temperature gauge, he noticed the needles were off the clock. The little Sokol retired from the race, having made a gallant effort in the face of strong opposition.

All eyes now turned to entries for the High Speed Handicap. The prizes were the Hythe Aero Trophy and £50 presented by the Borough of Hythe, plus a trophy donated by *The Aeroplane* magazine for the winner, and a trophy given by Gp Capt. Miles. Each pilot and co-pilot was presented with a souvenir silver tankard by Sqn Ldr D. C. Palmer and his wife. Geoffrey de Havilland entered the race in Vampire F Mk 1 TG285, Lt Cdr M. J. Lithgow flew the impressive-looking Seafang 32 VG475, W. Humble piloted Sea Fury NX802, and G. H. Pike flew Sea Hornet PX224. Bill Humble in his Fury led the start, followed by the Seafang, Hornet and Vampire.

The Fury was over the airfield within an amazingly short period of time, hotly pursued by the Seafang and the Hornet. The silver Vampire appeared and was gone. Both Seafang and Hornet could not take the turns so dramatically, so Geoffrey de Havilland finished first – or did he? Not so, as an error in the timekeeper's stopwatch had resulted in a faulty start; thus Humble in his Fury claimed first place. Despite this setback, De Havilland had impressed the crowds, as he had overtaken three aircraft in turn.

Other aircraft visiting Lympne were DH Leopard Moth G-ACTJ, DH Hornet Moth G-AFRE, Miles Magister G-AHNW, DH Dove G-AHRH, Vickers Viking G-AHON, and Miles M.65 Gemini G-AIDO. Aviation companies that entered aircraft had also brought their 'hack', DH Rapides, the successful twin-engine biplanes, two of which belonged to Arabian Airways Ltd and were named 'Balka' and 'Raghaden'. Another visitor, an Auster Autocrat, had spare main-wing spars lashed to the underside of the fuselage, just in case.

In the summer of 1947, the Lympne International Air Races included some record-breaking achievements. On 30 August, the heats were held for the Folkestone Aero Trophy, which took place the following day over

Lt Cdr Mike J. Lithgow sitting on the wing of the Supermarine Seafang F.Mk.32 which took fourth place in the Lympne High Speed Handicap on 1 September 1946.

three laps of a 19.5-mile course, Capel–Hythe–Lympne, and was won by Lt Cdr Paul Godfrey in B.A. Swallow 2 G-AELG at 99 mph. Second was J. Moseley at 101 mph in Tipsy Trainer 1 G-AISA, Ranald Porteus coming third in Chilton DW.1A G-AFSV. At the same time, Porteus and his aircraft established two new 100 km closed-circuit records at 123.72 mph during the race for 2 litres capacity and under, and for 2-4 litres capacity in Class C.I/IV. In the same event, W. P. I. Fillingham set up a new 100 km closed-circuit record of 178.33 mph for aircraft of 4-6 litres capacity, with DH TK.2 G-ADNO.

The Siddeley Challenge Trophy was awarded in conjunction with the Folkestone Aero Trophy to the highest placed club pilot, the winner being Lt Cdr Godfrey of the South Coast Flying Club at Shoreham. In the Lympne High Speed Handicap, four circuits of the course were made by the six competitors. First was Lt Cdr L. Peter Twiss in Fairey Firefly FR Mk 4 VG979 at 305.93 mph, with Gp Capt. Charles Flood in Blackburn Firebrand TF Mk V second, Gp Capt. R. G. Slade in Fairey Firefly Trainer T Mk I third, Sqn Ldr W. J. Guy Morgan flying the yellow Type 502 Spitfire VIII Trainer G-AIDN fourth, W. Humble in Hawker Fury F Mk I NX802 at 358.14 mph fifth, and Gp Capt. John Cunningham in DH.100 Vampire F Mk 1 VF332 at 494.63 mph sixth. The Tiger Moth Scratch Race was run over four laps of a ten-mile course with five simultaneous

Group Captain John Cunningham flew DH.100 Vampire F.Mk.1 VF332 in the Lympne High Speed Handicap race on 30 August 1947, establishing the closed circuit record of 496.88 mph.

starters, F. Kirk coming first with G-AINW. During the meeting on 31 August, Cunningham established a new Class C.I/I unrestricted world 100 km closed-circuit record of 496.88 mph with VF332.

The following year, on 28 August 1948, several races were run at Lympne. There were four starters in the Tiger Moth race for three laps of a five-and-a-half-mile course, the winner over sixteen and a half miles being W. P. I. Fillingham at 86 mph in G-AHXC. Derek J. Jemmett led all the way in the Hawk Trainer race to win at 103.25 mph with G-AKPE. Four Spitfires, three F Mk XVIs and one F Mk 22, participated in the RAuxAF Squadron race over 100 miles, first place going to Sqn Ldr H. S. L. Dundas of No. 601 (County of London) Squadron in an F Mk XVI. Three entrants – all from Fairey – took part in the Tipsy race, the winner being Flt Lt David James Masters at 76.25 mph in G-AISC. In second place was Lt Cdr Twiss in G-AFWT, and third was Gp Capt. R. G. Slade in G-AFSG. The High Speed Handicap provided plenty of noise and excitement, Flt Lt J. Colquhoun winning in Spitfire VIII Trainer G-AIDN, with Gp Capt. Cunningham in second place in Vampire F Mk 3 VV190 and J. O. Matthews third in Firefly FR Mk 4 Z1835. Sqn Ldr J. D. Derry was fourth in Vampire F Mk 5 VV217, and Miss Lettice Curtis was fifth flying a blue Spitfire PR Mk XI, N74138. Also competing were Sqn Ldr W. J. G. Morgan in Spitfire F Mk 24 VN324, and Sqn Ldr T. S. Wade in Fury F Mk I NX802. After the race, Miss Curtis, the famous ATA pilot, flew Spitfire PR Mk XI over the 100 km closed-circuit course to set a new international record in its class at 313.208 mph.

The previous year, Lympne had played a role in a tragic aircraft incident. On the afternoon of 11 January 1947, a message was received by air traffic controllers at RAF Manston: 'We are short of fuel, what is your weather report? – Hurry, please.' Capt. I. R. Goalen was in trouble and time was running out for BOAC Dakota G-AGJX on flight 21W/255. The aircraft was in fact a Douglas C-47A-1-DK Skytrain, previously USAAF 42-92236. It had later joined the RAF and was registered as FL604, having flown with several OTUs before being bought by BOAC on 7 July 1944. Low on fuel, the pilot was desperate to land his aircraft. Shortly after Manston received the call, the radio operator of the BOAC Douglas C-47/, hurriedly exchanged messages with Lympne Airport:

> Will you give me a fix? Send your call sign for sixty seconds, followed by a dash for ten seconds. Your true bearing in relation to me is 128 degrees. Weather report? Weather report where? Weather report you. Acknowledged. I will call back. Your true bearing in relation to me is 127 degrees Lympne.

The last message sent was intercepted by Central Air Traffic Control, Uxbridge: 'Fuel for thirty-five minutes.' Then later, at approximately 4 p.m., 'Fuel nearly out', followed by 'SOS, SOS.' At approximately 4.06 p.m. the aircraft hit high ground at Barley Hill, close to Highfields Farm at Stowting near Lympne. The aircraft struck at a shallow angle and then bounced for fifty yards before crashing into trees. Owing to the empty fuel tanks, there was no fire. The forward fuselage as far back as the cabin door was torn open, as was the starboard side of the fuselage when the aircraft swung violently to port, but the tail of the aircraft was largely undamaged. All seats were torn from their anchorages, although seat belts remained fastened. Two crew and three passengers were killed in the crash, which was the first for BOAC since 1944, three others subsequently dying as a result of their injuries.

This scheduled flight had been bound for Lagos in West Africa from London with five crew and eleven passengers. The first stop was to be Bordeaux. Prior to departure, Capt. Goalen was given all the relevant weather reports, but said that he did not like the weather conditions in that area and suggested that he might proceed direct to Lisbon. Sometime between 8.15 and 8.30 a.m. on that fateful day he received further reports and then checked weather reports at Marignane, which were favourable. He might fly there if he could not reach Bordeaux, and Toulouse was on the flight plan as an alternative airfield. The radio operator, R. D. Sanford, was briefed for the flight and at 9.35 a.m. the doomed airliner taxied onto the runway, taking off at 9.48 a.m.

On reaching Bordeaux there were three other aircraft waiting in the circuit. G-AGJX would be the last to land, but at the same time an Avro York with engine trouble was cleared for landing. Capt. Goalen was told to wait at 2,000 feet because of the York's emergency landing. The Dakota was cleared to land but, according to Bordeaux Control, the pilot said he would proceed to Toulouse. One of pilots of an airliner in the vicinity who overheard part of the conversation stated that the pilot had said that he could not wait and had decided to return to London. Apparently Capt. Goalen had been told, 'You can land in just one minute.' His reply was, 'I am sorry …' but the rest was not heard. The French controller, convinced that G-AGJX was bound for Toulouse, phoned Orly to report the situation. In the event, the Dakota did not land at Toulouse, presumably because of the turbulent weather conditions. As there was no further communication received from the aircraft, control radioed to say that they could not land. The time was 1.08 p.m. The radio operator on G-AGJX sent a message to Gloucester saying that they were returning to the UK. However, on later investigation it was discovered that an estimated time of arrival (ETA)

The first fatal air crash of BOAC, took place at Stowing, near Lympne on 11 January 1947, when Dakota DC-3 G-AGJX, hit high ground in poor weather. This aircraft flew with the RAF, serial FL604 with 512 and 271 Squadrons, finally serving with 107 Operational Training Unit, joining BOAC on 7 July 1944.

of 3.18 p.m. had been worked out by the navigator but the captain then asked for an ETA for Le Bourget which was 1.30 p.m. According to the radio log, the operator tried unsuccessfully to raise Le Bourget, asking about weather conditions and stating that they were now going there.

Gloucester was not informed of the pilot's decision to make for Le Bourget, and by then the weather was deteriorating rapidly. Other aircraft were in the circuit waiting for permission to land, one of them being a DH Rapide, G-AGWC, which was low on fuel. Receiving no reply from Air Traffic Control as they were so busy, the unfortunate Goalen abandoned his attempt to land at Le Bourget and headed out towards the coast and home, contacting Manston at 3.45 p.m. A fix was obtained on the Dakota, showing that it was nine miles south-south-east of Cap Gris Nez. Lympne received a message at 3.52 p.m. that the aircraft had only twenty-five minutes of fuel left, but time and luck were running out for G-AGJX.

The pilot had sent out a Pan-Pan call, meaning 'I'm forced to land', and at 4.02 p.m. an SOS was heard, giving the aircraft's position as 50°55' N and 1°21' E. Further SOS calls were sent at 4.03 and at 4.04 p.m. The captain was heading for Manston, but changed his mind when he reached the coast of France and made for the shortest route across the Channel. A Belgian Dakota flying locally was asked by radio to keep a lookout for G-AGJX, and the Dungeness lifeboat was called out, as were the Deal and Ramsgate RNLS boats. In addition, two air sea rescue Ansons from RAF Thorney Island were alerted and sent on patrol. The weather was terrible – it was dark, raining and there was a thick mist – but not unusual for the time of year. Maurice Hammond, the owner of Highfields Farm at Stowting, was doing his usual daily chore of milking the cows:

> While we were milking, I heard an aircraft overhead, flying extremely low. A minute later I heard a sort of thud but I did not connect it with the aircraft. Within a few moments, I heard a cry. It sounded as if a huntsman was shouting to his hounds. I went out and a man came running through the fog towards the house crying, 'Help! Help! A plane has crashed.' His face was covered in blood. He was wearing a Mae-West and he thought they were crashing into the sea. I went back with him up the hill. It was difficult finding our way in the thick fog. Eventually I heard women crying. There were two women passengers standing by the aircraft, one with a baby in her arms. One of them aged about twenty-three was injured but active. She tried to rescue one of the men trapped in the cockpit. She was very courageous.
>
> The fuselage was burning slightly and I asked the pilot, who was conscious, if there was any danger of the aircraft blowing up. 'None whatever, the fuel is all gone,' was the reply.

They set about trying to rescue him; he complained that his leg was going numb and he passed out. By that time, local farmers and villagers had arrived on the scene and tried to free him with axes. Eventually they got him out of the wreckage, laying him on the ground clear of the aircraft, but it was obvious that both his legs had been crushed. The rescuers went back to help the others. At 5.12 p.m. Ashford police station received news that the Dakota had been located and were asked to help, and both Ashford and Folkestone fire brigades were on their way to the crash site. The first doctor to arrive was Dr Regan, who started to treat the injured. A local farmer, Mrs Ironside from Water Farm, climbed to the top of the hill with hot tea and much needed blankets. She and other villagers did a great job of administering first aid before the ambulances arrived. Eventually, with great difficulty, the dead and injured were stretchered to waiting ambulances. By then it was much darker, the fog having closed in, and it was very muddy and slippery on Barley Hill. Mrs Hammond found a mother with her baby:

> I picked up the baby and found that the mother was injured. Still carrying the baby I walked round the injured near the aircraft and wrapped them in blankets. I took the baby back to the farmhouse, gave her milk and a neighbour looked after her, and I returned to the crash site to help.

One of the survivors, Mrs Andrews, who was on the way to join her husband in Africa, said, 'Just before the crash we had been told to put on parachutes, but we thought the pilot would bring us safely back. I was thrown clear of the wreckage.' At 6 p.m. the first patient reached Ashford Hospital and by 7 p.m. all the dead and injured had been recovered. There was little more to be done. Mrs Hammond returned to her house to nurse the baby, which went to sleep in her arms. Her thoughts turned to her son, serving with the RAF: 'Could this happen to my son?' she wondered.

Standing on Barley Hill, you realise how close they were to Lympne. If only Capt. Goalen had been able to reach Lympne, this tragedy, the first major crash with fatalities for BOAC, could have been avoided. Some years ago, Mr and Mrs Hammond were visited by someone connected with the incident. Together they strolled up Barley Hill to the trees where G-AJGX met its end, where the stranger asked to be left alone for a while. Remembering his parents' account of the crash and those who lost their lives, they respected his wish to be alone and walked down the hill to their home.

CHAPTER 10

Compensation for wartime damage; learning to fly at Lympne in the 1950s; Silver City, Skyways and Air Kruise at the airfield

On 18 August 1945, the government had yielded possession of land and property held by Sir Hugh Haldin, resident at Lympne Place, particularly gardens, grounds and cottages that had been acquired under emergency powers during the war. As a result, Sir Hugh had applied to the General Claims Tribunal for compensation for damage to some 1,765 trees and land adjoining the main road (a width of 55 feet) extending south of the footpath towards Lympne Place. In response to the claim, a sum of £1,050 was offered, with the proviso that if it was not accepted within seven days it would be withdrawn. This settlement was not accepted and Sir Hugh took legal action, and following a lengthy dispute with the authorities, he was eventually awarded £1,433 under the Compensation (Defence) Act 1939 for damage to land and trees.

Early in 1948, Ronald Sneller, a sergeant in the RAF who lived in Bridge, contacted a Mr Thompson at Lympne Airport in connection with flying instruction. It was arranged that Thompson's aircraft should be used for the purpose and that Thompson would be paid £2 10s an hour. On 31 August, Sneller commenced a course of instruction with Jack Pittock in Tiger Moth G-AHLT, and by 16 September the pupil had benefited from some sixteen hours of flying instruction from Mr Pittock, who told Thompson that he was then ready for a solo flight. The test was taken but at the end of the flight, Thompson was non-committal and so Sneller had some further instruction from Pittock. An hour later, he told Thompson that the flight was satisfactory. The following day, Sneller's father approached Thompson and asked him what the problem was with his son going solo. The reply was that he was waiting for the insurance to come through. Later that day, the young pupil flew with

DH.82A Tiger Moth G-AHPZ was blown over during refuelling in 1946, it's a wonder that there was no fire. Even the car and the control tower were not seriously damaged, the Moth was still flying in 1952.

Pittock for another half hour. This was his last flight in Thompson's aircraft and he eventually qualified for an 'A' licence with the Kent Flying Club. It subsequently came to light that Thompson had broken the law by using his aircraft for hire and reward without the necessary insurance and authority, as had Pittock by giving flying instruction while being unqualified to do so. As it turned out, both parties involved in the alleged case of unauthorised flying were not prosecuted, although the Guild of Air Pilots and Air Navigators of the British Empire said that the Ministry of Civil Aviation should take steps to deter others from following this example.

Richard Badger was a wireless operator and air gunner on Lancasters during the war and afterwards got a civil radio licence. He joined a firm called British Aviation Services, delivering aircraft all over the world. This firm was associated with Silver City, which started a car ferry service and some charter services from Lympne, where Badger remained, on and off, until about 1953, flying from Blackbushe Airport in between on Hermes aircraft.

While at Lympne, he got a private pilot's licence on a Tiger Moth, G-AHND, and bought the aircraft from the instructor who was retiring. He flew it around locally, and to Le Touquet and Ostend, to increase his flying hours. One day the Lympne manager asked if he could fly with him

Hawker Hurricane F.Mk.VIII Trainer G-AMAU, flown by Group Captain Peter W. Townsend, the famous Battle of Britain pilot, in the 1950 National Air Races. Sporting an overall deep blue colour scheme, it must have been an impressive sight landing at Lympne.

DH.89A Dragonfly G-AMKE was destroyed by fire on 30 June 1950, when the aircraft caught fire during refuelling. To save the company some embarrassment as to who flew the aircraft, their name was painted over on the fuselage just under the cabin window.

locally, having apparently been asked by the company to look around for a possible site for a new airport. Badger recalls:

In 1951, I decided to try to obtain a private pilot's licence and commenced training on a DH Tiger Moth from Lympne Airport in Kent, where I was based (the Tiger Moth was a very basic aircraft, no brakes, a skid for a tail wheel, no radio only the most basic instruments). I obtained the licence in November of that year, then later got a twin rating on a Miles Gemini (limited to 12,500 lbs all up weight). As the instructor who had taught me was retiring, he offered me the chance of buying the Tiger Moth (G-AHND) for £250!

As my intention was to obtain a commercial pilot's licence eventually, this seemed a good way of building up some cheap flying hours to the amount required for the commercial licence. One of the local flights that I did was to fly the station manager at Lympne around the area to look for the most likely spot to build a new airport. With Lympne being high (about 350 feet) we were often stopped flying by fog and low cloud and it was decided to find, and build, a less weather prone airport. This is now Lydd Airport.

There was one incident I remember vividly, shortly after getting my PPL [private pilot's licence]. I decided I would try going across the Channel in the Tiger Moth to Le Touquet, in France. It was one of those golden days, where you couldn't see either the sea or the sky (no artificial horizon either), although I kept glancing over my shoulders to glimpse the white cliffs of Dover, but they soon disappeared and I soon began to feel the odd G forces on my sides. With no artificial horizon and only turn and slip, altimeter, and airspeed instruments, I realized that I was in a peculiar attitude in the sky and would have to do something pretty quickly.

DH.82A Tiger Moth G-AHND which Richard Badger bought and flew from Lympne where he learnt to fly in 1951. This aircraft which had also flown with the RAF serial T6913 remained flying until it was written off on 8 April 1966.

Fortunately, I remembered something my instructor had said once: 'If you ever get stuck and don't know which way up you are, look at the turn and slip meter and use your hands on the bottom needle and your feet on the top.' Well, I don't know if that was the right way, but I did it and managed to keep on an even keel until the French coast thankfully came in sight. It sure taught me a lesson to make sure that there was good visibility and a horizon before going across the Channel again.

Although I flew the Tiger Moth quite a lot locally, and to Ostend and Le Touquet, I never managed to get enough flying hours in. Plus, our company had now obtained a trooping contract using the Handley Page Hermes aircraft to transport troops to various bases around the world like Hong Kong, Aden, Lagos, Singapore and Nairobi. As I was quite busy on these trooping flights I had to give up the Tiger Moth and sold it to Ramsgate Flying Club for £150. If only I could have kept it, it would now be worth many thousands of pounds. The Hermes aircraft that we were using were four-engine planes but had to be modified to meet military requirements [for example, rearward-facing seats, and to be able to use 100 octane fuel, which was in general use then, and not the 115 octane that the Hermes had been using].

Silver City

At Lympne Airport on Tuesday 13 July 1948, a Bristol Freighter, G-AGVC, was loaded with a 16 hp Armstrong Siddeley Lancaster saloon. After the loading had been completed, it took off from Lympne and flew the forty-two miles across the English Channel to Le Touquet. This twenty-five-minute journey by the Bristol Freighter was the inaugural service of what was to become Silver City's most famous route. It was operated under a BEA associate agreement and also in conjunction with the two motoring organisations, the AA and the RAC.

The Bristol Freighter could carry up to two cars and their occupants at a cost of £32 per car and four passengers for a one-way trip. Although this was a good deal more expensive than the cost of the sea ferry, the swiftness of Silver City's operation ensured instant success for the airline in this enterprising venture. Silver City continued to operate the route for almost three months, until 7 October, when the airline ended the service for the duration of the winter. During its period of operation, some 174 cars and their occupants had been ferried safely across the Channel, and the success of this first short season meant that many more were to follow.

Another major occupation for Silver City's Bristol Freighter fleet was found with the advent of the Berlin airlift. On 12 September 1948, one of the airline's Wayfarer aircraft joined the airlift, followed by a second aircraft two days later. These aircraft flew their first sorties from the aerodrome at Wunstorf on the 18 September, and flying continued until 24 November 1948, when the Wayfarers were withdrawn from the airlift. However, the airline continued to take part in the airlift using pure Bristol Freighters.

These aircraft, the first of which had arrived in West Germany on 12 October 1948, continued to fly sorties into Berlin until being withdrawn on 5 February 1949. By this time, the four aircraft, G-AGVB, G-AGVC, G-AHJC and G-AHJO, had flown a total of 213 sorties, amassing some 620 hours of flying time, and were the only twin-engine aircraft still operating on the airlift. They had established for themselves an enviable reputation for reliability and efficiency. For example, on one day, 9 December 1948, G-AGVB had carried a total of 76,400 lb of food, machinery, Red Cross supplies and other goods from Wunstorf and Hamburg to Gatow Airport in Berlin.

With the return of its Bristol Freighters to England, Silver City Airways increased its charter activities with these aircraft, and during March several bloodstock flights were made by these freighters. One of these flights involved the carriage of three racehorses from Ireland to Whitchurch on behalf of the Curragh Bloodstock Agency. In April 1949, one of the freighters flew a cargo of livestock to Malta, and on its return flight it was chartered to transport two and a half tons of strawberries from Orange to Blackbushe on 24 April. The last flight in a series of four livestock charters to Malta was made by G-AICT on 10 May 1949. The livestock consisted of thirty-three pedigree cattle selected from British farms to enable Maltese farmers to establish stud farms and to provide the islanders with adequate milk supplies.

As well as cattle and horses, the Bristol Freighters undertook a number of charters carrying cargoes of pigeons. Four thousand were placed aboard two Bristol Freighters at Bovingdon and transported to Brussels on 17 June to take part in the Chronicle Cup race. By the end of the summer, Silver City's Bristol Freighters had made visits to Cambridge, Dublin and Paris on several occasions, carrying a number of racehorses, and this activity provided the airline with a regular source of income from British, French and Irish racehorse owners. Although these flights were confined mainly to Europe, the company's freighters did occasionally make trips to other parts of the world. On 14 November, one of these aircraft left London with five tons of DDT on board destined for Khartoum, and after unloading the DDT the aircraft took on a damaged helicopter and flew it back to Britain on behalf of its owners, Pest Control.

Early in January 1949, Silver City Airways received permission from the Ministry of Civil Aviation to resume the Lympne–Le Touquet vehicle ferry service. One difference compared with the previous year was that there were two rates for the carriage of cars – for vehicles up to 14 feet in length the cost was £27; for those longer than 14 feet the cost was £32. The route was reinstated during the week prior to Easter, the first Channel crossing being made by one of the Bristol Freighters on 13 April. In 1949, this service was run in co-operation with a French charter company, Société Commerciale Aérienne du Littoral (later to become Compagnie Air Transport). Initially, Silver City operated three services a day in each direction between Lympne and Le Touquet, but this was increased if there was sufficient traffic. It was an immediate success and over eight hundred cars had used the air ferry service to cross the Channel by the middle of June.

On 10 July, the airline carried the British Alpine Trials team, consisting of five cars, their drivers and co-drivers, from Lympne to Le Touquet. They were flown across the Channel on three of Silver City's normal flights. On 5 August, Silver City carried its thousandth car on the air ferry, and total bookings by this time exceeded 2,000. The busiest day of the summer was 28 July 1949, when four Bristol Freighters made a total of twenty-three round trips carrying a total of sixty-three cars. By the end of October, 2,400 cars, 10,000 passengers and thirty motorcycles had been carried between Lympne and Le Touquet. As a result of the almost overwhelming success of this service, Silver City Airways announced early in October that the air ferry would remain in operation throughout the winter. However, from 1 November 1949 onwards, the company ran only an on-demand service, although over the Christmas period up to three or four services a day were run until the middle of January 1950.

At the beginning of the 1949 season, most of the cars carried by Silver City were flown on the leg from Lympne to Le Touquet, and the airline found that there were fewer vehicles to carry on the return trip to Lympne. Rather than return empty to Lympne, the freighters carried various cargoes, including sixty tons of fruit on nineteen flights from Le Touquet. The success of this service was as much due to the high serviceability rate of the Bristol Freighter as it was to the hardworking and enterprising staff at both Le Touquet and Lympne. The general manager of Silver City's car ferry service was L. Thornhill, who had previously been with the Bristol Aeroplane Company and Flight Refuelling Ltd.

With the reduction in the number of car ferry flights during the winter months, Silver City was able to transfer the majority of its Bristol Freighters to charter work. On 23 January 1950, one of these aircraft carried a two-and-a-half-ton aero engine from Frankfurt to London on behalf of American Overseas Airlines. Numerous flights were still being made carrying racehorses around Europe, and the freighters were often hired to carry bulky or outsize loads. On 1 April, Silver City restarted its summer schedules on its vehicle ferry service to Le Touquet, and for the 1950 summer season the airline operated a fleet of six Bristol Freighters, including those flown by its French associates. The rates for cars were the same as those for 1949, and in order to try to increase aircraft utilisation, Silver City introduced a new motor-powered loading ramp driven by a 2 hp JAP engine.

At quiet times during the summer, Silver City's Bristol Freighters undertook a large number of charter flights. One such was on 11 June 1950, when three horses were flown from Le Bourget to Blackbushe, and a further three from Dublin to Blackbushe. On the 12th, three more horses were flown from Cormeilles to Blackbushe. During the following week, twenty-four cows were carried from Lympne to Le Touquet aboard three Bristol Freighters, and the airline subsequently made regular cattle-carrying flights across the Channel, so that by the end of the second year, 150 animals had made the crossing. Some had been bought by the Italian authorities, who insisted that the animals had to be in calf when they arrived in Italy, but difficulties arose as a result of this requirement and the shipments became irregular.

By July, the car ferry service itself was well under way and up to twelve services operated daily in each direction, rising to twenty-four by mid-August. Amongst the many interesting cargoes to be carried on the ferry route were ten polo ponies belonging to an Argentine polo team, which were flown from Le Touquet to Lympne prior to playing against an English team. One very enterprising London taxi owner, Leslie Wightman, operated a fleet of three taxis on a London to Paris car service, using the air ferry link between Lympne and Le Touquet for part of the journey.

Silver City Airways carried 3,950 cars and 900 motorcycles on its Lympne to Le Touquet route during the 1950 summer season. This represented an increase of 40 per cent on the total carried in 1949, and 30 per cent more flights were flown in 1950 as compared to the previous year. For the winter of 1950, however, the airline decided to suspend its vehicle ferry route and to transfer the Bristol Freighter fleet to charter work.

During October 1950, three Bristol Freighters completed a total of 40,000 miles on charter flights, including a series of six flights made to Berlin carrying British exhibits to the Berlin Trade Fair. Five charter flights involved the carriage of ship's crews to Alexandria, Antwerp, Gibraltar, Gothenburg and Malta. To undertake these flights, the freighters were fitted out with forty-four passenger seats and were chartered at rates comparable with those charged for Dakotas. Other Bristol Freighters made several trips from Amsterdam to London carrying tin cans on behalf of a soft drinks manufacturer. On each trip, a Bristol Freighter was able to uplift 1,500 cans. One important charter flight made by Silver City during the winter involved taking Winston Churchill from London to Marrakesh on 17 December 1950 aboard the airline's leased DC-l, the aircraft then remaining in Morocco with Churchill until early in the New Year.

For the 1951 Lympne to Le Touquet vehicle ferry service, Silver City Airways acquired two more Bristol Freighters in the spring to bring the fleet's strength up to five aircraft. A number of others of the type were flown by the company's French associate, Compagnie Air Transport. By the time that the summer schedules commenced in April 1951, Silver City had already received 2,500 advance bookings, and at the height of the season the company was making thirty round trips a day between Lympne and Le Touquet. However, by the end of August the ferry business was beginning to quieten down once more, so, as before, the airline transferred its Bristol Freighter fleet to other work.

A freighter was dispatched to Berlin to carry awkward and bulky cargoes out of the German city, while a second freighter flew a number of cargo services from Dublin to Liverpool and Manchester on behalf of Aer Lingus, following a shipping line dispute. On 18 September, a Silver City Bristol Freighter left Bourn, near Cambridge, for Khartoum with a helicopter on board. This flight, and a second undertaken four days later, was completed on behalf of Pest Control. October saw the operation of a number of cargo charter flights to Amsterdam, Antwerp and Paris, and the carriage by four Bristol Freighters of British equipment for display in Berlin.

In November 1951, Silver City Airways was awarded a contract for the airlift of 1,800 cows from Lympne to Le Touquet. For over six weeks, a Bristol Freighter took off from Lympne every ninety minutes throughout the day carrying these animals at the rate of 300 each week. Each Bristol Freighter took eight cows per flight, and this contract helped to keep the company's fleet busy for much of the winter. Early that month, Silver City negotiated a ten-year associate agreement for the continued operation of the Lympne to Le Touquet vehicle ferry link, and as a result the company acquired the three Bristol Freighters flown by Compagnie Air Transport. Another important contract awarded to Silver City in November was for the carriage of Rootes Group cars across the English Channel. Sunbeam Talbots, Hillman Minxes and Humber Snipes were all driven to Lympne, where they were loaded on board a waiting Bristol Freighter and flown to Le Touquet. From here the cars were driven to motor agents and car showrooms in Paris and elsewhere.

Silver City's vehicle ferry operations in 1951 had been more successful than ever before. For example, during August the airline had carried two and a half times as much cargo into Lympne as the combined totals of cargo handled at both Heathrow and Northolt airports. During that month alone, Silver City Airways had transported almost 3,000 cars across the Channel, and the airline's Bristol Freighters accounted for over 85 per cent of all the air transport movements at Lympne. During the whole of the 1951 season, the company carried a total of 13,000 vehicles and 30,000 passengers on the Lympne to Le Touquet route.

The company had also received permission to open a scheduled vehicle ferry route linking Eastleigh Airport, near Southampton, with Maupertus Airport at Cherbourg. Unusually, this route was inaugurated by the airline during the middle of the winter, with the first car being flown by a Silver City Bristol Freighter on 5 December 1951. However, a regular scheduled service did not commence until 10 January 1952, by which time the necessary radio equipment had been installed at Cherbourg. Two Bristol Freighters were based at Eastleigh for this route, and until the vehicle ferry business had substantially built up, these Bristol Freighters were engaged in the carriage of cheese from Cherbourg to Southampton. By the end of the year, the freighters were importing eighteen tons of French cheese into Britain every week, this service continuing well into 1952.

By 1952, Silver City Airways employed a staff of 167 people, including more than a dozen pilots. The airline had flown over half a million revenue miles for the first time ever in 1951, and with further expansion in view, it placed an order with the Bristol Aeroplane Company for six of its special Super 170 Bristols.

The board of directors now consisted of S. J. Gordon, Gen. Sir Edwin Morris, S. A. Tennant, Air Cdre G. J. Powell and M. W. G. Franklin. The

Bristol 170 Mk.IIA G-AIME of Silver City preparing to take on vehicles, at Lympne Airport in the early 1950s. This aircraft was restored on two occasions before being withdrawn from service in October 1953.

airline's chief pilot was Capt. J. Adams, while R. B. Clark was the chief engineer, ensuring the high serviceability rate of the Bristol Freighter fleet.

Throughout the winter of 1951/52, Silver City Airways continued to undertake a wide variety of *ad hoc* charter flights. On 2 February 1952, one of the company's aircraft flew three trailer fire pumps from Blackbushe to Cairo, and on the 11th one of the Bristol Freighters spent a particularly busy day carrying United Nations television equipment from Paris to Southend, four tons of aircraft spares from Southend to Amsterdam, and four tons of metal containers from Amsterdam to Lympne. The company now had two Bristol Freighters based in Berlin, which were carrying well over 500 tons of cargo every month to and from the city.

Bloodstock charters were still a major part of Silver City's programme. On 2 April, the airline's freighters transported two racehorses to Liverpool from Le Touquet to take part in the Grand National, and during Derby week the company was responsible for the carriage of no fewer than twenty racehorses from France to Britain. The spring brought two lucrative contracts for Silver City, and both began on the morning of 7 April. The first involved the carriage of seventy-five tons of office furniture and other equipment from Lympne to Cormeilles. Sixteen flights were needed to transfer all this furniture to France, which was carried on behalf of NATO, and the whole operation was successfully completed within two days. The second contract, for a series of fifty flights between Amsterdam and London carrying a total of one million Dutch lettuces, was completed by the middle of May.

Silver City Airways was one of the few charter companies in Europe with aircraft specially equipped for the transport of horses, and within the British Isles the airline held a virtual monopoly on such services. On 19 July, four horses belonging to the Canadian Olympic equestrian team were flown from Bristol to Helsinki. Four days later, the French equestrian team, consisting of eight horses, ten cavalry officers and a ton of saddles, was flown from Paris to take part in the Olympic Games. This charter was followed three days later by the airlift of the Egyptian equestrian team from Paris to Helsinki. Other livestock to travel aboard Silver City's freighters during 1952 were many thousands of pigeons, which the airline regularly transported between Antwerp, Brussels, Copenhagen, Nantes and Paris.

On 14 April, Silver City inaugurated its first scheduled service to Belgium, linking Southend with Ostend, its third vehicle ferry route, the others being Lympne to Le Touquet, and Southampton to Cherbourg. The airline also put forward plans for a fourth ferry service between Southampton and the Isle of Wight. For this fifteen-mile air ferry, Silver City proposed a fare £4 6s 0d for a car up to 12 feet in length, which was almost £1 more than the equivalent fare using the more traditional sea ferry between Southampton and Cowes. This route was not opened in 1952, but Silver City's other vehicle ferry routes flourished. In the week prior to the Le Mans twenty-four-hour endurance race, on the weekend of 14/15 June, Silver City carried ten British racing cars and their drivers from Southampton to Cherbourg. Also in June, Silver City added another Bristol Freighter to its fleet when it took over the operation of an aircraft previously used by BEA for emergency engine-carrying flights. Under an agreement with BEA, Silver City would provide an aircraft to carry spare engines at BEA's request.

On 1 July 1952, Silver City Airways completed its 10,000th crossing of the Channel without a single accident. By this time, the airline's Bristol Freighters had carried over 24,000 vehicles across the English Channel. During July, one and a half tons of ship's spares were flown from Copenhagen to Cardiff, two horses were carried from Manchester to Le Bourget, and a further four were transported from Düsseldorf to Blackbushe.

August saw one of Silver City's Bristol Freighters flying thirty-two Tropic Airways passengers from Malta to Johannesburg, and four Air Ministry charters involved the airlift of servicemen from Sylt in Germany to Renfrew and Aldergrove. On 2 August, one of the company's freighters, G-AIMH, carried two Hillman Minx export models and two Hercules bicycles from Lympne to Ypenburg, in Holland, arriving at this Dutch airfield during an air display. At the time, it was the largest aircraft ever to land there.

From Berlin, two of Silver City's Bristol Freighters continued to ply their way along the 160-mile-long corridor to Hamburg carrying cargo. During one two-week period early in September, these aircraft completed fifty round trips carrying almost 500 tons of cargo, while a number of other flights were made to Vienna carrying theatrical equipment. Also in September, three Connaught Formula 1 racing cars were flown from Lympne to Milan to participate in the Italian Grand Prix, and ships' crews charters were undertaken to Bilbao and Gibraltar. Throughout October and November, several flights were made between Blackbushe and Dukhan carrying cargo on behalf of the Iraq Petroleum Company, while on 29 October, two Bristol Freighters carried consignments of electrical coils from Manchester to Helsinki for a Finnish power station. Other charters made by the company during the autumn saw its freighters visiting Algiers, Ankara, Paris and Tripoli, carrying cargoes varying from general merchandise to gold bullion.

During 1952, Silver City Airways had carried a total of over 11,000 vehicles and 27,000 passengers on its scheduled vehicle ferry services across the English Channel. To achieve these figures, its freighters had taken off and landed more than 9,000 times without mishap. However, the company dropped the Southend to Ostend service from its network at the end of the season.

For winter 1952/53, Silver City sent five of its freighters to Berlin to operate the freight service to Hamburg, while a sixth aircraft was dispatched to East Africa to undertake a photographic survey contract. One of the Bristol Freighters sent to Berlin, G-AICM, was written off on 19 January 1953, when it force-landed on railway lines when entering Berlin. Although no one was injured in this accident, the aircraft was damaged beyond economic repair. G-AICM had left Berlin for Hamburg with three tons of cargo on board, but on arrival at Hamburg the captain discovered that a landing was impossible due to fog. The aircraft had then diverted to Bremen, but fog also precluded a landing at this aerodrome, so it had then been decided to return to Tempelhof Airport, Berlin. However, luck was not with the freighter because the ground control approach service at Berlin was not operating, and eventually the captain was forced to land the aircraft on railway lines outside the city.

It had been announced in late December 1952 that Silver City had won a contract to establish a network of air services within the new state of Libya. The new airline was partly capitalised by the Libyans and was managed by Silver City Airways. Two Bristol Freighters formed the basis of this new airline's fleet, and these aircraft started flying services within Libya on 1 February 1953. On this date, one of the freighters carried over a ton of mail, a Morris Minor and a handful of passengers from Tripoli to Benghazi. Flying in the colours of Libyan Airways, these freighters provided a daily service between the two Libyan cities. Weekly services were also flown from Tripoli to Sebha, and from Benghazi to Kufra. The Bristol Freighters were equipped to carry nine second-class passengers in the cabin usually used for car ferry passengers, while a further twenty third-class passengers were seated inside the after-part of the hold. The aircraft was also capable of carrying up to two and a half tons of cargo. When not required for these scheduled services, the freighters were used for flights from Tripoli to Malta and Tunis, carrying British troops normally stationed in Libya who wished to visit Malta and Tunis during their leave at a greatly reduced air fare.

The general manager of the company in Libya was Kenneth Jolly, who had previously been Silver City's freight officer. Jolly was based in Tripoli, while his deputy, F. O. Foster, was based in Benghazi. In addition to carrying passengers on these scheduled services within Libya, a camel or horse could travel between Tripoli or Benghazi for a single fare of £24, while a goat or sheep could make the same journey for only £4.

Returning to the company's situation in the United Kingdom, Silver City was busily preparing for its summer season, during which the airline hoped that it would carry four times as many cars across the Channel as it had done in 1952. For the 1953 season, the airline received approval to operate vehicle ferry services connecting Lympne with Le Touquet and Ostend, Southampton with Bembridge (Isle of Wight), Cherbourg, Guernsey and Jersey, and Gatwick with Le Touquet. Over the Easter period, six of the company's Bristol Freighters carried 252 employees of the Frigidaire Company from Lympne to Le Touquet for their annual factory outing. Silver City broke all its previous records that Easter, a total of 250 cars, 100 motorcycles and 150 bicycles being flown across the Channel, in addition to over 1,000 passengers.

By April 1953, two of the new larger series Bristol Freighter 32s had entered service with Silver City, and on the 15th of the month one of these aircraft inaugurated the airline's new scheduled air ferry service between Gatwick and Le Touquet. This route was flown twice daily throughout the summer, and these new Superfreighters could carry three small cars and twenty passengers, although if the bulkhead was moved then they could accommodate any three cars and twelve passengers. The same month also saw Silver City purchasing three Dakotas from the RAF for use on general passenger and freight charter work.

In 1953 Silver City opened the Lympne–Ostend route using the Superfreighter Mk.32 G-AMWA, maintaining close links with the AA and RAC using a line-up of their vehicles for publicity.

Late in June 1953, Silver City Airways took delivery of a Breguet Deux-Ponts on lease from its French manufacturer. Capt. C. I. Hopkins collected the aircraft at Toulouse and then flew it to Berlin to set it to work on the cargo run between Berlin and Hamburg. In the first five months of 1953, Silver City's Bristol Freighters amassed a grand total of 56,000 miles while engaged on these flights, and by June fifty round trips were being made every week from Berlin. The arrival of the Deux-Ponts in Berlin meant that the airline could return up to three of its Bristol Freighters to Lympne to assist in its vehicle ferry services across the Channel. However, at the end of September the Deux-Ponts was returned to France, although the airline had considered the acquisition of further Deux-Ponts to supplement its Bristol Freighter fleet. Proposals were also put forward for the introduction of several Blackburn Beverleys, but the latter would not have been available until 1955 at the earliest, all production being committed to the RAF, so Silver City elected to expand its Bristol Superfreighter fleet instead.

By the end of October, Silver City had carried 38,000 vehicles on its vehicle ferry routes during the previous ten months. During the same period in 1952, it had carried a total of 10,344 vehicles, which meant that the company had almost achieved its bold target of quadrupling its traffic in 1953. Altogether, its freighters had now carried 175,000 vehicles and 93,000 passengers across the English Channel.

One problem that Silver City had encountered during 1953 was the poor state of the airfield at Lympne after heavy rain. The company had persistently urged the authorities to improve the facilities at Lympne, but without success. Lympne Airport was operated by the Ministry of Civil Aviation, and Silver City was by a wide margin the Ministry's best customer at Lympne, having paid approximately £12,000 in landing fees in 1952. In February, torrential rain had rendered the airfield's grass surface almost totally unusable as aircraft dug deep ruts into the surface during taxiing and while carrying out power checks prior to take-off. As a result, Silver City temporarily transferred all of its flights to Southend. On 22 September 1953, further heavy rain again caused chaos and disruption at Lympne, and Silver City again moved its operations, this time to West Malling. To avoid any further problems of this nature, the airline announced plans for the construction of its own airport at a site near Dungeness.

Due for completion during 1954, the new airport was to have two concrete runways and a large terminal building to cope with the ever-increasing demands of the vehicle ferry routes. This airport, appropriately named Ferryfield, was opened to traffic on 13 July 1954, and very quickly Silver City transferred most of its services from Lympne. On 17 August, the first helicopter to land at Ferryfield (Silver City's own Westland-

Sikorsky S-51, G-ANLV) flew in from London's South Bank. Ferryfield was soon the busy hub of Silver City's vehicle ferry operations, becoming only the second airfield in the country to install a Decca 424 approach radar system, which remains in use at the time of publication of this book.

With the opening of Ferryfield, it was only a matter of time before Silver City would suspend all of its services at Lympne. Thus, on Sunday 3 October 1954, Bristol Freighter G-AGVC flew the company's last service out of Lympne. This last historic flight was bound for Le Touquet, and among the passengers on board were M. D. Morrissey, the BOAC's cargo manager, his wife and their car, and E. C. Mekie, the chairman of Silver City Airways. The freighter used for this final service was also the aircraft that had operated the company's inaugural Lympne to Le Touquet service more than six years earlier. During its six years and almost three months of vehicle ferry operations from Lympne, Silver City Airways' Bristol Freighters had carried a total of 54,600 cars and 208,457 passengers from the Kent airfield.

Skyways

The idea of operating coach-air services between London and various towns on the Continent was first put forward by Eric Rylands in 1953. Rylands was the managing director of both the Lancashire Aircraft Company and Skyways, and in 1954 he applied to the Air Transport Advisory Council (ATAC) for permission to open services from Lympne to Beauvais and Brussels using Dakotas. These services were approved in the spring of 1955, and in July of that year it was announced that Skyways would inaugurate a daily service between Lympne and Beauvais in the autumn. This service was flown in association with a number of long-distance coach operators. Passengers were driven from Victoria coach station in a thirty-two-seat coach and on arrival at Lympne boarded a thirty-two-seat Dakota. This aircraft then flew them to Beauvais, where they boarded a second coach and were driven to Paris.

The airfield at Lympne was acquired by Skyways on a long-term lease from its owner, J. M. Beecham, the airline being responsible for the provision of all the facilities there. Rylands later purchased Lympne Airport after persuading various local farmers to part with some of their land. On 26 September 1955, the inaugural service to Beauvais was flown by two Dakotas, G-AMWV and G-ANAE, piloted by Capts Morgan and Stamp, but for the remainder of the winter just one Dakota maintained this air link. The route had been introduced at a quiet time of the year to enable Skyways to iron out any problems during the winter, thus allowing

A typical scene at Lympne Airport during the 1960s, as passengers leave their coach
to join Avro G-ARMV which crashed in 1965.

it a greater chance of providing the best possible service to the customer
throughout the following summer.

For the summer of 1956, Skyways used two of its own Dakotas on its
coach-air services, together with a third aircraft operated on a two-month
lease from Airwork. The route to Beauvais was a tremendous success from
the outset, and early in 1957 it was announced that Skyways would shortly
open a link between London and Nice. Again, passengers were driven from
Victoria coach station to Lympne, before boarding a Dakota to Lyons.
From Lyons they completed their journey to Nice by means of a coach
driven via the *Route des Grandes Alpes*. The first service to Lyons was due
to be flown by a Skyways Dakota on 9 May 1957, but the introduction
of this route was delayed until May of the following year. However,
throughout the summer of 1957, Skyways maintained a frequency of no
fewer than sixteen return flights per day between Lympne and Beauvais,
and during the year a second coach-air service was introduced, linking
London with Vichy and flown weekly.

The third coach-air service to be started linked London with Brussels.
This route was inaugurated on 17 April 1958 to coincide with the opening
of the Brussels International Exhibition. A twice-daily service was flown
between Lympne and Antwerp for the 1958 season only, passengers
continuing their journey to Brussels by luxury coach. In May, another

coach-air service started, linking London with Montpelier, but the most popular coach-air routes were those to Beauvais and Lyons, and subsequently both of these routes were flown throughout the year, other routes being flown only seasonally. By 1958, licences were also held by Skyways for similar services to Dijon, Fréjus and Tours. A reorganisation within Rylands' companies in the autumn of that year led to the formation of a separate company to operate these coach-air services. This new company, appropriately named Skyways Coach-Air, was registered as an airline company on 9 October 1958 with an initial capital of £1,000 (which was later increased substantially). The coach-air services to Montpelier and Vichy, however, remained the responsibility of Skyways itself, Skyways Coach-Air operating the services to Beauvais and Lyons.

Throughout 1959, 1960 and 1961, services continued for the most part unchanged, although Skyways Coach-Air's Dakotas now regularly flew charters from Gatwick to Beauvais and Le Bourget. During the first week of July 1960, all of the company's Dakotas were present at Gatwick while operating flights to Beauvais and Le Bourget. Many flights were operated to Gatwick when poor weather at Lympne necessitated a diversion to an airport near London in order to reduce the inconvenience to passengers.

In 1960, an annual meeting of the Aerodrome Owners' Association was held to discuss subjects of common interest and to visit local airfields

The East Kent Hunt met at Lympne Airport on the invitation of Skyways. Passengers about to take off were greeted with the sound of hunting horns. The aircraft is C-47B G-AMWX in Skyways of London livery, note the control tower to the right.

to see how owners ran their affairs. The venue was Folkestone, and 100 members and guests were present. Emphasis was on the passenger and freight services that Kent provided to the Continent from Dover harbour and from Lympne and Lydd (Ferryfield) airfields.

The first morning, on 11 October, was spent at the conference headquarters, the Grand Hotel, with a busy agenda covering such subjects as the Ministry of Aviation, customs, aircraft fire-fighting and helicopter transport. One speech was given by AVM Sir Laurence Sinclair, who had left the RAF three months before to become controller of ground services at the Ministry of Aviation. He made no specific statement of ministerial policy towards non-state airfields, but told the delegates that if any of them had any particular suggestions he would like to hear them. He received one from C. M. Newton of Sywell that the Ministry should hand over more of its airfields to the municipalities and use some of the money saved on ground services. Sinclair told his audience that the Ministry was carrying out an intensive study of air traffic control problems, and gave the conference an encouraging speech, saying, 'I really believe civil aviation is on the flood tide; it has at last made an impact on the British public and mass air travel is now a reality.' The remainder of the two-day event was spent visiting local venues, including a tour of Dover docks and a flight to Le Touquet and back.

At Lympne the delegates were welcomed by Skyways' managing director and were shown its facilities for aircraft and passenger handling. An impressive demonstration of firefighting by means of dry chemicals was staged by John Kerr and Company, the Liverpool-based fire equipment company, quickly subduing burning petrol and contaminated alcohol set up in different forms, both static and sprayed. The firm's managing director, H. G. Clements, had spoken at the previous day's lecture session of the merits of dry chemicals in firefighting, emphasising that the risk of explosion was significantly reduced by the use of a dry powder.

A number of financial reorganisations during the 1950s had provided the funds for a major expansion of the Skyways' activities and fleet, culminating in the buy-out of the company in 1961 by Rylands. To accommodate the expanding aircraft fleet and facilities, the older hangar was moved and re-erected by the old fire depot, and was to be used for storage. This was followed by the construction of an attached pair of replacement hangars. It was also suggested at this time that Skyways might use Lympne as a maintenance base for Lockheed Constellations, but the scheme was abandoned because even the new hangars could not accommodate a 29-metre-long aircraft. Despite this, rails were sunk into the hangar floor to enable Constellations to be pushed in sideways using trolleys, but of course these were never used.

Having decided to invest in larger aircraft, Skyways Coach-Air announced that the new Avro 748 would replace its existing Dakota aircraft, Rylands agreeing to purchase three of these forty-four-seater twin-engine turboprop aircraft at a cost of £750,000. The contract was signed in May 1961, and the company's first Avro 748, G-ARMV, arrived at Lympne on Thursday 2 November, commencing a 160-hour certification programme of route flying four days later. This programme was conducted in two nine-day instalments, with a one-day break in between for maintenance. Flown by Skyways' own pilots, this brand-new aircraft visited Beauvais, Lyons, Montpelier and Vichy, visits also being made to Gatwick and Manston after dusk as there were no night flying facilities available at Lympne. At the end of the month G-ARMV was returned to Woodford for pre-delivery checks to be completed in time for its formal hand-over to Skyways on 1 March 1962. This aircraft was scheduled to enter service with the airline on 1 April 1962, but delays occurred and it was not until Tuesday 17 April that Skyways operated its first commercial service with G-ARMV. The airline was therefore not the first company to operate a revenue service with this type of aircraft, this honour going to Aerolíneas Argentinas, which operated its first 748 commercial service on 2 April 1962 between Buenos Aires and Bahía Blanca.

On 17 April 1962, G-ARMV carried thirty-nine passengers and a crew of three from Lympne to Beauvais. This historic flight was piloted by the airline's chief pilot and operations manager, Capt. Morgan, and although it had been hoped to have three 748s in service by the middle of June, only two aircraft served with the company during that year. For the 1962 season, Skyways was also awarded licences to operate inclusive tour charter flights from Lympne to Barcelona, Basle, Luxembourg, Lyons, Palma, Perpignan, Pisa and Venice. The airline also received approval for a twice-daily, all-cargo scheduled service between Lympne and Beauvais using Dakotas. Subsequent applications included requests for winter inclusive tour services from Southend, Manston and Lympne to Barcelona, Basle, Palma and Tenerife using Dakotas, 748s, Constellations, Hermes, DC-3s and DC-6s at a daily frequency. Skyways Coach-Air's associate company, Skyways, was taken over by Euravia in September 1962, but Skyways Coach-Air remained independent of this take-over. Its board of directors now consisted of the chairman Sir Wavell Wakefield, Eric Rylands, Charles F. Dickson and David Gaunt, while the company's senior executives included D. J. Davies (secretary), V. J. Doel (financial controller), J. L. Clarke (traffic and sales manager), Capt. J. S. Morgan (chief pilot) and Mrs. E. Whittaker (public relations officer).

In April 1963, Skyways Coach-Air took delivery of its third Avro 748, and at the end of the season two of the Dakotas, G-AGYZ and G-AMVW, were withdrawn from passenger service to be converted to freighter configuration for operation on the all-cargo route from Lympne to Beauvais. The spring of 1964 saw the introduction of this freight service, but few other significant events took place during the year. However, in 1965, a Castle Donington–Lympne–Beauvais service was introduced at the end of April and the 748s began to operate coach-air services from Lympne to Tours and Vichy in June. Initially, this route was flown once weekly, but for the following season the frequency was increased to provide a daily service. During the spring of 1965, one of the 748s was leased to Leeward Islands Air Transport.

In order to allow Skyways to cope with the heavy Easter traffic, a Schreiner Airways Fokker F.27 Friendship, PH-SAF, was leased for a short period. However, the Friendship was not at home on the grass airfield at Lympne. As it taxied, one of the undercarriage legs sank into soft ground in the south-east corner of the airfield, known by staff as 'Wal's Hole', after Skyways pilot 'Wally' Hagger. Despite the best efforts of the staff it could not be moved, and X-rays were taken of the leg to check for stress fractures. The aircraft was subsequently operated from Lydd.

Perhaps the most notable event of 1965 was the crash of Avro 748 G-ARMV while on a scheduled flight from Beauvais to Lympne on 11 July. The pilot obtained a weather report from Lympne and took off from Beauvais at 3.51 p.m. As the aircraft passed Abbeville, radio contact was established with Lympne and a weather report was obtained that gave a visibility of 1,000 m in drizzle, the cloud ceiling being 200 feet, with a surface wind gusting to 26 knots. The pilot again checked landing conditions at Lympne before commencing an instrument approach and although conditions had not altered significantly since the previous report, he was informed of a slight improvement but that the wind was still gusting. The final instrument approach to runway 20 using radar began four miles from touchdown. The aircraft was in cloud, flying at 1,100 feet in turbulent conditions. Three-and-a-half miles from touchdown, the pilot began to descend at 350 to 400 feet per minute, the equivalent of a three-degree glide path in prevailing conditions. As there was no radar glide path at Lympne, the controller advised the pilot of the height that the aircraft should have been at each mile before touchdown. When G-ARMV was nearly a mile from touchdown the radar controller gave a final heading correction, and at the half-mile point, when the talk-down finished, he told the pilot that the aircraft was lined up with the right-hand edge of the runway.

The rest of the approach was made visually, but the controller continued to track the Avro. He saw it deviate further to the right of the extended centreline as it neared the touchdown point, the pilot reporting that he could see the far boundary of Lympne through heavy drizzle. After maintaining an altitude of 220 feet for a few seconds, the descent was continued and at a quarter of a mile from touchdown at 150 to 200 feet, full flap was selected and power reduced. With the turbulence becoming worse, the pilot realised the aircraft was drifting to the right of the runway but decided not to try to regain the centreline as this would require a turn at low altitude. As G-ARMV approached the airfield boundary the airspeed indicator was fluctuating and an attempt was made to maintain 92 knots, the starboard wing being held down slightly to compensate for port drift. The pilot began the flare out 30 to 40 feet above the ground and as he closed the throttles the starboard wing went down suddenly. Although aware that his aircraft was descending rapidly, the pilot was initially more concerned about restoring lateral level, only at the last moment attempting to check the rate of descent with elevator control, but the aircraft struck the ground heavily on its starboard undercarriage.

After the initial impact, the starboard wing, engine nacelle and undercarriage became separated from the aircraft, which rolled over to starboard and slid along the grass inverted, coming to rest after having swung through approximately 180 degrees. An inspection of the crash scene revealed that G-ARMV first struck the ground on its starboard undercarriage in a starboard wing-down attitude, 150 feet inside the airfield boundary and 170 feet to starboard of the right-hand edge of the runway. There was no fire, and the rescue vehicles and personnel were quickly on the scene, but there was some delay in getting all the passengers out since many of them, disregarding the risk of fire, would not leave the aircraft cabin without their belongings. Fortunately, there were no fatalities and only three of the forty-eight passengers were slightly injured. The four-man crew also escaped injury. Runway 20 had a published landing distance of 2,625 feet and it was 300 feet wide, its direction and outline having at one time been marked out by rectangles cut into the surface to expose the chalk subsoil. At the time of the accident, most of these marks were obliterated, having been overgrown by grass, and there was no approach or runway lighting for this runway, but there were two marker boards indicating the commencement of the landing threshold area. The northern approach, where the accident took place, fell away into a valley for about half a mile at a gradient of about one in forty. At the time, pilots were able to land anywhere on Lympne airfield and were not necessarily confined to the designated runways, provided the direction chosen did not invalidate performance requirements and that reasonable lateral clearance to any obstruction could be maintained.

The undercarriage was down and locked, examination of the port and starboard flap mechanism showing that both flaps were fully extended and capable of normal operation before the wing became detached. It

Wreckage of Avro 748 G-ARMV which crashed at Lympne on 11 July 1965, fortunately there were no fatalities, but it highlighted the need for a concrete runway.

was concluded that the accident was not caused by any structural failure or systems malfunction, and no evidence of bird strike was found. One suggestion was that the aircraft had been the victim of turbulence and wind shear, causing the aircraft to stall, from which the pilot was unable to recover, but there was insufficient evidence to support this idea. The pilot had made the approach to the right of the runway but had not intended to land so far to the right. At the time of the accident, with poor visibility in heavy drizzle and without runway markers or lighting, a precise visual approach would not have been an easy matter. This, together with the added severe turbulence, could have made excessive demands on the pilot's attention, so perhaps it would have been wiser to abandon the approach and overshoot the runway.

Both the pilot and co-pilot were experienced, the captain having a total of 6,799 flying hours, of which 2,732 were as pilot-in-command. On the day of the crash he had been on duty for nine hours. The documentation of the aircraft was in order and it had been properly maintained in accordance with an approved maintenance schedule, its weight and load distribution being within authorised limits and there being no evidence of pre-crash failure or malfunction. It was concluded that the accident resulted from a heavy landing following a steeper than normal approach.

Everyone knew that the surface of the airfield at Lympne was inadequate.

Although the Dakotas had little problem, the heavier Avro 748 did cause some damage to the surface and this led to the temporary closure of the airfield, Rylands managing to get planning permission to lay a concrete runway. Prior to its construction, parallel runways were established. As one became rutted through use, a second parallel runway was used, goose-neck flares being positioned on either side in order to assist aircraft landing and taking off.

Two Avro 748s were acquired from BKS Air Transport in March 1967, and in October the state-owned Transport Holding Company purchased a 50 per cent interest in Skyways, with the remainder of the shares being retained by Rylands. Late in 1967, work began on the new 4,500-foot-long concrete runway at Lympne. It is interesting to note that despite the Bomb Disposal Unit's efforts to clear the site of pipe mines five years earlier (see Chapter 11), yet another was dug up, Independent Television News reporting that 'the mine is thought to be German and dropped during World War 2'. The BDU arrived from their base at Horsham and carried out a controlled explosion. A new, cheap, construction technique – soil stabilisation – was used to lay the runway, which meant that much of the soil under the surfacing was injected with cement. It was supposed to solidify, achieving a firm base, but within a month the surface was subsiding in certain areas at the northern end, so repairs had to be made. Perhaps as a result of the experience at Lympne, this technique was not adopted for the construction of other runways. The new runway came into use for the first time on 11 April 1968, when an Avro 748 took off with a full load of passengers made up of airline employees and the contractors who had constructed it. In addition to the concrete runway, Skyways was also responsible for building taxiways and a new terminal building and the installation of a Decca 124 radar system at Ashford Airport.

In January 1969, the Ford Motor Company contracted Skyways to operate a regular service between Stansted and Cologne. This route was flown twice daily in each direction with 748s, Skyways supplying cabin service to first-class standard. Initially, both G-ARMW and G-ARMX were used for these flights, but in January 1970, G-AXVG took over, with a thirty-two-seat executive passenger configuration. These 748s also flew Ford personnel to Liverpool and Swansea. During 1970, Skyways introduced summer-only services from Luton and Ashford to Ostend, but neither of these proved to be particularly profitable and both were suspended at the end of the season. By this time, coach-air services were also flown to Clermont-Ferrand, but the services to Lyons, Tours and Vichy had been withdrawn.

The board of directors had changed considerably during the 1960s, and in 1970 the company's executives consisted of Eric Rylands (managing director), G. Sykes (secretary), J. Worrell (general sales manager), R. Chadwick (airport manager), J. Clarke (commercial manager), P. Davis (passenger service manager), J. McTaggart (technical manager), D. J. Clark (chief engineer), Capt. E. W. Havard (chief pilot and operations manager), K. Palmer (purchasing manager) and J. Stergard (manager of French operations). One Skyways Coach-Air employee, Dick Gilbert, who is the company's archivist, remembers his days at Lympne:

In the weeks of the summer of 1966, Lympne Airport was beautiful, as airports go. Perched on an escarpment above the old Kent fishing town of Hythe, the well kept flower beds opposite the senior air traffic controller's timber cottage guarding the gateway were bordered by the fading colours of the trees surrounding Lympne Country Club, spiritual home of the Cinque Ports Flying Club since the earliest days of British aviation, but now housing only memories of its former halcyon days. The airport was all grass, humped in the middle and very small. Skyways flew all their services from it, operated it and owned it. I arrived for my first day's work there as a flight dispatcher very wet behind the ears and somewhat surprised to find that the only other member of the department, the operations superintendent, had used my arrival as an excuse to catch up on three weeks long overdue holiday. I was straight in the deep end, but could not have wished for a more friendly and co-operative team to ease the way.

Skyways Coach-Air was the current operating arm of the long-established empire of Eric Rylands, Berlin Airlift entrepreneur and former managing director of Skyways of London, at one time the largest independent in the country with nearly a hundred transport aircraft wearing its colours over an eighteen-year post-war history. Skyways of London still existed as a name on the door of a tiny cobweb-strewn office in a corner of the hangar, containing piles of dusty ledgers and an ancient Dickensian figure whom nobody knew – he may very well have been dead for years. Lympne Airport Ltd, also part of the group, owned the airport. The vast hangar contained fascinating milestones of the organisation's history; dismantled radial-engined Lancashire Aircraft Prospectors, the none-too-successful agricultural aircraft derived from the Edgar Percival E.P.9 in the early sixties; a strange prototype hopper vehicle built by Blackburn Engineering; and G-AGPG, one of the very first Avro XIXs built, presented as a personal aircraft to Eric Rylands by Avro in recognition of the value of Skyways' order for the first three production 748s. I never saw it used until, in late 1967, it was wheeled into unaccustomed daylight and flew off to replace G-ALIH as the experimental ship for Ekco Electronics. It must have had very low hours for its age.

The prohibitive cost of the concrete runway and the airfield expansion led to a financial crisis at Skyways Coach-Air. Between 1967 and the end of 1970, the Transport Holding Company advanced loans of over £1 million, and in November 1970, Skyways requested a further loan of £300,000 to finance its operations through the winter months. The airline subsequently received two instalments of £100,000 each, but the permission needed to advance the remaining amount was not given by the Department of the Environment.

As a result, the airline announced that it was unable to continue operations, and on 20 January 1971, Skyways Coach-Air ceased operations. Its four 748s and three Dakotas were grounded at Ashford

A clear view of Ashford Airport during its occupancy by Skyways in the 1960s. To the top right of the scene is the runway. The terminal, gatehouse, hangars in excellent condition, parked are Avro 748s and the DC-3/C-47B of this successful company.

Airport while attempts were made to get the airline airborne again. At the end of January, a group of ten senior employees of Skyways Coach-Air led by John Knox (who had joined the company as commercial manager in November 1970) put in a bid for the airline. On the morning of 8 February 1971, the new airline, now known as Skyways International, resumed full scheduled operations when one of the 748s reopened the Ashford to Beauvais service. Knox became managing director of Skyways International, but in November his place was taken by two joint managing directors, Nigel Warshaw and Leonard Hastings, and in February 1972, Dan-Air began negotiations for the take-over of Skyways International. Contracts were exchanged with Sterling Securities on 11 February, followed by completion of the deal on 12 April, operations continuing under the (interim) Dan-Air Skyways name. The price paid for the airline was £650,000 – comprising £625,000 for the four 748s and £25,000 for various vehicles and ground handling equipment. The airport at Ashford was not included in the deal, although Dan-Air did take up the offer of a short-term lease on the airfield. Subsequently, Skyways International became known as Dan-Air Skyways and eventually all operations were fully integrated with those of Dan-Air.

One of the more unusual aircraft operated and owned by Skyways Ltd had been purchased in 1952. Avro Anson Mk 19 Series 1 G-AGPG, referred to by Dick Gilbert, had been built at Yeadon in June 1946. This aircraft remained with the company for sixteen years, converted by Avro to a Series 2. It was later sold to Ekco Aviation Ltd and used for evaluating radar equipment, which gave the aircraft an unusual appearance with its extended nose section.

Skyways Cargo Airline existed as the only surviving part of the once famous British airline company named Skyways. Skyways Cargo Airline's history can be traced back to April 1967 when a company named Air Freight was founded to act as general sales agent to Skyways Coach-Air at Lympne. This activity continued for three years until 1970, when Skyways' three Dakotas were transferred to Air Freight. However, these aircraft continued to fly all their freight schedules from Lympne to Beauvais in the colours of Skyways until Skyways Coach-Air was placed in liquidation and the Dakotas were painted in full Air Freight colours. On 21 February 1971, this company reopened the former Skyways scheduled cargo services from Lympne to Antwerp and Beauvais. The major shareholders in this company were Eric Rylands Ltd, Sea Freight Ltd and Beauvais Transit SA.

Throughout 1971, the three Dakotas plodded their way across the English Channel several times daily carrying cargo to Antwerp and Beauvais. Charter flights were also undertaken, including many on behalf of car manufacturers carrying vehicle components to Belgium and West

Germany. In October 1972, the company bought out the ailing South West Aviation, the purchase of this company adding a fourth Dakota to Air Freight's fleet. Few changes took place during the following two years, but with the ending of commercial activities at Lympne Airport in October 1974, Air Freight moved its operating base to Lydd on the last day of the month. By this time, Air Freight had also opened a freight office at Heathrow Airport, and cargo collected at this office was now driven to Lydd by lorry before being flown across the Channel.

Air Kruise

Wg Cdr H. C. Kennard formed Air Kruise in the summer of 1946. It started pleasure flying and charter flying from Lympne airfield with a Miles Messenger and Percival Q.6. Hugh Kennard had served throughout the Second World War in Fighter Command, and he now took up the position of chairman and managing director of Air Kruise. As a member of the RAuxAF, he had kept in close touch with military flying and on one occasion flew a Meteor F.3 into Lympne, an event which must have caused some heads to turn and from which the local aircraft spotters have probably never recovered.

An Airspeed Consul was added in February 1947, and during the summer months, in addition to pleasure flying at Lympne, Air Kruise operated many cross-Channel charter flights to towns in northern France and Belgium, these continuing over the next three years. In April 1950, the company acquired its first Dragon Rapide, and this aircraft opened a thrice-daily service from Lympne to Le Touquet on 15 July. This proved to be so popular that a second Rapide was soon acquired to help boost capacity, Capt. P. Cowell being appointed chief pilot. The company also took over the operation of Ramsgate Airport, reopening the airfield on 27 June 1953 under a lease from Ramsgate Corporation. From there, Air Kruise operated scheduled passenger services through Lympne to Le Touquet and Ostend from June onwards. These services were flown with Dragon Rapides under the title of Trans Channel Airways, the aircraft carrying both Air Kruise and Trans Channel Airways titling.

At Ramsgate, Air Kruise set up Ramsgate Flying Club, using an Auster Autocrat and a Tiger Moth, while another associate company, Skyfotos, used an Autocrat for aerial photographic work from Ramsgate. The Messenger was still used by Air Kruise for pleasure flying, the aircraft flying mainly from Ramsgate on this task, although Lympne still remained as Air Kruise's main base. During 1953, the company was taken over by British Aviation Services, which also operated services from Lympne under the guise of Silver City Airways. However, Air Kruise's operations continued unchanged except for the transfer of two Dakotas to the company for the operation of its scheduled services. Kennard remained with Air Kruise but also joined the board of directors of British Aviation Services. By 1954, Air Kruise was flying scheduled passenger services from Lympne to Ostend, Le Touquet, Basle, Birmingham and Zurich, carrying over 25,000 passengers on these services during the year.

The acquisition of further Dakotas in 1955 led Air Kruise to expand its inclusive tour charter services, which were now flown on behalf of several leading tour operators. By this time, all former Lympne services were being flown from Lydd and, in addition to the scheduled services to Le Touquet and Ostend, Air Kruise was flying summer services to Basle, Geneva, Turin, Venice, Salzburg, Copenhagen and Lyon. Inclusive tour charter flights were also made from Manchester to Ostend, and from Birmingham to Ostend and Basle, using Dakota aircraft. The Dakotas were also used for a limited amount of passenger and freight charter work, including the transport of many refugees to Britain after the Hungarian revolution.

Air Kruise's 1956 operations were further expanded by the transfer of three Bristol Wayfarers from Silver City, and these aircraft operated alongside the Dakotas on many of Air Kruise's inclusive tour services to the Continent, which by now were the most extensive of any British airline. One of the largest programmes flown by Air Kruise was on behalf of Blue Cars Continental Coach Cruises, using Dakotas. These services were flown from Lydd to Madrid, Barcelona, Palma, Turin, Venice, Basle, Salzburg and Jersey. In addition, numerous other flights were operated to other destinations including Perpignan, Copenhagen and Geneva on behalf of other tour companies. Services were also flown from Blackbushe, and Air Kruise's operations continued throughout 1957 and into 1958, but during that year the aircraft were gradually transferred to Silver City Airways and the name of Air Kruise disappeared.

In 1982, the airfield at Lympne, by then renamed Ashford Airport, was in use by Ashford Parachute Centre, with a Super Cub in residence in July 1983. The Eagle Parachute School also used Lympne before leaving for Headcorn, one reason for the club's move being on safety grounds. In a letter to *Flight* magazine, Terence Inch expressed his concern:

A potential source of danger to aircraft using the cross-Channel corridor to and from the French coast and to members of my parachute club at Lympne airfield is a promulgated drop zone with intensive parachuting operations taking place daily from ground level to 10,000 feet. Up to nine parachutists can be descending either in free fall or under canopy at the same time. The problems started with the closure of Lydd and

The airfield in 1948, and several of the wartime buildings are intact. Two Blister hangars, workshops and the wooden buildings by the main gate remain in use as are the huts to left of Otterpool Lane. The large house bottom left is 'Belle Vue', used in the war and still occupied today.

the suspension of the Lydd control zone and its associated local radio-radar coverage. Aircraft en route to the Continent are now advised either by London information or by Kent radar, who issue warnings of our location and operations to aircraft. Unfortunately, the pilots appear to ignore these warnings completely. At the moment, upwards of five or six aircraft a day fly directly over the drop zone when parachuting is taking place, culminating on Saturday, August 29 in a foreign-registered aircraft flying between two groups of parachutists' canopies. I appeal through your columns for pilots to remain clear of Ashford Airfield during daylight hours to prevent the almost inevitable accident if the current rate of incursions continues.

CHAPTER 11

Kent Gliding Club; reopening as Ashford Airport in 1969 and closure in 1974; Skyfotos; Luscombe Light Aircraft

At the beginning of 1959 it was clear to members of Kent Gliding Club, then currently operating from Detling, that they would have to find a new home – the landowner needed the field for growing hay. Arrangements had been made to take the gliders to Lympne where the club could continue to fly, albeit on a temporary basis, at a weekly cost of two and a half guineas (£2 12s 6d) for use of the facilities there. On 15 March 1959, Peter Gibbs towed the club's T21 and Olympia gliders to the new site behind his Tiger Moth, the remaining aircraft and trucks following by road on the Saturday. The club was, however, still allowed to use the clubhouse, hangar and repair huts at Detling for the time being.

The need for a new, permanent site became more pressing than ever, but certain criteria had to be taken into consideration. Air space was complicated by two main factors: West Malling, the disused RAF base near Maidstone, was due to reopen and would therefore impose restrictions on flying in that area, and the London Control Centre extended east as far as Maidstone. The idea of looking further east posed two major problems. First, too far to the east would result in sea breezes hampering soaring conditions; secondly, a site thus situated would be too far for some members to travel, many of whom lived in London. With these problems in mind, a general club meeting was arranged for 14 April 1959 to discuss the situation and was attended by about forty members. Fruitless efforts had been made to find a new home on the North Downs near Detling and all members were asked to join in the search. Financially, if the new land was to be leased, the rent was expected to come from revenue, but, if purchase was necessary, the capital sum would have to be borrowed. It was believed that certain industrial firms might be willing to lend the money at advantageous terms. For the duration of the club's stay at Lympne, country membership would be available for any member living over fifty miles away.

Operating from Lympne was not easy. Flying was hampered by a low cloud base on the first weekend there, but a week later conditions were much better and the first soaring flights from the new site were made. However, all flying and retrieving activities were under air traffic control, and a green light from the tower had to be seen before either could take place. If there was any mishap, a white light on the tower would summon a club representative to report to the controller. After a time, the club was no longer allowed to operate the trucks for retrieving, so work was started on a reserve using a Ford engine. Two-way radio communications between the tower and the launch point, to control flying, was also tried but was largely unsuccessful.

Meanwhile, the club had settled down to some good flying, and Roy Hubble, Philippa Buckley and Roger Neame (of Shepherd Neame Brewery) achieved Silver rating for distance flying. The annual general meeting was held on 11 July at Kent County Fire HQ at Tovil, near Maidstone, thanks to Commander Fordham, at which all the club's officers were re-elected for the following year.

Four holiday courses were arranged at Lympne for August and September. On 1 September, the weekly charge by Skyways of two and a half guineas for use of the facilities at Lympne was raised to seven guineas (£7 7s). However, it was decided to continue flying there on a monthly basis, subject to review at each committee meeting, especially because of the lower revenue during the winter months. The four courses proved very successful and showed a profit of over £300, which almost covered the club's deficit on flying since using Lympne. As the year ended, the clubhouse at Detling closed, which left them with no real home, and they faced an uncertain future in the next decade.

At the start of 1960, Lympne airfield was waterlogged to such an extent that all flying was prevented apart from on two days. However, the flying club managed to organise six courses for the summer, to bring in some much needed income, a situation not helped by the low attendance of members. The weather improved during the next two months, fifty glider launches being achieved on 13 March, but the club needed to recruit new members. In April, an experimental expedition was made to nearby Stowting Hill, using the club's Olympia glider and winch, and some good flights were achieved. All seemed to be going reasonably well during the spring and summer until local farmers complained to the council in September, leading to all gliding being banned from Stowting. The search for a new location continued, and two sites on the North Downs were being considered. There was good news when ninety acres of land became available at Challock, high on the North Downs, and a two-year struggle to raise enough money to purchase the land began. In November 1960, Roy Hubble introduced the Flying Progress Book, a move to speed up pilot training. However, this endeavour was set back for some time due yet again to poor weather conditions at Lympne. Another temporary site was needed until the site at Challock was finally ready to be handed over to the club.

By 1961, the position at Lympne was good, both financially and for flying, and permission for the club to fly at West Malling was given by the American naval flights now based at that airfield. Unfortunately, the hangar at Lympne and hut space had to be vacated, but this problem was solved when Maidstone Council allowed the flying club to carry out work at Mote Park. At the same time, permission to fly from Challock was progressing well. The severe snow conditions of 1962/63 did not help, although eight glider flights were made at Lympne, despite the big freeze, on 6 January 1963. In March, gliding began again, with a record number of launches. Finally, the club moved from Lympne to its new home at Challock, near Charing, on 15 June 1963, where it has remained ever since, and is one of the UK's most popular gliding clubs.

During 1940/41, lethal devices known as pipe mines had been buried at Lympne as an anti-invasion measure. It would seem that following the closure of RAF Lympne, an unknown number of such mines remained there –a clearance certificate at the time shows that 119 more mines were recovered than were recorded as having been laid by a Canadian unit in 1940 – and in March 1962, No. 2 Bomb Disposal Troop were assigned to recover the explosive devices and dispose of the potential hazards. It is incredible to think that such threats were still present on an active and busy airfield at this time. On 15 March, mine clearance began, the working party including ex-German PoWs who had become naturalised British subjects following the war and were employed by the War Department as civilian workers. Under the control of an Army sergeant, the civilians carried out any tasks necessary to assist the Bomb Disposal Unit personnel who located the end near the surface by means of an electronic instrument and excavated the mine by hand. It was then unscrewed into its separate sections and the pipe tilted to allow the cartridges to slide out before being taken away and destroyed by burning. Detonation of the mine occurred after the seal at one end of the pipe mine had been removed by one of the workers. On one occasion, as the sergeant in charge moved away to supervise the civilians, H. G. Borreck took hold of the end of a pipe and an explosion occurred, killing him and injuring P. Masur. There was no clear evidence as to what caused the accident, but it was thought that the nitroglycerine in the mine was in an unstable condition.

In fact, the first pipe mine dealt with by No. 2 Troop at Lympne had been reported in February 1961. It had been unearthed by a ploughing machine working on the airfield perimeter. Since that time about 25 per cent of the airfield perimeter had been swept and eight mines located and destroyed. Following the accident, an inquest was held at Ashford Magistrates' Court and aircraft traffic was restricted or stopped for some weeks during further checks. Skyways was informed that flight schedules were to continue, leaving one landing strip, 500 feet wide and 3,600 feet long, clear for this purpose. The checks for locating any remaining pipe mines started on 26 November for a period of up to ten weeks, after which the airfield was finally declared safe by the Bomb Disposal Unit. Any repair to disturbed areas of the airfield was left to Skyways, which had to employ skilled labour for this purpose.

In 1958, Sheila Scott took flying lessons at the age of thirty-six at Elstree airfield. Her instructor, David Ogilvie, confessed that he did not find her to be an easy pupil, as she was very nervous, with what he called 'an instability element'. Sheila had suffered from mental illness and, had Ogilvie known this, he would have been reluctant to take her on. Unfortunately, she failed her first attempt at obtaining a private pilot's flying licence, but at the beginning of the New Year 1959 she decided to try again, this time at Thruxton airfield in Hampshire. At the same time she learnt to drive, travelling to Thruxton nearly every weekend, and it was not long before her new instructor, John Heaton, considered her ready for a solo flight. Following an unfortunate fall, in which she broke an arm, she resumed flying lessons a week later, still in plaster, and it was the proudest moment of her life when her determination was rewarded and she eventually gained a licence. In the autumn of 1959, she bought a Tiger Moth on hire purchase. The aircraft had been converted with a covered rather than an open cockpit into a four-seater Thruxton Jackaroo, and she had it painted pale blue and silver, with white upholstery. Wanting to personalise her aircraft, registered G-APAM, she christened it 'Myth', the Greek word for a female moth.

Over the following months she gained much flying experience, revelling in the publicity generated and enjoying her new-found social life, and started to compare herself to her heroine Amy Johnson. In 1960, she entered for the National Air Races, having only six months in which to learn all the techniques of flying at speed over a set course, as well as familiarising herself with aerial racing regulations. However, she won her first trophy at a rally held on Jersey, a small reward presented by Lady Brabazon. Sheila remarked that it was 'Myth' that had won the race.

On 10 June 1969, Sheila was invited to be the first person to land at Lympne after the airfield was renamed Ashford Airport. At the time, Ashford was considered to be heading for a period of rapid growth and Lympne's fiftieth anniversary as an airfield seemed a suitable time for its rechristening. Its name had always been something of a drawback. When Eric Rylands acquired Lympne for Skyways Coach-Air he remarked, 'Americans used to say, "If you can't pronounce it, you can't spell it. If you can spell it, you can't pronounce it." ' The ceremony was conducted by the Conservative Party leader Edward Heath, who brought considerable pomp and publicity to the event. Sheila was expected to land with a flourish, creating even more publicity. It was a windy day as she arrived at Lympne in her record-breaking Piper Comanche, G-ATOY, 'Myth Too'. She taxied her aircraft up to the spectator line, but the strong crosswind pushed her aircraft out of sight of the crowd behind the trees, which enabled Heath to obtain maximum publicity. To commemorate the occasion, a plaque was unveiled by the leader of the opposition, which has since mysteriously disappeared, but in fact it was a pretence that Sheila had indeed been the first person to land at the newly named Ashford Airport.

Skyfotos was founded in 1947 by Ronnie Gott, who at the time had a contract to take aerial photographs of an industrial area on the Thames Estuary and took the opportunity to include extra shots of passing ships. Realising there was a market for this type of work, he formed Skyfotos and approached owners of ships and their crews in order to sell a number of his photographs. Sometimes such work was undertaken for a government agency, the exact reason not always being disclosed, but it could have been because the operator had been infringing maritime law or customs duties. An Auster Autocrat J/1, G-AIZZ, was soon purchased and Skyfotos began regular flights along the English Channel. The company later acquired a Piper Seneca and work expanded to cover flights around Gibraltar. Within three decades Skyfotos had a virtual monopoly in this segment of the commercial marine photography market and the company moved to its new location at Lympne.

On Saturday 2 June 1962, Skyfotos suffered a tragic loss when Piper Tri-Pacer PA-22 G-AREN took off from Lympne at 9.30 a.m. to survey and take aerial photographs of the *Pra River* in the English Channel. Pilot Peter Harrington and cameraman George Henderson were keen to locate the ship and estimated that the trip would take three hours. The Piper had enough fuel for almost a five-hour flight. By 2 p.m. they had not returned and a full search was in progress, but despite the best efforts of the RAF and HM Coastguard there was no sign of the missing aircraft. Wreckage was later found near Weymouth, but it was not from the Piper. The search continued into Sunday until the aircraft was discovered ditched off Beachy Head. Both crew members had been killed.

Piper Caribbean PA22 registration G-AREN of Skyfotos, piloted by Peter Harrington and assisted by George Henderson the cameraman, who lost their lives on a routine flight on 2 June 1962.

Skyfotos remained at Lympne until the 1970s. In the early 1980s, the company set up Andrews Professional Colour Laboratories under the name of Fotoflite and by January 1990, Skyfotos and Fotoflite shared a common archive of over 800,000 photographs. Moving first to New Romney, the two companies continued to use both names: Fotoflite covering the commercial market and Skyfotos turning to the field of collectors and enthusiasts. The company is now based in new premises at Ashford.

Business Air Travel had been operating a variety of services for many years in the South East. It was an associate company of the Cinque Ports Flying Club and Skyfotos, all three concerns working together for many years, and by the mid-1960s the company operated the occasional air taxi service with aircraft loaned from Skyfotos or the Cinque Ports Flying Club. Early in 1971, Business Air Travel bought a Cabair Apache specially converted to photograph shipping, having just a pilot's seat and one other seat. This activity was not the easiest of occupations, as the aircraft had to be flown at a very low speed due to the relatively slow speed of the ships that it was photographing. However, air taxi work suddenly became one of the company's major activities once again, because early in May 1975, a six-seat Piper Apache was acquired. This smartly painted aircraft, G-ARJW, flew many cross-Channel services to airports in northern France,

Belgium and Holland, as well as other services to airports within the British Isles. One of the company's first charters with this aircraft was to Lulsgate (Bristol) and Denham on 23 May 1975, and many other charters have been flown since then. During the summer of 1975, this Apache was used for pleasure flying at Lydd, and many flights of this nature were undertaken on weekdays, carrying schoolchildren aloft for a brief but no doubt enjoyable aerial geography lesson. On 19 July 1975, the aircraft carried a party of motor racing enthusiasts from Headcorn to Silverstone for the British Grand Prix, and the Apache has also been treated to the races at Doncaster on at least one occasion.

In April 1978, Alex Black, who lived in Sellindge, bought an E.P.9 Prospector, G-AOZO, advertised for sale by Sussex Agricultural Aviation Services in *Flight* magazine, for £12,500. The aircraft had been designed by Edgar Percival for crop spraying, and the type was used extensively in both Australia and New Zealand. Once at Lympne it was operated by the Eagle Parachute School. During take-off on 2 July 1980, G-AOZO crashed and burst into flames on impact. The aircraft had failed to gain circuit height and stalled before diving into the ground from approximately 500 feet, one mile west of the airfield, killing all six people on board, including the pilot Alex Black, the instructor Les Riley, a mechanic and three German parachutists. The subsequent Air Accident Investigation Board report attributed the crash to engine failure caused by water contamination in the fuel and the absence of a mandatory stall warning system. Sussex Agricultural Aviation Services operated another of this type, G-APWZ, from Lympne, and Skyways flew a third, G-APVX, moving another, G-ARLE operated by the Lancashire Aircraft Company, to Lympne from Stansted during July 1961.

Luscombe Light Aircraft and East Kent Memorial Flight, based at Lympne, was owned by ex-FAA pilot Pat Luscombe, who planned to restore aircraft and fly them from Lympne. The first of these aircraft awaiting restoration in a workshop on the industrial site was a Hawker Fury, but the business collapsed and the Fury was moved on. Luscombe had also acquired an Avro Anson Mk 19, G-AGPG, ex-Skyways, Ekco Aviation and Southend Aviation Museum. The Anson was later kept at Brenzett Aeronautical Museum before eventually being sold to Avro Aerospace, which had plans to restore the Anson and other classic aircraft.

In 1983, when Pat Luscombe was developing the Valiant, a two-seat canard microlight aircraft, and a military version, the Rattler, the Royal Ordnance Factories advised him on possible weapons. One 7.62 mm Hughes chain gun would have put the Rattler firmly into the serious category. Other war-load options included 14.2 inch unguided air-to-ground rockets, and a land-mine dispenser for rapid area-denial, carrying up to 144 anti-personnel mines.

Just inside Pat Luscombe's workshop/hangar stood the Hawker Sea Fury WJ288, civil registration G-SALY. This aircraft eventually went to Warbirds of GB Ltd. Biggin Hill, and is thought to be with the American Airpower Heritage Museum, Texas.

A view of Lympne airfield taken shortly after the war, with most of the buildings still intact. Note the aircraft in the area at the bottom of photograph. Otterpool Lane is seen to the left.

It would have been a cheap aircraft to assemble, operating from grass strips or roads on quick-reaction, close-support missions. Alternatively, the airframe could be equipped as a drone for reconnaissance of heavily defended targets. The boot-shaped fuselage had a welded three-inch aluminium tube mainframe, while the wing consisted of a box-section main spar and I-section rear spar with polyurethane foam interior filling. The fuselage and wing skins were of non-stressed glass fibre, with the metal hard-points for weapons glassed into the primary structure. Fuel tanks were in the wing-centre section and aircraft belly.

The cockpit was large and roomy, with a good view ahead, down, and to the sides, marred only slightly by the canard. A chiselled nose with an optically flat window allowed the fitting of electro-optical sensors, cameras, or a laser target marker. The 7.62 mm gun was to be mounted high on the starboard side of the fuselage with the 6 x 2,000 round magazine behind the pilot's seat, obviating trim changes as the magazine emptied. Take-off distance was predicted as 200 feet from a grass strip and 150 feet from tarmac. The reason for the demise of these projects is unknown, but it would have been a step in the right direction for the future of Lympne if Luscombe's plans had succeeded. By this time, the airfield was fast disappearing under development, with most of the original hangars and the control tower gone.

Lympne Control tower in 1983, surrounded by debris, with the upper floor already demolished. If it could have been protected it may have been a suitable location for a museum.

CHAPTER 12

An uncertain future; efforts to influence further development of Lympne

On a warm summer Saturday in 1983, members of the Kent Aviation Historical Research Society arranged to survey the site at Lympne airfield. They met at the control tower, one of the last original buildings, which has since been demolished. The society had been formed in 1977 by four established aviation historians – Roy Humphreys, David Collyer, Robin Brooks and Ray Munday – who had been researching the fascinating story of Kent's aviation for years. They were later invited to attend a meeting at Lympne to present the argument for saving the remainder of the site for posterity. Then, as today, there was no memorial.

Concerns were growing about the future of Lympne airfield. About seventy residents and other interested parties had turned up for the meeting, which had been arranged by the parish council to discuss several planning applications before making recommendations to Shepway District Council. One proposal was for a golf course, which it was thought would be a way of maintaining the site as a green area. Local residents felt that it was a good idea but were against it being located too near Lympne village. However, the accountant director of Lympne airfield's owners, Cheldale, stated that it could not be located anywhere else. The local councillor, Harry Margary, said that the applications did not conform with both the Kent County Area Plans and objected to a third proposal for an industrial estate on the site.

Cheldale had bought the site for £1.5 million. Keen to capitalise on their investment by developing the airfield, they felt that the best way to do this was to build houses, which would be good for the local community. However, a company representative made an unfortunate gaffe by saying, 'There is nothing in Lympne I would purchase!' As a result, Lympne

Former Southend Museum Fiat G.46 owned by Pat Luscombe in the Over Blister Hangar at Lympne in 1989, the hangar has since been demolished. Apart from the airframe, segments of moulds for the construction of a DH Sea Hornet were housed.

The parachute club used this Blister Hangar, as did Sir Paul McCartney with his band 'Wings' who made film and album recordings, whilst at Lympne Castle in September 1978. The hangar was the last to be demolished.

The entrance to one of the air raid shelters just off Otterpool Lane, looking somewhat overgrown, which with others, stands today on privately owned land.

airfield has finished up with an industrial estate. This, of course, has created jobs and helped local businesses, but there has been a price to pay, as heavy vehicles trundle up and down Otterpool Lane, the road leading to the airfield. There may be those who would have preferred the leisure centre option, but that is history. Today, what remains of the airfield site is under consideration for a large housing estate.

By the 1980s, all aviation had ceased at Lympne and the developers of the site had already started to churn up the runways of the late 1960s. Small business units appeared and were already occupied, such as Luscombe Aircraft Ltd. Lympne's new image was as the Eurobusiness Centre in response to business opportunities arising from the opening of Eurotunnel at Folkestone in 1992.

The Lympne Aero Classic, an event which began in 2010 and is the brainchild of John Simpson and his team of dedicated people, is held at the village hall and its grounds. The aim is to try and protect Lympne as a heritage site, and raise funds for the village hall. There are ideas for creating a permanent museum dedicated to the airfield, although nothing has yet been arranged. Already the event is well established and is sponsored by sympathetic companies who are aware of their historic surroundings on the airfield site. The Aero Classic event attracts restored military vehicles and re-enactment groups, and includes displays by local historians,

Huts close to the main gate at Lympne being demolished to make way for new buildings in the summer of 1989. Both the Dupe and Geal family had homes on the airfield, leaving Lympne in 1940. In this photograph, only the Gate House is still standing.

A view looking along what was left of the concrete runway in 1989. Today this is a pleasant area of open fields, possibly to be developed for housing.

Skyways and Silver City associations – a positive way of upholding the history of such an important airfield as Lympne, described by Skyways as Kent's Garden Airfield.

At the junction of Otterpool Lane with the A20 is a popular café bearing the appropriate name of Aerodrome Café. Most of the original buildings in the area have long since gone, but a few remaining airmen's huts and air-raid shelters can still be easily found. However, these are on private property so permission to have a look and take a photograph should first be sought. Also to be seen are the remains of firing butts, which are hidden amongst trees opposite to the 'The County Members' public house. Other reminders of Kent's aviation heritage are the sound mirrors or detectors that can still be seen on the slopes beneath Lympne – a reminder of the endeavours before the Second World War to create a defence system for detecting incoming German aircraft. It was these early experiments that led to the formation of the Royal Observer Corps and radar stations, both major factors contributing to Britain's survival.

Lympne Place, once home to Sir Philip Sassoon, whose tireless work for aviation and the RAF should not be forgotten, is now home to the son of Lord Aspinall and Port Lympne Animal Park. Lympne Castle is again

The plaque which commemorates the Jubilee and renaming of Ashford Airport on 10 June 1969 by Edward Heath MBE, MP. Sadly this has long since disappeared, its location unknown.

privately owned and closed to the public. Perhaps a visitor to The County Members public house should spare a thought for the airfield. At one time there was twin-bladed propeller above the bar, but enquiries have thus far failed to establish its present location. Close to the site of the airfield, tucked away behind trees on the escarpment that overlooks Romney Marsh, stands St Stephen's Church. It is a place of quiet and reflection, and if the visitor cares to look around he will find various headstones on graves of RAF personnel, pilots and victims of war and peace at Lympne airfield.

Cinque Ports Flying Club hangar packed with aircraft. Far left is Piper Trip-Pacer G-ARAH and in the centre Piper Aztec G-AREE. The Club was re-established in 1964 until 1968 when flying ceased.

Bibliography

Alington, Geoffrey, *A Sound in The Sky*, R. K. Hudson, 1994

Ashworth, Chris, *Action Stations 9: Military airfields of the Central South and South-East*, Patrick Stephens Ltd, 1985

Boot, Henry & Ray Sturtivant, *Gifts of War*, Air-Britain (Historians) Ltd, 2005

Caygill, Peter, *In All Things First: No. 1 Squadron at War 1939–1945*, Pen & Sword Aviation, 2009

Cole, Christopher & E. F. Cheesman, *The Air Defence of Great Britain 1914–1918*, Putnam, 1984

Collyer, David, *Lympne Airport in Old Photographs*, Alan Sutton, 1992

Cornwell, Peter D., *The Battle of France Then and Now*, After the Battle, 2007

Courtenay, William, *Airman Friday*, Hutchinson, 1936

Dagwell, Keith J., *Silver City Airways: Pioneers of the Skies*, The History Press, 2010

Docherty, Tom, *Swift To Battle*, Pen & Sword Aviation, 2010

Franks, Norman L. R., *RAF Fighter Command Losses of the Second World War Vols 1, 2, 3*, Midland Publishing, 1997–98

Freeman, Roger A., *The Mighty Eighth War Diary*, Arms and Armour, 1990

Gilbert, Nick, *Skyways at Lympne*, Nick Gilbert, 2013

Gillies, Midge, *Amy Johnson: Queen of the Air*, Weidenfeld & Nicolson, 2003

Graham, Peter, *Skypilot*, Pentland Books, 2001

Gray, Colin F., *Spitfire Patrol*, Hutchinson, 1990

Gull, Brian & Bruce Lander, *Diver! Diver! Diver!*, Grub Street, 2008

Hall, Peter, *No. 91 'Nigeria' Squadron*, Osprey Aviation, 2001

Johnstone, Sandy, *Where No Angels Dwell*, Jarrolds, 1969

Lewis, Peter, *British Racing and Record-Breaking Aircraft*, Putnam, 1970

Listemann, Phil H., *No. 453 (R.A.A.F.) Squadron 1941-1945*, Phil Listemann, 2009

Lomax, Judy, *Sheila Scott*, Hutchinson, 1990

Moulson, Tom, *The Flying Sword: The Story of 601 Squadron*, Macdonald, 1964

Ramsey, Winston G., *The Battle of Britain Then and Now*, After the Battle, 1987

Rawlings, John, *Fighter Squadrons of the RAF and Their Aircraft*, Macdonald, 1969

Reda, Helmut H. (ed.), *Because I Fly: A Collection of Aviation Poetry*, McGraw-Hill,

2002

Rochford, Leonard H., *I Chose the Sky*, William Kimber, 1977

Ross, David, *The Greatest Squadron of Them All: The Definitive History of 603 (City of Edinburgh) Squadron*, Grub Street, 2003

Shores, Christopher & Chris Thomas, *2nd Tactical Air Force Vol. 1*, Classic Publications, 2004

Simpson, Bill, *Spitfire Dive Bombers Versus the V2*, Pen & Sword Aviation, 2007

Spurdle, Bob, *The Blue Arena*, William Kimber, 1986

Sturtivant, Ray & Gordon Page, *The Camel File*, Air-Britain (Historians) Ltd, 1993

Sturtivant, Ray, John Hamlin & James J. Halley, *RAF Flying Training and Support Units*, Air-Britain (Historians) Ltd, 1997

Sturtivant, Ray & Gordon Page, *Royal Navy Aircraft Serials and Units 1911–1919*, Air-Britain (Historians) Ltd, 1992

Travers, C. T., *Cross Country*, Hothersall & Travers, 1989

Vasco, John J. & Peter D. Cornwell, *Zerstörer: The Messerschmitt 110 and its Units in 1940*, JAC, 1995

Warner, Graham, *The Bristol Blenheim*, Crecy Publishing Ltd, 2002

www.kentfallen.com

APPENDIX 1

Squadrons and units based at Lympne

Aircraft Erection Section – 1916
Aircraft Erection Park – 20 January 1917
Aircraft Acceptance Park – 1 September 1917 (formed from existing Aircraft
   Erection Park; redesignated 8 (Lympne) 8 AAP on 12 October 1917)
No. 8 (Lympne) Aircraft Acceptance Park (formed 12 October 1917 as AAP
   Lympne as collection point for aircraft en route to or from France; became No. 8
   (Lympne) AAP until at least November 1921, when disbanded.)
No. 1 (Auxiliary) School of Aerial Gunnery (formed January 1917 – ex-School of
   Aerial Gunnery Hythe/Dymchurch; detached to Lympne February 1917)
No. 64 Squadron, 14-15 October 1917
No. 69 (Australian) Squadron, 24 August 1917-9 September 1917 (3 Brigade)
No. 50 Squadron – 53 Wing, 1918 (used Lympne as ELG)
Technical Group – South East Area, 1918
No. 1 Group South East Area, November 1918
No. 83 Squadron, September 1919-15 October 1919, 82 Wing
No. 85 Squadron, 22 May 1918
No. 97 Squadron, 3-4 August 1918
No. 98 Squadron, 1 March 1918-1 April 1918
No. 102 Squadron, 26 March 1919-3 July 1919 (Cadre only) – disbanded
No. 108 Squadron, 16 February 1919-3 July 1919 (Cadre only) – disbanded
No. 120 Squadron, 17 July 1919-21 October 1919 (detached from Hawkinge)
Night Flying Flight (No. 6 Group), formed Biggin Hill 1 July 1923 in No. 6 Group
   detached to Lympne for acoustical manoeuvres during 1923, 1924, 1927, 1928.
   Moved 20 May 1926, returned to Lympne 28 May 1926
No. 21 (Bomber) Squadron, 3 November 1936-15 August 1938
No. 34 (Bomber) Squadron, 3 November 1936-12 July 1938
No. 51 (Army Co-operation) Wing
23 May 1940-8 June 1940 (Possibly re-formed No. 50 AC Wing)
No. 22 Group 16-59-2 & 226 Squadrons – moved to RAF West Malling 8 June
   1940

No. 1 Squadron, 15 March 1943-15 February 1944; 11 July 1944-10 August 1944
No. 2 Squadron, 20 May 1940
No. 16 Squadron, 19 May 1940-3 June 1940
No. 18 Squadron, 18 May 1940-21 May 1940
No. 26 Squadron, 22 May 1940-8 June 1940
No. 33 Squadron, 17 May 1944-3 July 1944
No. 41 Squadron, 11 July 1944-5 December 1944
No. 53 Squadron, 20 May 1940-21 May 1940
No. 59 Squadron, 20 May 1940-21 May 1940
No. 65 Squadron, 2 October 1942-11 October 1942
No. 72 Squadron, 30 June 1942-7 July 1942
No. 74 Squadron, 15 May 1944-3 July 1944
No. 91 Squadron (Nigeria), March 1941-2 October/9 October; 23 November
    1941-11 January 1942 and War Diary
No. 127 Squadron, 16 May 1944-4 July 1944
No. 130 Squadron (formed from No. 186 Squadron), 5 April 1944-30 April 1944
No. 133 Squadron, 30 June 1942-12 July 1942; 11 August 1944-22 August 1944
No. 137 Squadron, 14 December 1943-2 January 1944; 4 February 1944-1 April
    1944
No. 165 Squadron (Ceylon), 12 July 1944-10 August 1944
No. 186 Squadron, 1 March 1944-5 April 1944
No. 245 Squadron, 30 March 1943-28 May 1943 (Detached)
No. 310 Squadron No. 134 (Czech) Wing, 1 July 1944-11 July 1944
No. 312 Squadron No. 134 (Czech) Wing, 4 July 1944-11 July 1944
No. 313 Squadron No. 134 (Czech) Wing, 4 July 1944-11 July 1944
No. 350 Squadron (Polish), 29 September 1944-3 December 1944
No. 401 Squadron (RCAF), 14 August 1942-21 August 1942
No. 451 Squadron (RAAF), 6 April 1945-3 May 1945
No. 453 Squadron (RAAF), 6 April 1945-2 May 1945
No. 504 Squadron (County of Durham), 11 July 1944-13 July 1944
No. 567 Squadron, 14 November 1944-13 June 1945
No. 598 Squadron, 12 March 1945-30 April 1945 – disbanded
No. 609 Squadron (West Riding of Yorkshire), 18 August 1943-14 December 1943
No. 610 Squadron (County of Chester), 12 September 1944-4 December 1944
No. 601 Squadron (Summer camps, 1930s)
No. 659 Squadron, 4 July 1945-10 July 1945
No. 800 (FAA) Squadron, 9 July 1939-29 July 1939
No. 803 (FAA) Squadron, 9 July 1939-29 July 1939

APPENDIX 2

Miscellaneous units based at Lympne

No. 38 Works Flight
No. 70 Battalion Buffs (A Command)
No. 6 Battalion Yorks & Lancs, 138 Brigade
No. 459 RAA Battery
No. 175 Battery RA (B Troop)
Lympne K Site – dummy airfield
No. 3203 Servicing Commando Unit
No. 2744 AA Squadron
No. 2729 AA Squadron
No. 2798 Squadron RAF Regiment
No. 4 Works Squadron
No. 347 Searchlight Battery
No. 419 Battery (C & D Troops)
No. 3028 Servicing Echelon
No. 4006 AA Flight
No. 2823 Works Squadron
No. 3 Works Squadron
No. 2 AA Flight
No. 4133 AA Flight (2823)
No. 5003 RAF Construction Unit
No. 119 DE Section 11 Group Army Dispatch Rider Unit
No. 3053 Servicing Echelon
No. 3054 Servicing Echelon
No. 4659 Airfield Construction Flight
No. 13 Advanced Flying School
No. 5054 RAF Regiment
No. 2794 AA RAF Regiment
No. 2813 RAF Regiment
No. 2823 RAF Regiment
No. 3210 Servicing Commando
No. 5018 RAF Regiment

No. 3017 Servicing Echelon
No. 3102 Servicing Echelon (Re-formed as 6186 SE)
No. 7137 Servicing Echelon
No. 7130 Servicing Echelon
No. 2714 Squadron RAF Regiment
No. 2803 Squadron RAF Regiment
No. 4711 Airfield Construction Flight
No. 4731 Airfield Construction Flight
No. 2847 Airfield Construction Flight
No. 425 Refuelling & Rearmament Unit
No. 7137 Servicing Echelon
No. 6033 Servicing Echelon
No. 6074 Servicing Echelon
No. 6127 Servicing Echelon
No. 6310 Servicing Echelon
No. 6312 Servicing Echelon
No. 6313 Servicing Echelon
No. 2623 Squadron RAF Regiment
No. 6001 Servicing Echelon
No. 6165 Servicing Echelon
No. 3108 Squadron RAF Regiment
No. 6041 Servicing Echelon
No. 6065 Servicing Echelon
No. 6130 Servicing Echelon
No. 6350 Servicing Echelon
No. 6610 Servicing Echelon
No. 3054 Servicing Echelon
No. 334 Signals Unit
No. 2707 AA Squadron RAF Regiment
No. 2827 (D) Squadron
No. 2763 Squadron RAF Regiment
No. 2806 Squadron RAF Regiment
No. 5018 Regiment
No. 4085 Airfield Construction Flight
No. 421 Flight (Hawkinge)
No. 483 Group Control Centre
No. 5351 Wing
No. 24 Airfield Road Construction Co.
No. 141 RAAC (Ashford)
No. 4663 Airfield Construction Flight
No. 13 Works Unit
No. 2744 Squadron RAF Regiment
No. 4 Works Unit
No. 4006 AA Flight
No. 653 Works Unit
No. 5054 RAF Regiment
No. 5006 RAF Regiment
No. 425 Refuelling & Rearmament Unit
No. 5004 Airfield Construction Unit

No. 5010 Airfield Construction Unit
No. 2742 Squadron RAF Regiment
No. 272 Squadron RAF Regiment
No. 49 Maintenance Unit (Faygate)
No. 1334 Maintenance Unit (Hawkinge)
No. 46 Army Co-operation Flight (Hawkinge)

Select presentation aircraft operating from Lympne

Aircraft usually constructed by public subscription and fund-raising

'Spirit of Kent' – Lord Cornwallis – Spitfire Vc – Serial No. AR500
This aircraft, the second to be given this name, was allocated to No. 186 Squadron
at Lympne. No.186 Squadron was disbanded on 5 April 1944 and re-formed as No.
130 (Punjab) Squadron, AR500 joining the squadron on 18 April to fly bomber
escort from Lympne. It was shot down on 24 June 1944 by return fire from a Ju 88,
killing Flt Sgt William Frederick Hirock, aged twenty-one. He is remembered on Panel
218 of the Runnymede Air Forces Memorial. Spitfire AR500 also flew with Nos 313
(Czech), 131 (County of Kent), 412 (RCAF), 421 (RCAF) and 310 (Czech) Squadrons.

'Abbotshaugh Falkirk Bairn' – Spitfire Vb – Serial No. W3207
Presented by a donation of £5,000 through the Provost and Town Council
of Grangemouth in September 1940, it was allocated to No. 504 (County of
Nottingham) Squadron, left behind at Lympne and taken over by No. 310 (Czech)
Squadron on 15 July 1944. It was struck off charge on 23 October 1945, having
flown with Nos 609 (West Riding), 222 (Natal), 317 (Polish), 412 (RCAF), 132
(City of Bombay), 41 (Army Co-operation) and 61 (OTU) Squadrons.

'Aberford' – Spitfire Vb – Serial No. P8640
Named after village of the same name in Yorkshire, it was initially with No. 186
Squadron before joining No. 130 (Punjab) Squadron at Lympne on 3 April 1944
on bomber escorts and patrols. It was damaged on landing at Lympne on 28 April
1944, the pilot being Flt Sgt C. H. T. Clay. The aircraft also flew with Nos 609
(West Riding), 92 (East India), 610 (County of Chester), 308 (Polish), 302 (Polish),
416 (RCAF) Squadrons and No. 1 (Air Gunnery School).

'Bauchi Province' – Spitfire Vb – Serial No. W3132
Presented by the *Nigeria Daily Times* Win the War Fund, it was allocated to No. 91
(Nigeria) Squadron on 8 May 1941, being based at Hawkinge and Lympne. W3132

was lost on shipping patrol on 8 February 1942, when piloted by Flt Lt John Denys Fletcher. He is buried in Row A, Grave 5, Middelkerke Communal Cemetery, Belgium.

'Bombay City 4' – Spitfire Vb – Serial No. BM252
On 27 April 1944 the aircraft was passed on to No. 130 (Punjab) Squadron from No. 186 Squadron at Lympne, flying bomber escort and ASR practice. Damaged on 27 October 1944 when based at B82 (Grave) airfield in Belgium and struck off charge on 9 March 1945, it had also flown with Nos 122 (Bombay), 222 (Natal) and 316 (Polish) Squadrons.

'Holt III' – Spitfire Vb – Serial No. W3825
One of fourteen Spitfires funded by Sir Herbert Holt, New York donated £72,000 through the Wings for Britain fund. Serving with No. 316 (Polish) Squadron, Plt Off. J. Piotrowski crash-landed it at Lympne on 27 March 1942. It also flew with Nos 130 (Punjab), 308 (Polish) and 316 Squadrons, 2nd Squadron 52nd Fighter Group USAAF, and Nos 65 and 349 (Belgian) Squadrons and was struck off charge on 8 January 1945.

'Katsina Province' – Spitfire Vc – Serial No. AB248
Presented by the *Nigeria Daily Times* Win the War Fund, it was allocated to No. 91 (Nigeria) Squadron at Hawkinge and Lympne, and was flown by Flt Lt Robert Spurdle from Lympne in May 1942. AB248 was assigned to No. 315 (Polish) Squadron on 13 May before being struck off charge on 23 May 1942.

'Muntok' – Spitfire Vb – Serial No. BL646
Presented by the Netherlands East Indies, it was named after a place on the island of Banka. Although not based at Lympne during wartime, it is interesting to note that this aircraft was collected from Dunsfold on 14 April 1947 by Skyways, following restoration by Reid & Sigrist, and flown to Portugal to serve with Spitfire Fighter Aviation Group at Ota Air Force Base until scrapped in 1953.

'Watford' – Spitfire Vb – Serial No. W3456
The aircraft was presented by the Watford Spitfire Fund, Hertfordshire. On 1 April 1944, the port undercarriage collapsed prior to its move to No. 186 Squadron, W3456 eventually moving on 5 April to Lympne before being transferred to No. 130 (Punjab) Squadron on 18 April. It also flew with Nos 616 (South Yorkshire), 65, 302 (Polish), 303 (Polish), 308 (Polish) and 416 (RCAF) Squadrons, and No. 17 Service Flying Training School at Cranwell where it crashed, killing the pilot, on 10 November 1944.

'Zaria Province' – Spitfire Vb – Serial No. BM543
Presented by the *Nigeria Daily Times* Win the War Fund, the aircraft was allocated to No. 91 (Nigeria) Squadron at Hawkinge and Lympne, where it was flown by Flt Lts Robert Spurdle and Geoff Parnell. Also assigned to Nos 132 (City of Bombay), 122 (Bombay), 234 (Madras) and 350 (Belgian) Squadrons, it was struck off charge on 23 October 1944.

Air races at Lympne

Folkestone Aero Trophy

Date	Aircraft Registration	Pilot	Speed (mph)
25-08-1932	Comper Swift G-ABWH	A. J. Styran	141
26-08-1933	DH.60G Gipsy Moth G-ABOG	K. H. F. Waller	103
12-09-1934	DH.60X Moth G-AAMU	J. G. Brown	101.25
14-09-1935	DH.60G III Moth G-ABVW	L. Lipton	112
01-08-1936	Aeronca C-3 G-ADYR	R. R. Grubb	84.75
31-07-1937	Percival Mew Gull G-AEXF	A. Henshaw	210
30-07-1938	DH.87B Hornet Moth G-ADMT	H. Buckingham	123.25
05-08-1939	Chilton DW.1A G-AFSV	Hon. A.W. H. Dalrymple	126
01-09-1946	Supermarine Walrus G-AHFN	J. Grierson	121
31-08-1947	B.A. Swallow G-AELG	Lt Cdr P. Godfrey	99

Grosvenor Challenge Cup

23-06-1923	Sopwith Gnu G-EAGP	Flt Lt W. H. Longton	87.60
04-10-1924	Avro 562 Avis G-EBKP	H. J. L. Hinkler	65.87
03-08-1925	RAE Hurricane G-EBHS	Sqn Ldr J. S. Chick	81.19
18-09-1926	Blackburn Bristol I G-EBKD	Sqn Ldr W. H. Longton	84.95
01-08-1927	DH.60 Moth G-EBMV	Mrs. S. C. Eliott-Lynn	88.50
05-10-1929	DH.60 Moth G-EBPT	G. S. Kemp	98.00
06-09-1930	DH.60 Moth G-EBQV	L. Turnbull	95.00
22-08-1931	Blackburn Bluebird IV G-AAUU	Sqn Ldr J. W. Woodhouse	102.50
02-07-1932	Westland Widgeon III G-AADE	G. S. Napier	98.00
13-07-1935	DH.60G III Moth G-ACBX	Lt Cdr C. W. Phillips	109.25
01-08-1949	Auster J/1B Autocrat G-AGXK	D. A. Archer	112.50
29-07-1950	Tipsy Trainer I G-AFJT	K. C. Millican	97.50

11-07-1952	Avro 638 Club Cadet G-ACHP	D. F. Ogilvy	106.50
20-06-1953	Moth Minor G-AFPN	D. R. Robertson	111.00
20-08-1955	Auster Aiglet G-AMMS	D. Westoby	119.00
21-07-1956	Chipmunk I G-AKDN	J. N. Somers	146.00
14-07-1957	Miles Monarch G-AIDE	W. P. Bowles	131.50
12-07-1958	Tiger Moth G-AIVW	J. H. Denyer	115.63
11-07-1959	Tiger Moth G-ANZZ	B. J. Snook	118.50
19-08-1967	Tiger Club A Team	Hon. J. Baring	178.00
		F. O. Marsh	
		J. Stewart-Wood	
11-07-1969	Comper Swift G-ABUU	J. Pothecary	117.50

RAF and civilian casualties buried in St Stephen's churchyard, who lost their lives serving or working at RAF Lympne 1939-45

Sidney Herbert Bell – Leading Aircraftman
Died Monday 12 August 1940. Aged 38. Son of William and Emmeline Bell.
Husband of Kathleen Agnes Bell of Winchester, Hampshire. Grave 11D.

Frederick Charles Thomas Burvill – Leading Aircraftman
Died Friday 30 August 1940. Aged 54. Born Folkestone, Kent, 1886.
Resided at 7 Beach Street, Folkestone, Kent. Son of Jeremiah and Elizabeth Burvill.

William Eric Davis – Secretary/Manager Cinque Ports Flying Club
Died 12 March 1938 in local flying accident. Aged 34. Born Birkenhead, Cheshire,
25 August 1903. Although not a casualty of the Second World War, Bill Davis will
always be associated with the flying club and Lympne airfield.

William George Diwell – Home Guard
Died Friday 30 August 1940. Aged 56. Husband of Alice Diwell of 47 Walton
Gardens, Folkestone, Kent

Joseph Down – Civilian
Died Friday 30 August 1940. Aged 48. Resided at Postling Vents Cottage, Postling,
Hythe, Kent. Son of the late Beeching and Eliza Down of Westenhanger Brickyard,
Stanford, Hythe, Kent.

Reginald Frederick Cyril Dupe – Sergeant Pilot
Died Saturday 10 February 1940. Aged 28. Son of Sgt Maj. S. J. Dupe (Airfield
Manager, Lympne) and Clara Annie Dupe. Grave 16C. Commemorated on the
Lympne (Second World War) civic war memorial.
George Macklin – Civilian
Died Friday 30 August 1940. Aged 55. Resided at 4 Bonsor Road, Folkestone, Kent.

Alfred Salmon – Civilian
Died Friday 30 August 1940. Aged 56. Resided at 57 Linden Crescent, Folkestone, Kent.

Frederick Charles Townsend – Civilian
Died Friday 30 August 1940. Aged 62. Resided at 66 Dover Street, Folkestone, Kent.

Albert Emmanuel van den Hove d'Ertsenryck – Pilot Officer
Died Sunday 15 September 1940 in combat. Aged 32. Buried with full military
honours at St Stephen's and later moved to the lawn of honour at Evere Cemetery
in Brussels, Row 2, Grave 13. Commemorated on the Battle of Britain Memorial on
the Thames Embankment, London.

APPENDIX 6

Aircraft incidents connected with Lympne

Espenlaub E14 D-185
Having arrived at Lympne on 5 December 1930 with Mr Farquharson and its designer, on 8 December it took off in a gusty wind, stalled when climbing and crashed on the airfield fence. The pilot received facial injuries but the passengers were uninjured.

Goliath F-AEGP
On 7 May 1923, having developed engine trouble over the Channel, the pilot turned back to Lympne and hit a searchlight platform on landing. There were no injuries to the crew or passengers.

Gipsy Moth I G-AADV
Registered to John Scott-Taggart on 21 January 1929 at Stag Lane, it crashed at Bolton after a Swiss tour on 3 March 1929 and was rebuilt by Short Bros. It flew at Lympne following conversion to a single-float amphibian and was displayed on Shorts' stand at the Olympia Aero Show in July 1929. G-AADV crashed on 24 December 1929, attempting to land in rough seas one mile off Sandgate; it was salvaged and towed into Folkestone harbour.

DH.60 Moth G-AAKP
Bought by the Cinque Ports Flying Club (CPFC) at Lympne on 29 August 1939, it was impressed into the RAF on 6 June 1940.

Cirrus III Moth G-AAKR
Registered on 7 August 1930 at Lympne to Nigel B. Cohen, who died when the aircraft crashed near The Royal Oak at Newingreen near Lympne.

Gipsy Moth I G-AALM
Registered to Malcolm Campbell (London) 1927 Ltd, it departed from Lympne on 23 March 1930, crashing in fog thirty-five miles north-east of Paris.

Gipsy Moth II G-AAMU
The aircraft was a Folkestone Aero Trophy winner at Lympne during September 1934 with J. G. Brown.

Gipsy Moth I G-ABEN
Registered to Flt Lt Cedric W. Hill of RAF Henlow and flown by him to Australia, it left Lympne on 5 October 1930 and arrived on 10 December. It was impressed into the RAF as A7-81 in January 1940.

B.A. Swallow G-ADJM
Based at Croydon and owned by E. S. Baker, who force-landed in the Channel en route between Ostend and Lympne on 14 May 1938.

B.A. Swallow II G-ADJN
Owned by W. S. Shackleton Ltd, it was destroyed by enemy action at Lympne on 11 June 1941.

B.A. Swallow II G-ADLD and G-ADSF
Owned by CPFC at Lympne, both aircraft were destroyed there by enemy action on 11 June 1941.

Monospar ST-25 G-AEAT
Mr Willows took off from Lympne for Heston on 16 March 1938 and was reported one hour overdue. The pilot rang Croydon to say he had landed twelve miles south-west of Croydon and that the aircraft was damaged, but in fact he had landed at Brasted, Kent, and G-AEAT was written off.

Currie Wot G-AFCG and G-AFDS
Both these aircraft were destroyed in May 1940 during an enemy raid on Lympne. The name 'Currie Wot' was carried on the side of G-AFDS, which was the prototype.

B.A. Swallow II G-AVEC
Bought by CPFC at Lympne on 29 August 1939, it was destroyed by enemy action on 11 June 1941.

Cirrus I Moth G-EBNN
Registered to CPFC 24 October 1928, and destroyed in a crash at Lympne on 27 March 1929.

DH.60 Moth G EBPM
Owned by the Hon. G. Cunliffe from 27 January 1927 and last owned by CPFC at Lympne from June 1929, it crashed on 27 February 1930 at Smarden, and was the first production Cirrus II Moth.

DH. 60 Moth G EBSA
Owened by Major G.C Maxwell.Last owned by CPFC at Lympne from May 1930. Crashed and cancelled in October 1930.

Cirrus II Moth G-EBRI
Sold to the Duchess of Bedford at Woburn, it was later with CPFC on 17 December
1928. It was impressed into the RAF as X5128 on 12 February 1940 and taken
to No. 5 Maintenance Unit at RAF Kemble. Allocated to Sound City Films Ltd on
30 November 1940 and used as a decoy aircraft on dummy airfields, it was struck
off charge on 1 January 1941.

DH.60 Moth G-EBSS
Owened by William Whitley Ltd. Named 'Jeunesse' by Viscount de Sibour, sold to
CPFC
July 1928.Sun into ground at Selby Farm, near Lympne on 13 October 1928, G.T
Skinner killed.

DH.60X Moth G EBTD
Owned by CPFC at Lympne from October 1935, it was impressed into the RAF by
No. 40 Group on 26 June 1940 and allotted the service serial AW153, later being
scrapped at RAF St Athan in 1941.

DH.60X Moth G-EBVD
Owned pre-war by Christopher M. C. Turner at Lympne from July 1933, on 24 July
1939 its licence expired and it was stored during the war, being re-registered by
R. K. Dundas Ltd on 7 June 1945. The remains were sold to C. J. Packer Burton,
Wiltshire, in November 1945 and ended up at Coulsdon, being scrapped in 1949.

DH.60X Moth G-EBWC
The aircraft was bought by CPFC at Lympne on 27 March 1928, but the letters
'WC' were objected to by lady members of the club, resulting in the new registration
G-EBZN being allotted. However, it was damaged beyond repair in a collision with
a hangar wall at Lympne on 7 July 1928 and the new registration was not used.

No. 8 Air Acceptance Park, Lympne 1917–19

Serial numbers of De Havilland DH.4s handled by this unit prior to moving to France or other units

This aircraft proved very effective as a daylight bomber, with a bomb load of 545 lb. It was fitted with a Vickers gun fixed forward and two Lewis guns in the rear cockpit, and had a crew of two (its widely spaced cockpits causing communication problems between them). Fitted with a 375 hp Rolls-Royce Eagle engine, it could reach a speed of 136.5 mph at a height of 6,500 feet, remaining airborne for 3.75 hours, with a ceiling of 17,500 feet.

A2171, A2712, A7402, A7403, A7404, A7439, A7474, A7480, A7483, A7507, A7510, A7529, A7533, A7547, A7551, A7555, A7566, A7562, A7590, A7598, A7613, A7633, A7657, A7660, A7670, A7719, A7747, A7767, A7769, A7807, A7808, A7815, A7816, A7920, A7937, A7943, A7979, A7981, A8014, A8016, A8018, A8026, A8027, A8035, A8045, A8047, A8049, A8074, A8086, A8088, A8089, A8090, B2064, B2066, B2068, B2115, B2133, B3955, B3987, B9439, C4523, D8363, D8378, D8381, D8382, D8384, D8385, D8386, D8387, D9244, D9252, D9255, D9279, F2652, F2654, F2658, F5700, F5729, F5733, F5735, F5744, F5745, F5748, F5760, F5761, F5762, F5763, F5781, F5782, F5783, F5784, F5786, F5787, F5788, F5789, F5790, F5791, F6222, F6234, H7148, H8263

Serial numbers of De Havilland DH.9s handled by this unit

This aircraft was a new version of the DH.4, designed to improve the speed of production, but all it achieved was an aircraft of inferior performance albeit with an increased bomb load of 931 lb. As with the DH.4, it was fitted with one forward-firing Vickers gun together with two Lewis guns in the rear cockpit. It could attain a speed at 6,500 feet of 136.6 mph, with a ceiling of 22,000 feet.

B7638, B7660, C1342, C2195, C2199, C2216, C2217, C6092, C6210, C6247, C6314, C6315, D470, D555, D558, D607, D609, D613, D1049, D1086, D1089, D1112, D1122, D1165, D1171, D1664, D1688, D1727, D1728, D2778, D2779, D2799, D2855, D2856, D2857, D2859, D2860, D2874, D2875, D3036, D3039, D3045, D3046, D3047, D3048, D3051, D3056, D3057, D3058, D3059, D3060, D3065, D3078, D3082, D3084, D3085, D3088, D3093, D3097, D3106, D3107, D3113, D3122, D3244, D3253, D5576, D5688, D5838, D5845, D7203, D7243, D7245, D7250, D7341, D7353, D7357, D7361, D7470, E622, E664, E666, E668, E692, E726, E733, E734, E735, E5435, E8422, E8429, E8494, E8495, E8528, E8861, E8862, E8864, E8867, E8868, E8869, E8880, E8919, E8923, E8956, E8957, E8959, E8962, E8984, E9007, E9015, E9016, E9026, E9030, E9036, E9046, E9698, F1085, F1086, F1090, F1091, F1092, F1095, F1151, F1167, F1190, F1200, F1279, F6072, F6113, H4218, H4245, H4275, H4277, H4289, H4296, H4309

Serial numbers of Sopwith Camels handled by this unit prior to moving to France or other units

The Sopwith Camel F.1 was a welcome sight on the Western Front, a great favourite with scout and fighter pilots, destroying more enemy aircraft than any other type. It was highly manoeuvrable but was unforgiving to an inexperienced pilot. With two Vickers guns, a maximum speed of 121 mph at a height of 10,000 feet, a ceiling height of 20,000 feet, and a climb rate of 995 feet per minute, the F.1 was truly the Spitfire of the First World War.

B2322,B2323, B2344, B2358, B2395, B2404, B2442, B2499, B3815, B3816, B3823, B3824, B3825, B3826, B3827, B3828, B3836, B3837, B3838, B3874, B3875, B3876, B3890, B3898, B5122, B5153, B5172, B5173, B5238, B5239, B5241, B5402, B5403, B5404, B5405, B5583, B5599, B5608, B5631, B5633, B5643, B5649, B6212, B6267, B6372, B6384, B6404, B6411, B6412, B6423, B7156, B7174, B7180, B7231, B7292, B7295, B7307, B7309, B7316, B7365, B7384, B7394, B7404, B7407, B7760, B7777, B9136, B9139, B9166, B9192, B9255, B9290, B9296, B9300, B9301, B9308, B9315, B9325, C1653, C1655, C1665, C1667, C3293, C3324, C3379, C6783, C8201, C8204, C8232, C8241, C8253, C8256, C8267, C8272, C8273, C8308, C8347, D1791, D1792, D1812, D1813, D1815, D1889, D1891, D1900, D1901, D1911, D1927, D1931, D1964, D3358, D3367, D3374, D3376, D3395, D3418, D6407, D6421, D6440, D6458, D6474, D6502, D6505, D6508, D6528, D6540, D6631, D6647, D6653, D6655, D6665, D6671, D6694, D6696, D8148, D8151, D8165, D9381, D9400, D9411, D9452, D9453, D9455, D9458, D9460, D9479, D9492, D9497, D9505, D9508, D9515, D9518, D9522, D9524, D9526, D9528, D9530, D9536, D9550, D9572, D9599, D9606, D9613, D9623, D9629, D9666, E1402, E1408, E1410, E1415, E1417, E1423, E1424, E1426, E1428, E1431, E1451, E1452, E1453, E1454, E1468, E1470, E1478, E1495, E1498, E1512, E1536, E1538, E1546, E1547, E1548, E1570, E1593, E4381, E4385, E4386, E4411, E4423, E5156, E5158, E5159, E7165, E7189, E7221, E7222, E7242, F1302, F1304, F1306, F1308, F1313, F1314, F1316, F1318, F1322, F1332, F1338, F1340, F1342, F1344, F1346, F1348, F1354, F1356, F1360, F1362, F1364, F1366, F1368, F1370, F1372, F1374, F1378, F1380, F1382, F1384, F1386, F1394, F1398, F1399, F1403, F1413, F1414, F1448, F1461, F1466, F1533, F1542, F1910, F1920, F1923, F1934, F2134, F2143, F2164, F2177, F3123, F6346, F6349, F6374, F6384, F8500, F8509, F9636

APPENDIX 8

Examples of aircraft operated by Air Kruise (Kent) Ltd between 1949 and 1962

Auster J/1 Autocrat G-AIZZ
Bristol B170 Freighter Mk 21 G-AIFM
Bristol B170 Freighter Mk 21 G-AIME
Bristol B170 Freighter Mk 21E G-AHJI
DH.89A Dragon Rapide G-AESR
DH.89A Dragon Rapide G-AEWL – 'Nicole'
Douglas C-47A Dakota G-ANLF
Douglas C-47B Dakota G-AMYV – 'City of Oxford'
Douglas C-47B Dakota G-AMYX – 'City of Rochester'
Douglas C-47B Dakota G-AMZB
Douglas C-53D Dakota G-AOBN
Miles M.65 Gemini 1A G AJWH

APPENDIX 9

Examples of aircraft operated by Silver City Airways between 1948 and 1962

Bristol B170 Freighter Mk IA G-AGVC – 'City of Sheffield'
Bristol B170 Freighter Mk IIA G-AHJC
Bristol B170 Freighter Mk IIA G-AHJG
Bristol B170 Freighter Mk IIA G-AHJO
Bristol B170 Freighter Mk 21 G-AGVB
Bristol B170 Freighter Mk 21 G-AHJD
Bristol B170 Freighter Mk 21E G-AHJI – 'City of Bath'
Bristol B170 Freighter Mk 21 G-AHJJ
Bristol B170 Freighter Mk 21 G-AHJP
Bristol B170 Freighter Mk 21 G-AICM
Bristol B170 Freighter Mk 21 G-AICS
Bristol B170 Freighter Mk 21 G-AICT
Bristol B170 Freighter Mk 21 G-AIFM – 'City of Carlisle'
Bristol B170 Freighter Mk 21 G-AIFV – 'City of Manchester'
Bristol B170 Freighter Mk 21 G-AIME – 'City of Exeter'
Bristol B170 Freighter Mk 21 G-AIMH – 'City of Birmingham'
Bristol B170 Freighter Mk 32 G-AMWA – 'City of London'
Bristol B170 Freighter Mk 32 G-AMWB – 'City of Salisbury'
Bristol B170 Freighter Mk 32 G-AMWC – 'City of Durham'
Bristol B170 Freighter Mk 32 G-AMWD – 'City of Leicester'/'City of Hereford'
Bristol B170 Freighter Mk 32 G-AMWE – 'City of York'
Bristol B170 Freighter Mk 32 G-AMWF – 'City of Edinburgh'/'City of Coventry'
Bristol B170 Freighter Mk 32 G-ANWG – 'City of Winchester'
Bristol B170 Freighter Mk 32 G-ANWH
Bristol B170 Freighter Mk 32 G-ANWI – 'City of Glasgow'
Bristol B170 Freighter Mk 32 G-ANWJ – 'City of Bristol'
Bristol B170 Freighter Mk 32 G-ANWK – 'Fourteenth of July – Le Quatorze Juillet'/'City of Leicester'
Bristol B170 Freighter Mk 32 G-ANWL – 'City of Worcester'
Bristol B170 Freighter Mk 32 G-ANWM – 'City of Aberdeen'

Bristol B170 Freighter Mk 32 G-ANWN – 'City of Hull'
DH.86A Express G-ACZP
DH.90A Dragon Rapide G-AKOE
DH.90 Dragonfly G-AEWZ
DH.104 Dove 1 G-AIWF
DH.104 Dove 1 G-AKJP
DH.104 Dove 1 G-AOYC
DH.104 Dove 2 G-AKJG
DH.104 Dove 2 G-ANGE
DH.114 Heron 1B G-AOZM – 'City of Bradford'
DH.114 Heron 1B G-AOZN – 'City of Belfast'
Douglas DC-2-115B G-AKNB – 'City of Bradford'
Douglas C-47A Dakota G-AIRG
Douglas C-47A Dakota G-AIRH
Douglas C-47A Dakota G-AIWC – 'City of Tripoli'/'City of Lincoln'
Douglas C-47A Dakota G-AJAU
Douglas C-47A Dakota G-AJAV – 'City of Hollywood'
Douglas C-47A Dakota G-AJZD
Douglas C-47A Dakota G-AKII
Douglas C-47A Dakota G-ALFO
Douglas C-47A Dakota G-ALPN – 'City of Belfast'
Douglas C-47A Dakota G-ANLF – 'City of Cambridge'
Douglas C-47B Dakota G-AGND
Douglas C-47B Dakota G-AMJU – 'City of Leeds'
Douglas C-47B Dakota G-AMPZ – 'City of Dublin'
Douglas C-47B Dakota G-AMRA
Douglas C-47B Dakota G-AMVC
Douglas C-47B Dakota G-AMWV – 'City of Lancaster'
Douglas C-47B Dakota G-AMYV – 'City of Oxford'
Douglas C-47B Dakota G-AMYX – 'City of Rochester'
Douglas C-47B Dakota G-AMZB – 'City of Guildford'
Douglas C-47B Dakota G-ANAE – 'City of Newcastle'
Douglas C-53D Dakota G-AOBN – 'City of Canterbury'

Examples of aircraft operated by Skyways between 1961 and 1972

Airspeed AS.57 Ambassador G-ALZZ
Airspeed AS.65 Consul G-AJXF
Auster J/5L Aiglet Trainer G-ANWX
Avro 19 Series 2 G-AGPG; Southend museum; Brenzett museum; Woodford
  museum; Hooton Park, dismantled
Avro 748 Series 100 G-ARAY
Avro 748 Series 101 G-ARMV; crashed at Lympne on 11 July 1965
Avro 748 Series 101 G-ARMW
Avro 748 Series 101 G-ARMX
DH.89A Dragon Rapide G-AGOJ; bounced and swung on landing at Lympne on
  1 May 1961; badly damaged
Douglas Dakota C-47A G-AMGD
Douglas Dakota C-47A G-APUC
Douglas Dakota C-47B G-AMPY
Douglas Dakota C-47B G-AMSM; USAAF 43-49948 26 January 1945; nose section
  at Brenzett Aeronautical Museum
Douglas Dakota C-47B G-AMWV
Douglas Dakota C-47B G-AMWW
Douglas Dakota C-47B G-AMWX
Douglas Dakota C-47B G-ANAE
Douglas Dakota C-47B G-AOUD
Douglas Dakota C-47B G-APBC
HS.748 Series 106 G-ARRW
HS.748 Series 108 G-ASPL – 'City of Berne'
HS.748 Series 225 G-ATMI
HS.748 Series 226 G-AXVG
HS.748 Series 232 G-AZSU (Dan-Air Skyways); briefly at Lympne, August 1972
Lancashire Aircraft E.P.9 Prospector G-APWX
Taylorcraft Auster AOP.V G-AKTF; crashed near Beachy Head on 7 February 1960

Details of V-1s destroyed by pilots operating from Lympne 1944

Squadron and aircraft, date, pilot and locality

74 Squadron (Spitfire LFIX) 29-06-44
Flt Lt D. E. Llewellyn NH468/4D-N – Lympne
Sgt J. Dalzell RR207/4D-T – Lympne

310 (Czech) Squadron (Spitfire IX) 08-07-44
Flt Lt O. Smik EN527/NN – Ashford, Battle and Tenterden

312 (Czech) Squadron (Spitfire IX) 08-07-44
Sqn Ldr M. A. Liskutin MK670/DU-V – Ashford/Maidstone

310 (Czech) Squadron (Spitfire IX) 09-07-44
Flt Sgt F. Mares EN526/NN – Exploded

312 (Czech) Squadron (Spitfire IX) 09-07-44
Sgt J. Pipa NH692/NN – Folkestone
Sqn Ldr M. A. Liskutin MK670/DU-V (shared) –Rye

313(Czech) Squadron (Spitfire IX) 09-07-44
Sgt K. J. Stojan ML145/RY – Romney Marsh

41 Squadron (Spitfire XII) 12-07-44
Flt Sgt P. W. Chattin EN602/EB – Ashford

486 (RNZAF) Squadron (Spitfire XII) 13-07-44
Plt Off. J. C. J. Payne MB804/EB-T – Battle

1 Squadron (Spitfire LFIXb) 14-07-44
Flt Lt E. N. W. Marsh MK423/JX – Cap Gris Nez
Flt Lt P. W. Stewart NH253/JX – Tenterden

41 Squadron (Spitfire XII) 14-07-44
Flt Lt K. F. Thiele (RNZAF) MB856/EB-X – Cliff End

165 Squadron (Spitfire IX) 14-07-44
Flt Sgt C. R. Bundara (RAAF) MJ580/SK-Y – Exploded

1 Squadron (Spitfire LFIXb) 15-07-44
Flt Sgt H. J. Vassie MJ422/JX – Detling

1 Squadron (Spitfire LFIXb) 16-07-44
Flt Lt T. Draper ML423/JX-S – Maidstone

41 Squadron (Spitfire XII) 16-07-44
Plt Off. D. P. Fisher MB798/EB-U – Beachy Head

165 Squadron (Spitfire IX) 16-07-44
Flt Lt J. K. Porteous (RNZAF) ML242/SK-A – Hythe
Plt Off. A. Scott ML204/SK-N – Dungeness

1 Squadron (Spitfire LFIXb) 18-07-44
Flt Lt D. H. Davy ML119/JX-B – Channel

165 Squadron (Spitfire IX) 18-07-44
Flt Lt I. A. StC. Watson MK425/SK-V – Maidstone
Flt Lt J. K. Porteous (RNZAF) MK738/SK-L – Tenterden
Flt Sgt L. Wright MK401/SK-M – Staplehurst

41 Squadron (Spitfire XII) 19-07-44
Flt Lt M. A. L. Balasse (Belg.) MB880/EB – Lamberhurst

41 Squadron (Spitfire XII) 20-07-44
Flt Sgt I. T. Stevenson MB878/EB – Channel

165 Squadron (Spitfire IX) 20-07-44
Flt Lt J. K. Porteous (RNZAF) MK425/SK-V – Exploded
Flt Sgt C. R. Bundara (RAAF) ML139/SK-Q – Tenterden

41 Squadron (Spitfire XII) 21-07-44
WO A. S. Appleton EN602/EB – Hastings

1 Squadron (Spitfire LFIXb) 22-07-44
Flt Lt J. O. Dalley MJ422/JX – Lamberhurst/Hawkhurst
Flt Lt D. H. Davy ML117/JX-D – Exploded

165 Squadron (Spitfire IX) 22-07-44
Flt Lt T. D. Tinsey ML175/SK-P – Sittingbourne
Flt Sgt R. J. Hughes MK480/SK-F – Tonbridge

41 Squadron (Spitfire XII) 23-07-44
Flt Lt M. A. L. Balasse (Belg.) MB798/EB-U – Rye
Plt Off. J. C. J. Payne MB880/EB – Exploded
WO A. S. Appleton MB882/EB-B – Bexhill

1 Squadron (Spitfire LFIXb) 24-07-44
Flt Lt F. W. Town MK926/JX – Ashford
Plt Off. K. R. Foskett MK986/JX-V – Ashford

1 Squadron (Spitfire LFIXb) 26-07-44
Flt Lt I. P. Maskell NH466/JX – Maidstone
Flt Lt D. H. Davy ML117/JX-D – Folkestone
Flt Lt D. H. Davy ML117/JX-D (shared) – Lympne
Flt Sgt G. Tate MK987/JX- (shared) – Lympne

41 Squadron (Spitfire XII) 26-07-44
Flt Lt M. A. L. Balasse (Belg.) EN609/EB – Beachy Head
Flt Lt E. B. Gray EN605/EB – Exploded

165 Squadron (Spitfire IX) 26-07-44
Flt Lt C. M. Lawson (RAAF) ML175/SK-P – Ashford
Plt Off. A. Scott MK514/SK-Z – Maidstone
Flt Sgt P. T. Humphrey (RNZAF) ML175/SK-P – Ashford
Flt Sgt G. S. Cameron NH401/SK-M – Robertsbridge

41 Squadron (Spitfire XII) 27-07-44
Flt Sgt C. S. Robertson (RAAF) EN602/EB – Dungeness

165 Squadron (Spitfire IX) 27-07-44
Flt Lt T. D. Tinsey MK514/SK-Z – Faversham
Flt Sgt G. S. Cameron ML139/SK-Q – Staplehurst
Flt Lt B. J. Murch NH401/SK-M – Exploded
Flt Lt G. P. Armstrong (RAAF) MJ221/SK-T – Exploded

1 Squadron (Spitfire LFIXb) 28-07-44
Flt Lt. J. O. Dalley MK987/JX – Cap Gris Nez
Flt Lt F. W. Town MK919/JX – Staplehurst and (shared) Lenham

165 Squadron (Spitfire IX) 28-07-44
Flt Lt S. R. Chambers ML139/SK-Q – Ashford

41 Squadron (Spitfire XII) 29-07-44
Flt Lt M. A. L. Balasse (Belg.) EN609/EB – Le Touquet and Romney Marsh

165 Squadron (Spitfire IX) 29-07-44
Flt Sgt A. F. A. McIntosh (RCAF) ML204/SK-N (shared) – Wadhurst

1 Squadron (Spitfire LFIXb) 03-08-44
Flt Lt D. R. Wallace MK919/JX – West Malling

165 Squadron (Spitfire IX) 03-08-44 Plt Off. J. V. Tynan MK738/SK-L – Ashford
Flt Lt T. A. Vance ML418/SK-G – Robertsbridge

1 Squadron (Spitfire LFIXb) 04-08-44
Flt Lt W. J. Batchelor MJ481/JX – Ashford

41 Squadron (Spitfire XII) 04-08-44
Flt Lt T. A. H. Slack EN238/EB-Q – Isle of Oxney

165 Squadron (Spitfire IX) 04-08-44
Plt Off. J. M. Walton (RCAF) MK801/SK-E – Tunbridge Wells
Flt Lt J. K. Porteous (RNZAF) MK854/SK-E – Exploded
Flt Lt B. J. Murch NH401/SK-M – Robertsbridge

41 Squadron (Spitfire XII) 05-08-44
Flt Lt I. T. Stevenson MB795/EB – Maidstone

165 Squadron (Spitfire IX) 05-08-44
Flt Lt C. M. Lawson (RAAF) ML175/SK-P – Robertsbridge and Tunbridge Wells
Plt Off. A. Scott MK752/SK-W – Dungeness
Plt Off. T. P. G. Lewin MJ580/SK-Y – Boulogne

1 Squadron (Spitfire LFIXb) 09-08-44
Flt Lt J. J. Jarman MK659/JX – Hailsham

41 Squadron (Spitfire XII) 09-08-44
Flt Lt T. Spencer MN875/EB – Wadham
Flt Lt H. Cook MB878/EB – Channel

41 Squadron (Spitfire XII) 11-08-44
Flt Lt J. F. Wilkinson EN609/EB – Brabourne

41 Squadron (Spitfire XII) 15-08-44
Flt Lt C. J. Malone (RCAF) EN622/EB – Ashford
WO P. T. Coleman MB875/EB-G – Ashford
Flt Lt R. P. Harding MB795/EB – Ivychurch

41 Squadron (Spitfire XII) 16-08-44
Flt Sgt V. J. Rossow (RAAF) MB857/EB – Ashford
Flt Lt P. B Graham MB831/EB – Wrotham

41 Squadron (Spitfire XII) 17-08-44
Flt Lt R. P Harding MB854/EB-Z – Brenzett
Flt Lt P. B Graham MB831/EB – Ashford

130 Squadron (Spitfire XIV) 17-08-44
Sgt P. E. H. Standish RM744/AP – Exploded and Dover

130 Squadron (Spitfire XIV) 17-08-44
Flt Lt K. M. Lowe (RAAF) RM757/AP – Wye
Plt Off. F. C. Riley (RAAF) RM760/AP – Brook

41 Squadron (Spitfire XII) 18-08-44
Plt Off. E. Gray (RAAF) EN228/EB (shared) – Hollingbourne
WO J. P. N. Ware (RAAF) EN228/EB

41 Squadron (Spitfire XII) 19-08-44
Flt Lt T. Spencer MB875/EB-G – Appledore

130 Squadron (Spitfire XIV) 19-08-44
Flt Lt K. J. Matheson RM760/AP (shared) – Boulogne
Plt Off. R. J. Martin (RCAF) RM760/AP
Flt Sgt G. W. Hudson RM744/AP – Channel and (shared) Ashford
WO D. H. White RM744/AP

41 Squadron (Spitfire XII) 20-08-44
Plt Off. E. Gray RAAF EN228/EB – Folkestone

130 Squadron (Spitfire XIV) 20-08-44
WO J. Edwards RM693/AP (shared) – Dover
Plt Off. J. P. Meadows RM693/AP

41 Squadron (Spitfire XII) 23-08-44
Flt Lt T. Spencer MB882/EB-B – Ashford and Harrietsham
Flt Lt D. J. Reid (RAAF) MB853/EB– Ashford
Flt Sgt V. J. Rossow (RAAF) MB857/EB – Cap Gris Nez

130 Squadron (Spitfire XIV) 23-08-44
Sgt P. E. H. Standish RM744/AP – Dover
Flt Lt K. J. Matheson RM760/AP – Exploded
Plt Off. W. Dobbs (RCAF) RM756/AP – Channel
Flt Sgt G. Lord RM749/AP-B – Exploded

130 Squadron (Spitfire XIV) 24-08-44
Plt Off. J. P. Meadows RM693/AP – Dungeness

41 Squadron (Spitfire XII) 28-08-44
Flt Lt T. Spencer EN229/EB-K – Rye